HEALTHISM

Can an employer refuse to hire someone who tests positive for nicotine or alcohol? Can an airline or movie theatre require overweight customers to purchase two seats? Can a health insurance company refuse to sell policies to those most in need of medical care? Can the government condition public assistance on wellness program participation or work activity? In this illuminating book, Jessica L. Roberts and Elizabeth Weeks consider these and similar questions, offering readers a nuanced analysis of when and why discrimination based on health status – or "healthism" – should be allowed, and when it should not. They provide a methodology to distinguish desirable health-based classifications from the undesirable and propose law and policy solutions to encourage the former and limit the latter. This work should be read by anyone concerned with how government does – and does not – regulate based on health.

Jessica L. Roberts directs the Health Law & Policy Institute at the University of Houston Law Center. A noted expert on diverse issues of health law, she has been interviewed by the BBC World Service, the *New York Times*, the *Houston Chronicle*, and National Public Radio. She has participated in a congressional briefing on the Genetic Information Nondiscrimination Act, presented at NASA, and served as a consultant for the Football Players Health Study at Harvard. Professor Roberts is also a Greenwall Faculty Scholar in Bioethics and a Health Policy Scholar with Baylor College of Medicine's Center for Medical Ethics & Health Policy.

Elizabeth Weeks is Associate Dean for Faculty Development at the University of Georgia School of Law. In addition to numerous law review articles and book chapters, she is coauthor of *The Law of American Health Care*. She is past Chair of the Association of American Law Schools Section on Law, Medicine & Bioethics, and has received numerous awards and honors, Health Law Scholars Award, giving by the American Society of Law, Medicine & Ethics, University of Kansas Docking Faculty Scholar Award, and University of Kansas School of Law Immel Teaching Award.

Healthism

HEALTH-STATUS DISCRIMINATION AND THE LAW

JESSICA L. ROBERTS
University of Houston Law Center

ELIZABETH WEEKS
University of Georgia School of Law

CAMBRIDGE
UNIVERSITY PRESS

CAMBRIDGE
UNIVERSITY PRESS

University Printing House, Cambridge CB2 8BS, United Kingdom

One Liberty Plaza, 20th Floor, New York, NY 10006, USA

477 Williamstown Road, Port Melbourne, VIC 3207, Australia

314–321, 3rd Floor, Plot 3, Splendor Forum, Jasola District Centre, New Delhi – 110025, India

79 Anson Road, #06–04/06, Singapore 079906

Cambridge University Press is part of the University of Cambridge.

It furthers the University's mission by disseminating knowledge in the pursuit of education, learning, and research at the highest international levels of excellence.

www.cambridge.org
Information on this title: www.cambridge.org/9781107160385
DOI: 10.1017/9781316675601

First published 2018

Printed and bound in Great Britain by Clays Ltd, Elcograf S.p.A.

A catalogue record for this publication is available from the British Library.

Library of Congress Cataloging-in-Publication Data
NAMES: Roberts, Jessica L., author. | Leonard, Elizabeth Weeks, author.
TITLE: Healthism : health-status discrimination and the law / Jessica L. Roberts, Elizabeth Weeks.
DESCRIPTION: Cambridge, United Kingdom ; New York, NY: Cambridge University Press, 2019. | Includes bibliographical references and index.
IDENTIFIERS: LCCN 2018012839| ISBN 9781107160385 (hardback : alk. paper) | ISBN 9781316613429 (paperback : alk. paper)
SUBJECTS: | MESH: Healthcare Disparities—legislation & jurisprudence | Social Discrimination—legislation & jurisprudence | Privacy—legislation & jurisprudence | Insurance, Health—legislation & jurisprudence | Health Status Disparities | United States
CLASSIFICATION: LCC RA412.3 | NLM W 33 AA1 | DDC 368.38/2—dc23
LC record available at https://lccn.loc.gov/2018012839

ISBN 978-1-107-16038-5 Hardback
ISBN 978-1-316-61342-9 Paperback

For DF and LJF
And JDW, GGW, and EJL

The State of Nature has a Law of Nature to govern it, which obliges every one: And Reason, which is that Law, teaches all Mankind, who will but consult it, that being all equal and independent, no one ought to harm another in his Life, Health, Liberty, or Possessions.

John Locke, *Second Treatise*, § 6

Contents

Preface

The US Constitution requires that people receive equal protection regardless of their race, ethnicity, national origin, or religion, absent a compelling governmental interest. To a somewhat lesser degree, the government is prohibited from discriminating on the basis of gender, illegitimacy, and sexual orientation. By statute, the US Congress also has limited certain private actors from discriminating in certain contexts on the basis of race, age, disability, pregnancy, genetic information, immigration status, or military affiliation. Conspicuously absent from this list of protected statuses is health. This book proposes a new protected category – the unhealthy – and a new form of discrimination – healthism.

"Healthism," like the other, previously recognized "isms," describes socially undesirable differentiation on the basis of a particular trait, in this case, health status. So used, the term carries a pejorative meaning. But not all differentiation on the basis of health necessarily constitutes healthism. In fact, differentiating on the basis of health can be neutral and, in some cases, even desirable. Hence, our project is to distinguish the "good" health-based distinctions from the "bad," or "healthist," ones. This book surveys and evaluates the legal regulation of health in a variety of settings, both historically and following comprehensive federal health-care reform. The Patient Protection and Affordable Care Act of 2010 (ACA) signaled a sea change in the public's and lawmakers' tolerance for health-status discrimination. The ACA aspires to end discrimination against the unhealthy, at least with respect to access to health insurance. No longer may public or private insurers deny coverage or charge more to the unhealthy. As we discuss, however, the ACA's gains are limited by various exceptions and vulnerable to shifting political winds. As of this writing, Congress has eroded significant components of the ACA that may well reintroduce health-status discrimination in health insurance.

Our survey of health-status discrimination is by no means limited to federal health reform or health insurance. The following chapters catalog the many ways that government and private entities differentiate based on health status and the implications of those policies. We explore examples from a wide range of contexts, including employment, medical care, commercial goods and services, judicial rules and remedies, public benefits, housing, and public and political discourse. We explain the inadequacy of existing disability and other antidiscrimination laws to fully protect the unhealthy from unfavorable treatment, thus justifying the need for our new paradigm.

We recognize that the law can be a powerful tool to promote wellness and encourage healthy lifestyle choices. But such differentiation can also perpetuate stigma and compound other disadvantages. Accordingly, our thesis is that differentiation on the basis of health status is desirable when it promotes responsible, healthy behaviors, yet undesirable when it perpetuates or exacerbates existing health disparities and social disadvantage. Our approach is distinct from other scholarship in this area, which tends to focus on the potential for health-based distinctions to infringe on personal liberty. Instead, we view the issue through the lenses of social advocacy and health promotion, allowing that even some arguably paternalistic laws, policies, and practices may not be "healthist" inasmuch as they encourage and support healthier lifestyles. We conclude that sometimes the law should permit – or even encourage – health-based distinctions and sometimes it should prohibit them. Although it challenges the tidiness of our methodology, we maintain that this equivocal stance more accurately and honestly captures the wide range of contexts that health touches.

The book concludes by offering a roadmap for navigating the treacherous terrain of health-status discrimination. In some instances, we advocate legal responses to healthist practices and policies, identifying gaps in existing protections for the unhealthy and proposing appropriate reforms. In other instances, we endorse laws that promote healthier behaviors and conduct, with a cautionary eye toward the potential for those laws to perpetuate discrimination and stigmatization of disfavored groups. Most importantly, our book introduces the concept of healthism into the lexicon and invites an ongoing dialogue about the merits and demerits of treating individuals differently based on their health statuses.

Acknowledgments

The authors wish to acknowledge and thank Ifeoma Ajunwa, Kent Barnett, Josh Blackman, Cyndi Canup, Kyle Chapel, Danielle Charron, Jessica Clarke, Dave Fagundes, Elaine Fiala, Jacqueline Fox, Caroline Jozefczyk, Emily Lawson, Brendan Maher, April Moreno, James Nelson, Paul Secunda, Jennifer Shinall, Lauren Wallace, Mike Wells, Lindsay Wiley, Mary Dovel, Bradley Tipper, Hannah-Alise Rogers, Mark Rothstein, Kate Thorne, and T. J. Striepe.

1

What Is Healthism?

1.1. INTRODUCTION

The American Health Care Act of 2017 will

> allow insurance companies to require people who have higher health care costs to contribute more to the insurance pool. That helps offset all these costs, thereby reducing the cost to those people who lead good lives, they're healthy, they've done the things to keep their bodies healthy. And right now, those are the people – who've done things the right way – that are seeing their costs skyrocketing.
>
> U.S. House of Representatives, Mo Brooks (Republican – Alabama), May 4, 2017

People who "lead good lives" and "who've done things the right way" deserve to pay less for health care. But people who lead "bad lives" and have done things the "wrong way" deserve to pay more. That attitude is the essence of healthism: permitting – and even *encouraging* – discriminatory treatment based on an individual's health status.

Health status, like many prohibited bases for discrimination, often is not the result of good or bad living, or of doing things the right or wrong way. Even conduct that appears voluntary at first blush, in fact, may be the product of myriad interconnected factors. This book comprehensively examines the pervasiveness of health-status discrimination in law and society and urges that, at least in some instances, such discrimination should not be tolerated.

US law recognizes a number of "protected categories," or bases on which individuals may not be treated unfavorably. Current federal law prohibits discrimination (to varying degrees, and in varying contexts) based on race, color, national origin, sexual orientation, sex/gender, pregnancy, disability, genetic information, religion, military service, immigration status, and age.[1] Conspicuously absent from this list of protected statuses, though, is health. Should the law allow unhealthy individuals to be treated less favorably than healthy ones? Or should we recognize a new category of impermissible discrimination?

This book is about discrimination on the basis of health status, or, as we will call it, "healthism." Political scientists in prior work have used the term *healthism* to refer to the government's establishment of coercive health norms.[2] Under that view, human activities are categorized as healthy or unhealthy, with preference given to the former. Healthy is moral and patriotic, while unhealthy is immoral and polluted. We do not adopt that meaning of the word healthism but instead repurpose it to refer to health-status discrimination by government and private actors. It is a discriminatory "ism" akin to racism, sexism, ageism, and ableism.[3] Distinct from those other protected categories, however, health status does not presently garner independent legal protection.

Once attuned to the concept of healthism, it is easy to spot examples. Employers, insurers, health-care providers, retailers, manufacturers, airlines,

[1] The US Constitution prohibits discrimination on the basis of race, national origin, religion and – to a somewhat lesser degree – gender, illegitimacy, and, perhaps now, sexual orientation. The Equal Protection clause of the US Constitution states that no state shall "deny to any person within its jurisdiction the equal protection of the laws." US Constitution amend. 14, § 1. Courts have interpreted this provision with varying levels of scrutiny depending on the impacted group. *See* 3 Treatise on Const. L. § 18.3(a). While discrimination on the basis of sexual orientation is not officially deemed a suspect class, US Supreme Court jurisprudence may open the door to heightened scrutiny of possible cases of such discrimination. *See* Mark P. Strasser, *Obergefell's Legacy*, 24 *Duke J. Gender L. & Pol'y* 61, 88 (2016). ("Perhaps in light of *Romer*, *Lawrence*, *Windsor* and *Obergefell*, the Court will soon announce that orientation is suspect or quasi-suspect.") The First Amendment outlaws religious discrimination by forbidding any law "respecting an establishment of religion, or prohibiting the free exercise thereof." US Const. amend. 1. By statute, Congress has limited certain private actors from discriminating also on the basis of disability, pregnancy, genetic information, immigration status, or military affiliation. *See* Pregnancy Discrimination Act of 1978, Pub. L. No. 95-555, 92 Stat. 2076 (codified at 42 U.S.C. § 2000e-(k)) (1976 & Supp. II 1978); Americans with Disabilities Act of 1990, Pub. L. No. 101-336, 104 Stat. 327 (codified as amended at 42 U.S.C. §§ 12101–213 (2013)); Genetic Information Nondiscrimination Act of 2008, Pub. L. No. 110-233, 122 Stat. 881 (codified as amended in scattered sections of 26, 29, and 42 U.S.C.); Immigration and Nationality Act § 247B, 8 U.S.C § 1324b (1996); Uniformed Services Employment and Reemployment Rights Act of 1994, 38 U.S.C. §§ 4301–35 (2012).

[2] Jessica L. Roberts, *"Healthism": A Critique of the Antidiscrimination Approach to Health Insurance and Health-Care Reform*, 2012 *Univ. Ill. L. Rev.* 1159, 1171 (2012). ("The traditional concept of healthism involves the government's promotion of coercive health norms, and its attempts to impose lifestyle choices deemed 'healthy' on its citizens.")

[3] Jessica L. Roberts and Elizabeth Weeks Leonard, *What Is (And Isn't) Healthism*, 50 *Ga. L. Rev.* 833, 838 (2016); *see also* Jessica L. Roberts, *Healthism and the Law of Employment Discrimination*, 99 *Iowa L. Rev.* 571, 592 (2014).

regulators, and public officials increasingly probe our personal lives and data sources for information that they deem relevant to their operations and interests. Health information is of particular and increasing interest. Both private and public actors make decisions about which opportunities to offer – or to deny – to groups or individuals based on their perceived health, or otherwise disadvantage subject people labeled as unhealthy.

Consider one university's plan to require all freshmen to wear Fitbits to track their steps, heart rates, and fitness activities.[4] The data are then sent directly to a central computer at the university, accessible by administrators and faculty. Oral Roberts University hails the program as a success and notes that seventy employers have followed suit.[5] Similarly, retailers and employers may be able to learn about a woman's pregnancy, or even her plans to become pregnant, based on her buying patterns or changes in pharmaceutical purchases.[6] Those examples involve use of otherwise private health information to invite a host of potentially discriminatory policies. Other examples reveal outright bias against individuals based on health status. During the 2016 presidential campaign, now President Donald J. Trump commented pejoratively on private individuals' disabilities and physical appearances.[7] Physicians decline to treat high-need patients. Employers adopt policies against hiring individuals who engage in health-risky behaviors, such as tobacco use. Reproductive biologists specifically select against certain chromosomal traits or abnormalities.

Although health-status discrimination is not yet formally recognized, allegations of healthism have generated their fair amount of litigation against a variety of different kinds of defendants, including employers, health-care providers, and businesses. Consider six-year-old Mackenzie Gonzalez, who was

4 Jessica Chasmar, *Oklahoma University Requires Freshmen to Wear Fitbit, Track 10K Steps per Day, The Washington Times* (Jan. 11, 2016), www.washingtontimes.com/news/2016/jan/11/oklahoma-university-requires-freshmen-to-wear-fitb/; Elizabeth Chuck, *Oral Roberts University to Track Students' Fitness Through Fitbits, NBC News: College Game Plan* (Feb. 3, 2016), www.nbcnews.com/feature/college-game-plan/oral-roberts-university-track-students-fitness-through-fitbits-n507661.

5 Bill Sherman, *Fitbit Fitness Monitoring Program a Hit at ORU, Tulsa World* (Mar. 20, 2017), available at www.tulsaworld.com/homepagelatest/fitbit-fitness-monitoring-program-a-hit-at-oru/article_eae41a5e-830a-5270-98de-c1aa62aac28d.html.

6 Kashmir Hill, *How Target Figured Out a Teen Girl Was Pregnant before Her Father Did, Forbes: Tech* (Feb. 16, 2012), www.forbes.com/sites/kashmirhill/2012/02/16/how-target-figured-out-a-teen-girl-was-pregnant-before-her-father-did/#202639476668.

7 Jenna Johnson, *Trump Attacks Former Miss Universe Who "Gained a Massive Amount of Weight" and Had "Attitude," The Washington Post: Post Politics* (Sept. 27, 2016), www.washingtonpost.com/news/post-politics/wp/2016/09/27/trump-attacks-former-miss-universe-who-gained-a-massive-amount-of-weight-and-had-attitude/?utm_term=.0701dec95454; www.nbcnews.com/politics/2016-election/trump-s-worst-offense-mocking-disabled-reporter-poll-finds-n627736.

diagnosed with cancer in December 2008.[8] At the time, her father, Yovany Gonzalez, worked for Wells Fargo in Palm Beach, Florida, as a mortgage consultant. Like many Americans with health insurance, Gonzalez held a policy through his employer. In August 2010, however, the bank fired Gonzalez, a mere three days before Mackenzie was scheduled to go into surgery. Along with his job, Gonzalez and his family also lost their health insurance, leaving them unable to afford the costly treatment. As a result, the hospital canceled the surgery. In March 2011, just seven months later, Mackenzie died. In August 2012, Gonzalez filed suit against his former employer, arguing that Wells Fargo terminated him because his daughter's health-care costs were too high.

In 1994, Sidney Abbott got a cavity. Like most people with cavities, she decided to go to the dentist. She chose Dr. Randon Bragdon. On her new patient intake form, Abbott indicated that she was HIV-positive, though asymptomatic. As a result, Dr. Bragdon refused to treat her in his office. Instead, he agreed to fill her cavity in the hospital, but Abbott would have to cover those additional expenses herself. She sued, alleging discrimination on the basis of her HIV status, and took her case all the way to the US Supreme Court.

Kenlee Tiggeman, who weighed about 300 pounds, was shocked when she tried to board her Southwest Airlines flight in 2011 and was told she needed to purchase a second ticket.[9] According to Tiggeman, Southwest employees humiliated her in front of other passengers by laughing at her and asking for proof of her weight. One gate agent apparently told Tiggeman that she was "too fat to fly." Tiggeman filed a lawsuit against the airline, which was eventually thrown out for procedural reasons.

You will learn more about these and many other stories as you read this book. Were the policies and decisions described fair or rational? Or were they unjust or intrusive? And what, if anything, should the law do to regulate these practices? These are the questions that judges, legislators, and policy-makers must ask themselves. Among developed countries, America spends inordinately on health care, yet our people suffer poorer health status comparatively.[10] The implications for health-status discrimination, thus, are widespread.

[8] Bonnie Kavoussi, *Yovany Gonzalez's Wells Fargo Lawsuit Alleges Bank Fired Him, Cut Dying Daughter's Health Insurance, Huffington Post* (Aug. 7, 2012), www.huffingtonpost.com/2012/08/07/wells-fargo-yovany-gonzalez_n_1751461.html; Christine Roberts, *Florida Man Says Wells Fargo Sacked Him Over Daughter's Cancer Treatment Cost, NY Daily News* (Aug. 12, 2012), www.nydailynews.com/news/national /florida-man-wells-fargo-sacked-daughter-cancer-treatment-costs-article-1.1134828.

[9] Associated Press, *Judge Rejects Woman's 'Too Fat to Fly' Lawsuit, Times-Picayune* (Nov. 1, 2012), www.nola.com/crime/index.ssf/2012/11/judge_rejects_womans_too_fat_t.html.

[10] David Squires and Chloe Anderson, *U.S. Health Care from a Global Perspective: Spending, Use of Services, Prices, and Health in 13 Countries* (The Commonwealth Fund, Oct. 2015),

Our book catalogs the many ways that government and private entities differentiate on the basis of health status and the implications of those policies. It draws examples from a wide range of contexts, including the protections offered by civil rights and privacy laws; the Patient Protection and Affordable Care Act's rejection of health-status discrimination in private health insurance sales and pricing; and the potential for personal injury law to disfavor the unhealthy.

We recognize that the law can be a powerful tool to promote wellness and encourage healthy lifestyle choices. Yet classifying people based on their perceived health can also lead to stigma and compound other disadvantages. Accordingly, we argue that distinctions based on health are desirable in some contexts, but problematic in others. Viewing this issue through the lenses of social advocacy and health promotion, we conclude that sometimes the law should permit or even encourage health-based distinctions, and sometimes it should prohibit them as unlawful. We maintain that our approach more accurately – and more honestly – captures the wide range of concerns facing law and policy-makers.

This book provides a roadmap for navigating the treacherous terrain of health-status discrimination. Chapters 1 and 2 define key terms, explaining more precisely what we mean by the term healthism – answering initial objections to recognizing new prohibited bases for discrimination, and outlining a theoretical framework for approaching the problem – which recognizes that not all forms of differential treatment based on health status are necessarily healthist.

Chapters 3–5 provide real-world examples. We survey key categories of existing US laws that partially, but incompletely, address healthism, thus highlighting the need for a new conceptual framework. In particular, existing laws protecting privacy or prohibiting discrimination based on disability and genetic information fail to capture all instances of health-status discrimination that we would deem undesirable. Health insurance law, much of which is in flux under a new presidential administration, leaves gaping holes through which insurers may discriminate based on health status, as in the Mackenzie Gonzalez example above. Judge-made private law, namely torts and contract, contain ample opportunities for health-status discrimination.

Chapter 6 outlines a framework, containing a set of factors, for distinguishing between "good" (or health-promoting) distinctions and "bad" (or healthist) ones. Thus, the final chapter draws together a critical insight from Chapters 1 and 2

---

www.commonwealthfund.org/~/media/files/publications/issue-brief/2015/oct/1819_squires_us_hlt_care_global_perspective_oecd_intl_brief_v3.pdf.

that not all instances of health-based differentiations are undesirable or normatively wrong and applies our framework to the various examples of health-status discrimination from Chapters 3 through 5. Indeed, one of the challenges of recognizing a new "ism" based on health is that treating individuals differently based on health is not necessarily harmful. In fact, in some cases, health-status discrimination may benefit the individual or society. Thus, we provide a blueprint for drawing those distinctions and navigating the divide.

Here, in Chapter 1, we begin with the concept of healthism. We contend that an entity discriminates on the basis of health status when it distinguishes – intentionally or unintentionally – based on health in such a way that produces a normative wrong. Drawing from antidiscrimination theory, we unpack essential elements of that definition, including "health," "health status," and "normative wrong." This clear definition of healthism allows us to distinguish between socially harmful and socially beneficial differentiations based on health status in later chapters.

1.2. HEALTHISM: THE CENTRAL CONCEPT

The fact that healthism has not already been the subject of widespread legal regulation begs the question: Why is it problematic? We propose that healthism matters for at least two main reasons. First, people perceive many healthist practices to be unfair. In other words, while much of healthism is legal, it still may raise important – and legitimate – moral concerns. Second, healthist practices threaten to exacerbate existing social inequalities, including health disparities.

People face real disadvantages based on their health-related attributes. Rates of weight discrimination – particularly among women – rival those of race discrimination and permeate all aspects of life, including education, health care, public life, and employment.[11] This negative differential treatment has financial as well as psychosocial implications, with weight discrimination linked to depression, anxiety, social rejection, suicide, avoiding medical treatment, and unhealthy behaviors.[12] Perhaps not surprisingly, this widespread discrimination likely stems from negative stereotypes that heavier individuals are lazy, stupid, undisciplined, sloppy, and at fault for their weight.[13] Yet despite these beliefs, the support for laws prohibiting weight discrimination has continued

[11] Jennifer L. Pomeranz and Rebecca M. Puhl, *New Developments in the Law for Obesity Discrimination Protection*, 21 *Obesity* 469, 469 (2013).

[12] Ibid.

[13] Rebecca M. Puhl, Young Suh, and Xun Li, *Legislating for Weight-based Equality: National Trends in Public Support for Laws to Prohibit Weight Discrimination*, *Internat'l J. Obesity* 1, 1 (2016).

to increase among liberals and conservatives alike. A 2016 survey found that 78 percent of respondents support laws forbidding weight discrimination in employment.[14]

In fact, eighty-eight percent of Americans believe that employers should not make hiring decisions based on whether an applicant smokes or is overweight.[15] Yet despite public opinion, a wide range of employers have adopted policies that ban hiring nicotine users. Not surprisingly, many viewed the policies as unfair. One public health professor called nicotine hiring bans "a form of employment discrimination," in part because they involve an employer "making a hiring decision based on a group someone belongs to, not his or her qualifications for the job."[16] And a state politician stated that "[e]ven if [the obesity ban] wasn't *illegal*, the policy was *discriminatory*."[17]

In addition to being discriminatory, critics also described the nicotine hiring ban as "an invasion of privacy and really overreaching"[18] and as "a step too far" that "extends far too deeply into the private lives of prospective workers."[19] Commentators feared that those policies were the tip of the iceberg and could lead to even more intrusive kinds of actions by employers. One editorial inquired: "If employers routinely reject people who engage in risky, but legal, behavior on their own time, what about such things as overeating or drinking too much alcohol?"[20]

Permitting healthism could eventually lead to restrictions on all kinds of private actions because so much of our conduct affects our health,[21] including

14 Ibid.

15 Rebecca Riffkin, *Hiring Discrimination for Smokers, Obese Rejected in U.S., Gallup* (July 22, 2014), www.gallup.com/poll/174035/hiring-discrimination-smokers-obese-rejected.aspx.

16 Roberts, note 3, at 571, 592 (quoting Renée C. Lee, *Hospitals Turn Away Applicants Who Smoke, Hous. Chron.* (Oct. 19, 2012) (quoting Michael Siegel), www.chron.com/news/houston-texas/houston/article/Hospitals-turn-away-applicants-who-smoke-3988931.php).

17 Ibid. at 593 (quoting Erin Pradia, *Citizens Medical Center Reverses Ban on Hiring Obese People, Victoria Advoc.* (Apr. 12, 2012) (quoting Alex Hernandez), www.victoriaadvocate.com/news/2012/apr/11/ep_citizens_health_041212_173212).

18 Ibid. at 592 (quoting Renée C. Lee, *Hospitals Turn Away Applicants Who Smoke, Hous. Chron.* (Oct. 19, 2012) (quoting Dotty Griffith), www.chron.com/news/houston-texas/houston/article/Hospitals-turn-away-applicants-who-smoke-3988931.php).

19 Ibid. at 592 (quoting *Editorial: Not Hiring Smokers Crosses Privacy Line, USA Today* (Jan. 29, 2012), http://usatoday30.usatoday.com/news/opinion/editorials/story/2012-01-29/not-hiring-smokers-privacy/52874348/1).

20 Ibid. at 593 (quoting *Editorial: Not Hiring Smokers Crosses Privacy Line, USA Today*, Jan. 29, 2012, http://usatoday30.usatoday.com/news/opinion/editorials/story/2012-01-29/not-hiring-smokers-privacy/52874348/1).

21 Lewis Maltby, president of the National Workrights Institute, has observed: "The more we learn about the relationships between behavior and health, the more we realize that everything we do in our private lives affects our health. If employers are permitted to control private behavior when it is related to health, virtually every aspect of our private lives is subject to employer

our eating choices, sex lives, recreational conduct, and sleep patterns. Thus, in addition to fairness, opponents of healthism also raise related concerns about protecting privacy, respecting autonomy, and avoiding paternalism. Unchecked, healthism could threaten our ability to freely make decisions about our private lives.

Healthist practices also demand legal attention because they disproportionately impact certain historically disadvantaged populations.[22] Health disparities research from 2016 found that non-white and low-income populations have reduced health-care access, are less likely to have health insurance, and are more likely to encounter barriers when seeking health care.[23] Likewise, people with disabilities are less likely to receive preventative care, and are more likely to have poor health outcomes and to engage in unhealthy behaviors.[24] Because members of those groups are in poorer relative health, policies that discriminate based on health status will inevitably have a greater impact on them. Thus, in addition to the challenges that they already face, these populations have the added disadvantage of discriminatory treatment on the basis of health, whether it is in the context of health insurance, employment, health-care access, public health, government programs, or commerce. Accordingly, facially neutral policies, such as taxes on tobacco products or sugary soft drinks, may disparately impact certain already-disadvantaged groups.

Further complicating matters is the reality that disadvantaged populations encounter greater structural barriers to adopting health-promoting behaviors.[25] People need resources to purchase healthy food, find opportunities to exercise, quit smoking, and even get enough sleep. Existing literature on social determinants of health reveals that certain populations encounter roadblocks on their paths toward healthy living.[26] Common structural barriers include

---

control." Lewis Maltby, *Whose Life Is It Anyway?: Employer Control of Off-Duty Smoking and Individual Autonomy*, 34 *Wm. Mitchell L. Rev.* 1639, 1641 (2008).

22 Roberts, note 3, at 616–18.

23 Agency for Healthcare Research and Quality, National Healthcare Quality and Disparities Report: Chartbook on Access to Healthcare (2016).

24 Disability and Health, Healthy People 2020, www.healthypeople.gov/2020/topics-objectives/topic/disability-and-health.

25 Roberts, note 3, at 616–18; Jessica L. Roberts and Leah Fowler, *How Assuming Autonomy Undermines Wellness Programs*, 27 *Health Matrix* 101 (2017).

26 For example, medical ethicist Harald Schmidt explains: "A law school graduate from a wealthy family who has a gym on the top floor of his condominium block is more likely to succeed in losing weight if he tries than is a teenage mother who grew up and continues to live and work odd jobs in a poor neighborhood with limited access to healthy food and exercise opportunities. And he is more likely to try." Harald Schmidt, Kristin Voigt, and Daniel Wikler, *Carrots, Sticks, and Health Care Reform – Problems with Wellness Incentives*, 362 *New Engl. J. Med.* e3(1) (2010).

living in a food desert (or a fast food swamp); lacking access to safe, affordable opportunities to exercise like parks or public pools; and not being able to pay for the child care necessary to make time to exercise or sleep. Rationalizing healthism as a means to encourage people to be healthy assumes that they are in poor health for reasons within their control. We explore the limits of personal autonomy to achieve optimal health status throughout this book.

Thus far we have established that healthism is not only potentially stigmatizing, unfair, and intrusive but also may perpetuate – or even fortify – existing social disparities, creating further impediments for already-disadvantaged populations. If we wish to regulate healthism, however, we will first need a clear definition of precisely which kinds of distinctions based on health status may constitute discrimination. Explanations of key components of our definition – including discrimination, healthy, health status, and normative wrong – follow.

1.2.1. *Discrimination*

The first step to a working definition of healthism is to spell out precisely what we mean by "discrimination." In the simple, dictionary sense, to discriminate simply means to differentiate.[27] People then discriminate on a daily basis. Insurers discriminate based on risk, lenders discriminate based on financial history, and employers discriminate based on education and experience. We even discriminate when we choose friends and romantic partners. This definition of discriminate is what forms the root of adjective *indiscriminate*, meaning not selective.[28]

In that sense, prohibiting people from discriminating, or differentiating, altogether would be not only undesirable but also nearly impossible. Consequently, when we talk about antidiscrimination law, we are inevitably talking about a particular subset of discriminatory actions. Yet which ones? The answer is the types of differentiation that violate certain important social norms, typically, fairness and equality. While discrimination has a value-neutral meaning, frequently when people say an action is "discriminatory"

[27] *See The Oxford English Dictionary* 757–8 (Oxford University Press, 2nd edn., 1989) (defining "to discriminate" as "to divide, separate, distinguish"); *see also* Robert K. Fullinwider, *The Reverse Discrimination Controversy: A Moral and Legal Analysis* 10–11 (Roman & Littlefield Publishers, 1980) (explaining that the term "discrimination" is "morally neutral"); *see also* Roberts, note 2, at 1163; Roberts, note 3, at 591; Jessica L. Roberts, *Protecting Privacy to Prevent Discrimination*, 56 *Wm. and Mary L. Rev.* 2097, 2109 (2015); Roberts and Leonard, note 3, at 838–9.

[28] "Indiscriminate," *The Oxford English Dictionary* (3rd edn., 2010) (defining an indiscriminate person as "not using or exercising discrimination").

they mean that the differentiation is somehow wrong or unfair.[29] In other words, there is an inherent value judgment. In fact, the legal and political meaning of discrimination is so widely accepted as pejorative that merely *calling* something discriminatory may be enough for some people to consider it problematic. Discrimination is the kind of distinction that goes against the way at least some people think the world *should* be. We refer to these violations of social mores as "normative wrongs." Thus, for differentiation to be "discrimination" it must result in a normative wrong. We further consider the meaning of normative wrong below and in Chapter 2.

Importantly, discrimination is not limited to differentiations that *intentionally* produce disadvantage. Discrimination can also encompass disadvantage that is unconscious or otherwise unintentional. Antidiscrimination law sometimes allows people to sue for "disparate impact," when an action or policy disproportionately harms a particular group, regardless of intent.[30] Disparate impact signifies discrimination by result, not by design.[31] Height requirements provide a prototypical example. While an employer that requires its employees to be 5′77″ so that they can properly operate equipment does not intend to exclude women, more men than woman will be eligible for the position simply because men tend to be taller.[32] With respect to healthism, weight requirements disparately impact overweight people, and occupational standards may screen out people who have health conditions like hepatitis that make them more vulnerable to toxicity. We explore how these kinds of cases have played out in the courts in Chapter 3.

Next, consider how socially undesirable differentiation operates. One popular set of frameworks for understanding discrimination is anticlassification versus antisubordination.[33] On one hand, discrimination can mean merely *classifying* people based on a particular protected status – for instance, race, sex/gender, or disability. On the other hand, discrimination can also signify *subordinating*

[29] Roberts, note 2, at 1172–4; Roberts, note 3, at 591; Roberts, note 27, at 2109–12; Roberts and Leonard, note 3, at 839.

[30] *See* Lex K. Larson, *Employment Discrimination*, ch. 20: The Basics of Disparate Impact Theory 2–20 (Matthew Bender, 2nd edn., 2016); *see also* Roberts, note 2, at 1172–3; Roberts, note 27, at 2120–1; Roberts, note 3, at 617; Roberts and Leonard, note 3, at 840.

[31] *Alexander* v. *Choate*, 469 U.S. 287, 292 (1985).

[32] *See e.g., Boyd* v. *Ozark Air Lines*, 568 F.2d. 50, 53 (8th Cir. 1977) (holding that a height requirement of 5'7" has a disparate impact on women and instituting a 5'55" requirement as a less discriminatory alternative).

[33] Jack M. Balkin and Reva B. Siegel, *The American Civil Rights Tradition: Anticlassification or Antisubordination?*, 58 *U. Miami L. Rev.* 9, 9–10 (2003); *see also* Roberts, note 27, at 2123–5; Roberts and Leonard, note 3, at 839–40. There are of course other antidiscrimination paradigms. *See* Jessica A. Clarke, *Protected Class Gatekeeping*, 92 *N.Y.U. L. Rev.* 101, 145–55 (2017) (discussing the antiessentialism and anti-balkanization theories of antidiscrimination).

one particular group or groups – for instance, people of color, women, or people with disabilities – regardless of intent. Under either approach, healthism produces disadvantage related to a person's health status. As we will explain, our healthism rubric fits most comfortably under the antisubordination view.

Antisubordination focuses on group harm, seeking to raise the social status of historically subjugated populations. Antisubordination embraces both the disparate impact actions described above and positive differential treatment like affirmative action or accommodations for people with disabilities. By contrast, anticlassification centers on protected classes, prohibiting any intentional differentiation – good or bad – but not intervening in cases of inadvertent discrimination. Anticlassification does not, then, support claims for disparate impact or positive differential treatment.

In the case of healthism, we can either describe the socially undesirable differentiation as classifying on the basis of health status or as subordinating people deemed unhealthy.[34] Antisubordination would seek to combat the social subjugation of people labeled as unhealthy, allowing claims for disparate impact and supporting positive differential treatment. Anticlassification would simply outlaw all intentional health-based distinctions, taking a "health-blind" position.

Both paradigms have their challenges. With respect to antisubordination, people with disabilities, overweight people, smokers, people with elevated levels of genetic risk, and individuals who are HIV-positive have surely faced discrimination in one form or another. It is unclear, however, whether people perceived to be unhealthy, as a collective group, have been the victims of widespread social subjugation. Thus, simply making "unhealthy" a prohibited basis for discrimination may not be workable or desirable. By way of comparison, however, "disability," which is a legally protected category, is a similarly broad umbrella that encompasses people with a wide range of impairments. Therefore, the heterogeneity of the proposed protected status does not in and of itself rule out possible antidiscrimination protection.

Anticlassification raises its own issues. First, as we explain in Chapter 2, not all intentional health-status differentiations are discriminatory. Universally prohibiting public and private institutions from considering health could undermine efforts to promote and improve health and other social goods. Moreover, anticlassification's exclusion of unintentional discrimination and aversion to positive differential treatment are also not well-tailored for healthism. As we

[34] *See* Roberts, note 2, at 1174 (explaining that "health-status discrimination can be thought of in two ways: discrimination on the basis of a protected trait [health status], or alternatively as discrimination against a particular disadvantaged group [the sick]"); Roberts and Leonard, note 3, at 841.

will explain, a number of policies could have a harmful disparate impact. Moreover, certain kinds of positive differential treatment related to health status may be socially desirable. For example, it may be good policy to facilitate smokers' access to resources to quit smoking, to provide Medicaid benefits to pregnant women, and to prioritize sicker patients over healthy ones in donor organ–allocation decisions. By the same token, insurance coverage policies covering longer post-partum hospital stays following a caesarean, as opposed to vaginal delivery, could be said to be healthist despite good, rational, medically appropriate reasons for the differentiation.

Between the two views of discrimination, our definition of healthism most clearly tracks antisubordination, but neither is a perfect fit.[35] While antisubordination and anticlassification are foundational ways of understanding discrimination, other theories have also been influential. For example, antiessentialism rejects the notion that there are essential attributes to any particular identity category, like race or sex.[36] For example, someone who essentializes sex would assume that all women's experiences of raising children are largely the same. In reality, however, all of our social statuses – race, sex/gender, education, class, religion, and so on – shape our lives in interrelated and overlapping ways. Consequently, there is no "woman's experience" or "black person's" experience that can be separated from a person's other identities. To reduce a person to a single aspect of her identity engages in essentialism. Antiessentialism, then, seeks to dismantle essentialism and to treat individuals as whole, multifaceted persons.

Essentialism can also occur regarding health. For example, a person with schizophrenia becomes "a schizophrenic." Illness involves its own culture and social meaning. Medical sociologists have long identified the concept of the "sick role," which carries with it customary rights and obligations.[37] Adopting the sick role exempts a person from normal social roles and absolves her of personal responsibility for her condition, while obligating her to try to get well and to seek treatment. If people are blamed for their ill health, however, they may not be accorded special solicitude or relief when ill. Also, people may reject the sick role by not wanting to be dependent or to become a "passive patient."

When we reduce a person to a single health-related attribute – weight, smoking, HIV, mental illness, or even cancer – we are engaging in health

[35] Roberts and Leonard, note 3, at 856–7.

[36] Trina Grillo, *Anti-Essentialism and Intersectionality: Tools to Dismantle the Master's House*, 10 *Berkeley Women's L.J.* 16, 17 (1995).

[37] *See* Talcott Parsons, *The Social System* (2nd edn., 1991) (first published 1951) (introducing the concept of the sick role).

essentialism. Hence, our theory of healthism is committed to ensuring that we treat people as full human beings, not simply as their health status.

1.2.2. *Health*

In considering whether to prohibit health-status discrimination, we must have a good sense of what health means in the first place. The World Health Organization (WHO) defines health as "[a] state of complete physical, mental and social well-being and not merely the absence of disease or infirmity."[38] The WHO definition is a broad, aspirational standard, which we do not find workable on a practical level. If we base our definition of health on WHO's idea of health, then many of us have never been healthy a day in our lives!

Health has both descriptive and normative elements.[39] On the descriptive level, definitions of health frequently refer to how well a body functions. Under this definition, disease or ill health is a functional limitation. For example, someone with diabetes is ill because her body does not efficiently break down sugar. A person with cancer is ill because her body produces too many malignant cells. However, thinking of health in those terms requires agreeing on a baseline level of functioning. That is, it requires a concept of normalcy.[40] If I tell you that your blood pressure is 129/82, you have no way of knowing whether that number is "high" without the added information that "normal" blood pressure is under 120/80. However, what is normal inevitably shifts. Humans tend to live longer and to be taller and stronger than we were a century ago. Thus, the center of the bell curve always moves, making functionalism as a means of defining health less stable than it might initially appear.

Additionally, functional limitation alone may not always result in a person being labeled "unhealthy." Para-athletes experience functional limitations related to their disabilities, but because they are world-class athletes one would be hard-pressed to call them unhealthy. Likewise, a relatively minor functional problem, like a blister or a cavity, is not typically considered a sign of ill health.[41] Definitions of health, therefore, have normative elements. As a result, whether a particular condition or state is labeled unhealthy will depend, at least in

[38] Constitution of the World Health Organization (New York, July 22, 1946), 14 U.N.T.S. 185, entered into force Apr. 7, 1948 www.who.int/governance/eb/who_constitution_en.pdf; *see also* Roberts and Leonard, note 3, at 853.

[39] *See* Christopher Boorse, *On the Distinction between Disease and Illness*, 5 *Phil. & Pub. Aff.* 49, 52–3 (1975); *see also* Roberts and Leonard, note 3, at 853–5.

[40] Jessica L. Roberts, *Health Law as Disability Rights Law*, 97 *Minn. L. Rev.* 1963, 1978 (2013).

[41] *See* Roberts and Leonard, note 3, at 855.

part, on the perceived desirability of that status.[42] Consider an overweight person with no accompanying health issues. She may be considered "unhealthy" based on her weight even without any functional limitations, simply because society deems being overweight undesirable. The "Health at Every Size" movement is a reaction to the common conception that being overweight in and of itself constitutes poor health. Health is, at least to some extent, in the eye of the beholder. It bears emphasis that all definitions of health (including functionalist ones that require setting a norm) are socially constructed.

But the fluidity of what constitutes health aside, our project requires us to have a workable definition. Because we all experience unwanted bodily malfunctions – such as acne, headaches, occasional insomnia, or situational anxiety – we also include an element of *severity* to provide clearer boundaries for the degree of poor health that may be the basis for antidiscrimination claims. Combining both descriptive and normative elements, we define "unhealthy" to mean having a condition – typically related to a functional limitation of a certain degree of severity – that the individual or society regards as undesirable.[43] For example, suppose a person is infertile, meaning that person's reproductive system is not functioning properly; however, we would not consider her unhealthy unless she desires to bear children, or society deems it undesirable to be infertile. The social undesirability of certain conditions may vary by culture, geography, or point in time.

1.2.3. *Health Status*

Healthism includes discrimination against people labeled as unhealthy, under the definition above. A more radical feature of our healthism project is extending our definition to include discrimination on the basis of "health status," including not only individuals suffering from recognized, "static" health conditions but also individuals who engage in *behaviors* associated with poor health. Expanding the scope of our project in this way presents challenges because any number of behaviors, habits, conditions, opportunities, experiences, and exposures may bear on our health. Thus, to say that a particular entity adopts a policy that discriminates based on "health status" in this more inclusive sense, we must clearly define that term and its boundaries.

As noted, our definition of health status includes both health-related traits and health-related conduct.[44] Health-related traits, as we use the term here,

[42] Christopher Boorse, *On the Distinction between Disease and Illness*, 5 *Phil. and Pub. Aff.* 49, 50–7 (1975); *see also* Roberts and Leonard, note 3, at 853–6.

[43] Roberts and Leonard, note 3, at 855.

[44] Roberts, note 3, at 604–7; Roberts and Leonard, note 3, at 858–61.

mean static conditions. Diagnosed conditions, medical records, and genetic test results are all traits. Nicotine use – particularly smoking, which has been linked to so many potential health problems – is the paradigmatic health-related conduct. By the same token, drinking alcohol, not wearing a seatbelt, skiing, mountain climbing, tanning, and having stressful jobs or relationships may also expose individuals to greater health risks. Accordingly, all these habits, behaviors, and activities may be considered "health statuses" for purposes of our definition.

Indeed, the modern understanding of health recognizes that virtually everything we do impacts our health. If nutritionists and physicians recommend drinking eight glasses of water a day, but I do not follow this advice, should I be considered "unhealthy"? If I could prove that I was discriminated against based on my low water consumption, would I have a case for healthism? We think not. Just as we qualify our definition of "unhealthy" based on severity (thereby generally excluding conditions such as cavities and acne), we also limit the category of health-related conduct to activities tending to correlate with serious health conditions deemed undesirable by the individual or society. Accordingly, working in stressful or high-risk workplaces could be considered health-related conduct for purposes of our definition. Stress can lead to debilitating anxiety, heart disease, and general reduction in immune system functioning – conditions that most people consider undesirable. A more dramatic example is a victim of an abusive relationship, the stress of which can lead to a range of physical and psychological health conditions.

Including health-related conduct is consistent with modern antidiscrimination theory. Historically, antidiscrimination law has been largely trait-centric, focusing protecting characteristics deemed "immutable." The rationale is that it is unfair to disadvantage someone for something outside of her control.[45] If a person chooses, causes, or could change the attribute, however, that trait would not warrant antidiscrimination protection. Whether intentional or not, focusing on immutability encourages people to alter their behavior or to assimilate to avoid facing disadvantage. We join leading scholars in rejecting immutability as a justification for antidiscrimination law.[46]

Immutability does not lend itself to healthism because so much health status relates to conduct and, therefore, is potentially mutable. Despite the challenges that our expanded definition presents, including conduct is essential to our project. Drawing a line between traits and conduct would be difficult and artificial. Health-related traits and health-related behavior necessarily overlap; many of our traits are the results of our conduct. Smoking may lead to lung

45 Jessica A. Clarke, *Against Immutability*, 125 *Yale L.J.* 2, 4 (2015).

46 Ibid.

cancer. Eating sugary foods may lead to diabetes. Drinking alcohol may lead to liver disease. The connection between traits and conduct could even extend to the cellular level. We all acquire our DNA by chance from our parents. This genetic information is then a static trait. But it is not that simple. Although much of our genetic information is fixed at birth, our conduct can also affect our DNA. It can impact both our gene structure through epigenetic changes and mutations and how our genes function (or malfunction).[47] Differentiating the trait from the underlying conduct can present a serious challenge.

We also reject perceived voluntariness as a touchstone for protected status. While holding people accountable for their health-related conduct resonates with the American ideal of personal responsibility,[48] the social determinants of health and the limits of autonomy demonstrate that not all actions are truly voluntary.[49] Returning to the domestic violence victim: If she stays in the abusive relationship, is that voluntary? Should she be denied any protection from discrimination for the resulting health conditions? If someone remains in a high-stress job due to financial and job-market constraints, is that voluntary? If a person cannot lose weight because she cannot afford healthy food and lacks time and access to safe exercise options, is she overweight by choice? Additionally, even voluntary conduct might warrant protection if it is private, legal, and does not affect others.

1.2.4. *Normative Wrong*

We have now almost arrived at a workable definition of healthism. Healthism, as we define it, means both intentional and unintentional differentiations that disadvantage people based on either their health status or their perceived unhealthiness. We focus on a broad range of disadvantaging treatment, including policies, practices, or patterns of behavior that are part of an organization's structure, such as an employer's general refusal to hire elderly or overweight workers. But even these limitations are not enough. People who have not graduated from college face clear disadvantages in employment, but few would call that discrimination. And it is not about being rational either. An employer who refuses to hire graduates of the University of California–Los Angeles because the company's president went to the University of Southern California would be discriminating arbitrarily, yet the policy would violate no

[47] *See* Mark Rothstein, Yu Cai, and Gary E. Marchant, *The Ghost in Our Genes: Legal and Ethical Implications of Epigenetics*, 19 *Health Matrix* 1 (2009).

[48] Roberts and Fowler, note 25.

[49] Ibid.; Roberts and Leonard, note 3, at 893–4.

law.[50] Here we return to the meaning of discrimination, focusing now on its normative implications. We ask, what makes disadvantaging people based on health status wrong?

Often the distinguishing factor between wrongful discrimination and socially acceptable differentiation is the basis of the discrimination itself. Whether a status warrants antidiscrimination protection is highly contextual, and dependent on culture and history.[51] Prohibited bases for discrimination usually have personal or social significance or have been the foundation of past subordination.[52] Race and ethnicity, sex/gender, religion, age, and disability are well-accepted antidiscrimination categories.[53] The question then remains, should the law prohibit discrimination based on health status?

It would be easy to fall back on the disparate impact that healthism has on other protected bases like race or disability to justify antidiscrimination protection. That approach, however, does not require looking to health status as an independent basis. In other words, the fact that certain groups are disparately impacted because of their health status does not answer the question whether healthism constitutes its own independent form of discrimination.[54] Importantly, health-status discrimination does not always overlap with already-recognized forms of discrimination.

As explained earlier in this chapter, existing antidiscrimination theories do not neatly apply to healthism. Healthism is not categorically undesirable in the same way racism is. Moreover, health status encompasses not only groups and traits – the familiar territory of antidiscrimination laws – but also conduct. Yet just because healthism does not fit squarely into an existing antidiscrimination paradigm does not mean that it fails to generate a normative wrong. In fact, as we discuss at length in Chapter 2, healthism can violate important values

[50] This example originally appeared in Roberts, note 27, at 2110.

[51] Larry Alexander, *What Makes Wrongful Discrimination Wrong?: Biases, Preferences, Stereotypes, and Proxies*, 141 *U. Pa. L. Rev.* 149, 153 (1992) ("[T]he line between wrongful and acceptable discrimination is, in most cases, difficult to locate with precision because it is historically and culturally variable."); *see also* Roberts, note 2, at 1172–3 (providing various illustrations of how the distinctions among discrimination rely on culture and history); Roberts, note 27, at 2110 ("Often the determination of whether a practice is discriminatory in the pejorative sense turns on whether the conduct in question leads to disadvantage on the basis of a characteristic that either has personal or social relevance, or has been the basis for systematic social subjugation in the past."); Roberts and Leonard, note 3, at 854.

[52] Roberts, note 27, at 2110–12; Roberts and Leonard, note 3, at 839.

[53] Roberts, note 27, at 2110 (citing Civil Rights Act of 1964 § 703(a), 42 U.S.C. § 2000e-2(a) (2006); Americans with Disabilities Act of 1990 § 102(a), 42 U.S.C. § 12112(a) (2006); Age Discrimination in Employment Act of 1967 § 4(a), 29 U.S.C. 623(a) (2006)).

[54] Roberts and Leonard, note 3, at 856.

related to welfare, equality, liberty, and justice. Running afoul of these values is precisely what makes a health-based differentiation "wrong."

1.3. ANTICIPATED OBJECTIONS TO HEALTHISM

We recognize several important challenges for a theory of healthism, including some issues that we have already flagged: the heterogeneity of "health status" or the "unhealthy"; the inclusion of arguably voluntary behaviors bearing on health and the associated difficulty of determining what conduct is truly voluntary; the intersectional nature of health and health-status discrimination with other traits and bases for discriminatory treatment; and the existence of established legal protections for overlapping conditions, including – but not limited to – disability, pregnancy, genetic information, and age. Perhaps the biggest challenge to our project, however, is the fact that differential treatment based on health-status, in more than a few cases, will not be deemed normatively wrong.

Consider an employer's policy to refuse to hire tobacco users or obese workers. The employer undoubtedly singles out groups of potential workers, based on their health status, for less favorable treatment – namely, refusal to hire. Thus, there is (1) differentiation (2) based on health status. The harder question is whether there is a normative wrong. The employer may argue that its hiring policy is utterly rational because it could readily anticipate that workers with those particular health statuses will be more expensive to insure; more likely to become ill and miss work; and less productive due to slower mobility, physical discomfort, and the need for smoke (or other) breaks. Because there are good reasons for the discriminatory treatment, the employer might assert that the policy should not be deemed healthist. As we discuss in Chapters 3 and 6, under our four guiding principles of health welfare, health liberty, health equality, and health justice, we reach a different conclusion for this example.

By the same token, the long-standing practice of health insurers before the Patient Protection and Affordable Care Act of 2010[55] (ACA) – the signature congressional health reform law enacted under President Barack Obama, discussed in depth in Chapters 3 and 4 – was to make decisions about which individuals to cover and how much to charge in premiums, based on individual risk profiles. Risk profiles include detailed personal information about existing health conditions, genetic predispositions, age, sex/gender, geography, weight,

[55] Patient Protection & Affordable Care Act of 2010, Pub. L. No. 111-148, 124 Stat. 119 (2010), available at www.gpo.gov/fdsys/pkg/PLAW-111publ148/pdf/PLAW-111publ148.pdf.

employment, education, and other demographics – essentially, any data that would help an insurer predict an applicant's likelihood of using covered medical care. This practice of "experience rating" is commonplace in insurance. To issue a life insurance policy, for example, insurers typically require a physical exam. The insurer bases its decision of whether the person is an insurable risk and how much to charge in premiums on its estimate of life expectancy relative to the term of coverage. Likewise, automobile insurance policy premiums are lower for individuals with safe driving records, and auto insurers use statistical predictions based on age, sex/gender, and other demographics. Flood insurance may be unavailable or very expensive for a homeowner living in a flood plain (absent federal subsidies[56]).

Experience rating seems eminently rational. To be sure, health insurers would prefer not to insure individuals who are already ill or who are very likely to become ill. Viewing insurance as financial protection against unexpected risk, such an individual would hardly be considered insurable. There is no longer an unexpected risk but, rather, a known need for medical treatment. Even if an insurer were to issue a policy to someone with a known health condition, the insurer would rationally prefer to charge higher premiums to cover the greater risk – or, in the case of someone who is already sick, the certainty – of using medical care. By contrast, health insurers would prefer to insure individuals with little risk of needing health care and could offer them policies that cost less because the predicted exposure is much lower.

For an insurance risk pool to function properly, insurance companies require a mix of "good" (or low) and "bad" (or high) risk individuals. The low-risk individuals pay premiums in an amount that may well exceed the cost of medical care that they end up using. But if they are risk-averse, they may prefer paying an amount certain on a monthly basis rather than facing the uncertainty of unexpected catastrophic costs. The high-risk individuals may well use more medical care than they have paid in premiums, but the surplus premiums from the low-risk individuals end up covering those costs, as well as the insurers' overhead and profit. Depending on the composition of the risk pool, the insurer may have to increase premium rates across the board to generate adequate reserves to cover the costs of medical care utilized by the insured individuals. Even with decently accurate risk predictions and corresponding premium rates, and a balance of good and bad risks, insurers

[56] *See, e.g.*, National Flood Insurance Program, 42 U.S.C. § 4011 (2012); The National Flood Insurance Program, FEMA, www.fema.gov/national-flood-insurance-program (last accessed June 28, 2017).

themselves may be concerned about unexpectedly high claims from the individuals whom they insure. Accordingly, they may purchase reinsurance or "stop-loss" coverage – essentially, "insurance for insurers" – to reduce their own financial uncertainty.

Another element of insurable risk is that the loss is outside the insured's control. For that reason, life insurance policies typically exclude coverage for suicide, and liability insurance policies typically exclude coverage for intentional harms. Insuring such actions may lead to "moral hazard," meaning the increased tendency of individuals to engage in certain activities if they know that they are insured. In health insurance, moral hazard may manifest as individuals seeking more medical care than they would if they were uninsured. That tendency may be desirable, as in the case of preventive or diagnostic treatment, or undesirable in the case of emergency room care for nonemergency conditions. Health insurers "check" moral hazard by requiring copayments from the insured at the time of service, or applying deductibles, which require the insured to cover a certain amount of cost before the policy coverage kicks in.

The point of this discussion is that there are ample rational reasons for health insurance companies to discriminate based on the health status of individuals whom they choose to insure. The prevailing model of insurance – described in more detail in Chapter 4 – has long allowed experience rating in health insurance, as in other insurance contexts. The common law of private contracts – discussed at greater length in Chapter 5 – also largely privileges such practices, allowing private individuals to choose with whom they do business. But an insurer's refusal to sell a policy to someone who is ill operates, quite explicitly, as (1) differentiation (2) based on health status. On the question of normative wrong, insurers and free-market libertarians would argue that there is none. First, a health insurer should not be expected to insure against known health conditions. Moreover, low-risk individuals should not be expected to subsidize medical care provided to high-risk individuals. Finally, charging the same premiums regardless of how much medical care an individual uses only exacerbates moral hazard. What incentive – aside from safety and some sense of moral or legal duty – do I have to avoid traffic law violations if my auto insurance rates will not rise as a result?

To argue that experience rating in health insurance is normatively wrong and, therefore, healthist, we must espouse a different view of health insurance, as the framers of the ACA did. Instead of health insurance being a way for individuals to protect themselves against unknown financial risks, health insurance instead is a way for society to provide access to essential medical care to a substantially larger portion of the population. By design, low-risk individuals subsidize high-risk individuals. Thus, this account of health insurance seeks to improve the health of the community and views access to health care as more of an entitlement than a privilege. Again, under our guiding theoretical principles, on balance, we deem experience rating in health insurance healthist.

Another argument against recognizing healthism is that policies that appear discriminatory may actually be health-neutral. For example, a commercial airline's decision to charge obese passengers for two seats may not discriminate based on health-status but, rather, is a health-neutral policy that charges passengers for the number of seats they occupy and are thereby unavailable to be sold to other customers. By the same token, it would not be discriminatory against parents to charge for two seats even if a toddler ends up in her parent's lap, instead of the seat purchased for her, during the entire flight. The charge for two seats merely reflects the lost opportunity to sell the child's seat to another customer. The reason for the differential treatment is about the number of seats, not about health status.

Similarly, in personal injury, or tort, law, we explore examples of unhealthy defendants who have injured another person by transmitting a contagious disease or who have performed a duty – such as medical treatment – with a health impairment. If those defendants are held liable for the harms that they inflict, one could say that they are treated unfavorably based on their health statuses. On the other hand, one could argue that they are being held to the same standard of care as a healthy person and fall short of that standard by failing to take reasonable precautions. The reason for the verdict in favor of the plaintiff is, therefore, not about the defendant's health status but her failure to exercise reasonable care under the circumstances. Recall that we include not only intentional, but also disparate impact discrimination in our definition. We explain whether, and why, some of these facially neutral examples nevertheless are healthist in Chapter 5.

Readers may also balk at including certain activities, in particular, smoking, as prohibited bases for discrimination. Our definition would seem to protect an adult engaged in a habit linked to a variety of serious health conditions for the individual and those around her, just as it would cover a child diagnosed with type 1 diabetes. Are we prepared to defend a civil rights law for smokers? Many may readily agree that the child should not be denied a health insurance policy or access to blood-sugar monitoring equipment. But should smokers receive similar protection? The short answer is – sometimes. We do not propose across-the-board legal protections for smokers but conclude that certain anti-smoking policies and laws are healthist. Specifically policies that are based on animus or unfair stereotypes, unduly infringe on private conduct, fail to improve health or promote healthier choices, reduce access to health care, or deepen disparities are normatively wrong and, therefore, healthist.

This discussion demonstrates that our approach to healthism is fluid. That fluidity may strike some readers as unworkable and hopelessly indeterminate. Stigma and stereotypes are social constructs that may change over time. Could a policy that is healthist today not be so tomorrow? Some of our factors turn on whether a particular law, policy, or practice is effective. Does smoking, in fact, decrease when taxes on tobacco products are increased? Must we then wait for scientific testing of that question before clearing the policy as non-healthist?

We recognize these and other challenges with applying our rubric, but we emphasize that what we offer are guideposts and factors for consideration, not a definitive, one-size-fits-all remedy. Our flexible framework is akin to the reasonable care standard in the law of negligence. Under tort law, a defendant may be deemed negligent, and therefore liable for injuring another, if she fails to exercise reasonable care under the circumstances. What counts as reasonable care, however, may be different from one place and time to another. Moreover, some formulations of reasonable care turn on a cost-benefit analysis, comparing the cost of prevention to the quantum of safety gained. Those elements may also change with new science and new technology, just as our conclusions about the health effects of various strategies to reduce tobacco usage may change. Nevertheless, courts and juries can – and do – draw conclusions about what constitutes reasonable care under the circumstances. The broad contours of tort law provide guidance for other actors aiming to conduct themselves in such a way to avoid liability. Similarly, we believe that our flexible approach to healthism will provide guidance to government and private actors seeking to avoid acting in healthist ways. To be sure, healthism is a complex, multilayered concept.

2

Understanding Healthism

2.1. INTRODUCTION

In Chapter 1 we considered both the reasons for and the major objections to recognizing healthism as a form of discrimination. While healthism can lead to a number of social ills, there are still many good reasons to differentiate based on health status. Must we forgo those potential benefits to avoid the potential harms? We respond with a resounding: "No."

As we explore in Chapters 3–5, current legal protections leave much socially undesirable healthism unaddressed. Yet we do not want to discount the value of some health-status differentiations. To that end, we believe it is possible to distinguish between "good" (or socially desirable) health-status distinctions and "bad" (or socially undesirable) health-status discrimination.

With respect to the "good" category, we recognize that health-status differentiations can generate welfare or utility, facilitate healthy decision-making, reduce health risks, lower costs, and lead to better health care and increased access. When individuals have the ability to make meaningful choices about their health and health care, distinguishing on the basis of health can actually have a positive impact. Namely, health-status differentiation can create incentives for people to improve their own – as well as society's – health.

"Bad," or healthist, distinctions can have serious negative consequences. Healthist laws and policies may be the result of animus, rather than thoughtful, evidence-based policymaking. Moreover, even if not motivated by animus, healthism can express a view that people who are unhealthy have lower social value, leading to stigma. Healthism can also worsen health outcomes and create or perpetuate health disparities. It can punish people for their private conduct. It can even impede access to health care or undermine the ability to make healthy decisions.

In this chapter, we provide a theoretical framework for distinguishing socially beneficial health-based differentiations from socially damaging healthism. This chapter describes the guiding principles underlying these subtle distinctions. In Chapter 6, we apply these principles to a working paradigm, testing it against discrete examples. In broad-brush terms, if distinguishing based on health actually improves health, lowers costs, and reduces disparities, it would be hard to judge that conduct as healthist, at least by our definition. Our approach permits and encourages health-status distinctions that promote wellness, healthy decision-making, and access to health care. On the other hand, our approach discourages health-status differentiations that are based in animus, create stigma, intrude on private conduct, limit access to health care, impede the ability to make healthier choices, generate poorer health outcomes, or exacerbate existing health disparities. When a health-status distinction neither harms nor helps, we remain neutral. But how are we to know the difference?

2.2. GUIDING PRINCIPLES

Our definition of healthism from Chapter 1 includes a normative wrong. In other words, a "healthist" law or policy must offend some core norm or value. We offer four governing principles to guide this analysis: (1) health welfare, (2) health liberty, (3) health equality, and (4) health justice. We do not attempt to rank these principles in terms of their relative importance.[1] To be sure, some people may believe that health liberty should always carry the day, while others may be strict health egalitarians. And certain circumstances may implicate one of these four principles over the others. If a particular practice violates *all* of these values, however, we can safely say that it is healthist. Likewise, if a health-status differentiation advances *all* of these values, that result is strong evidence that the policy is not only nondiscriminatory but also socially desirable. Of course, those examples are the easy cases; the hard cases are ones in which the guiding principles point in different directions. When these values conflict, the categorization as "healthist" or benign is less clear.

[1] It would appear that Cass Sunstein agrees with this type of approach to policymaking. *See* Cass R. Sunstein, *The Ethics of Influence: Government in the Age of Behavioral Science* 4 (Cambridge University Press, 2016) (explaining that "it is often possible to make progress by bracketing the deepest theoretical questions, and by seeing if some approaches compromise none of the values and can attract support from people who are committed to all of them, or who are uncertain of their relationship").

2.2.1. Health Welfare

One important consideration when distinguishing benign considerations of health status from socially damaging healthism is whether the health-based distinction benefits society as a whole. In other words, does it produce net social welfare?

Considering how something affects the common good is an example of one well-accepted form of welfarism: classical utilitarianism. The utility principle seeks to facilitate the greatest good for the greatest number. As Jeremy Bentham famously explained, an action is moral when its tendency to increase the community's happiness exceeds its tendency to lower the community's happiness.[2] Bentham further opined that the ability of a law or policy to generate utility is the "measure of the Government." For utilitarian welfarists, maximizing utility or welfare should be the ultimate goal of law- and policy-makers.

Conversations about welfare maximization frequently employ the notion of efficiency. While the utility principle describes how governments should function, efficiency captures the kinds of outcomes they produce. Utilitarians believe that regulations should put resources to their most efficient use: maximizing the benefit to society, while minimizing the costs. Cost-effectiveness is then a decidedly welfarist concern. A utilitarian view of tort law, for example, would impose liability only when the cost of additional precautions is cheaper than the amount of safety – or accident avoidance – to be gained. If we held people liable whenever they failed to take safety precautions, even when the amount of safety gained was relatively minimal, the result would be inefficient, wasting societal resources and, thereby, reducing overall social welfare. Accordingly, we do not require all cars to drive only twenty-five miles per hour. While that precaution might reduce the number and severity of automobile accidents, it would cost society in terms of other things we value, such as timely movement of goods and services, driving enjoyment, fuel efficiency, and time spent on other endeavors.

In the context of health, increasing social welfare might mean raising average life expectancies and improving quality of life, whereas minimizing costs would entail lowering risks and reducing expenditures. Thus, cost-effectiveness alone may not justify classification based on health status. With the relatively recent rise of neoclassical economics, monetary gain became a major criterion in the welfare calculus. Previously, utilitarians tended to focus on maximizing happiness and minimizing suffering.[3] Today, many welfarists look to whether a given

[2] Jeremy Bentham, *An Introduction to the Principles of Morals and Legislation* 7 (Clarendon Press, 1907) (1789).

[3] James Fieser, *Moral Philosophy through the Ages* (2001), www.utm.edu/staff/jfieser/class/300.

policy satisfies a person's preferences to determine whether it enhances welfare.[4] The idea is that if each individual maximizes her own welfare, then, in the aggregate, social welfare will be maximized. But regardless of how you define welfare, other competing yet important values still exist. As we discuss later in this book, even welfare-enhancing health-status differentiations may raise concerns related to privacy, autonomy, equality, and justice.

Another important consideration in welfare analysis is externalities. Externalities are costs or benefits that affect third parties.[5] For example, a factory located close to a residential area may produce pollution that bothers the neighboring homeowners. That pollution is a negative externality.[6] The factory may be increasing its and consumers' welfare by producing goods that consumers desire and purchase, but the residential neighbors' welfare is reduced because of the pollution. Unhealthy behaviors also can impose negative externalities, as others may be forced to bear the costs of another person's health-related decisions. M. Todd Henderson has argued that employees who smoke impose externalities on their coworkers, in the form of either higher health insurance premiums or lower wages.[7] Smoking may impose further costs on the corporation and its shareholders through reduced productivity and higher health-care costs. These externalities produce inefficiencies and reduce overall social welfare. The goal, then, of law- and policy-makers is to make sure that we all fairly bear – or, in the words of economists, *internalize* – the costs that we create. The factory, for example, would need to pay the homeowners an amount that represents the value of the pollution-free air that they are giving up and incorporate that cost into the price of its product.[8]

Because individual preferences are frequently the modern measure of welfare, it would seem that laws or policies that ignore individual preferences would undermine welfare. Sometimes policies designed to promote health will be contrary to the individual's – at least short-term – wishes, making the intervention arguably paternalistic.[9] For instance, while a person might crave

4 *See* Connie S. Rosati, *Persons, Perspectives, and Full-Information Accounts of the Good*, 105 *Ethics* 296 (1995) (defining preferentism); *see also* Matthew D. Adler, *Happiness Surveys and Public Policy: What's the Use?*, 62 *Duke L.J.* 1509, 1511 (2013) (defending preferentism); Daniel Haybron, *The Pursuit of Unhappiness* 34 (Oxford University Press, 2010) (describing preferentism as "the theory to beat").

5 John Black, Nigar Hashimzade, and Gareth Miles, *Externality*, A *Dictionary of Economics* (Oxford University Press, 5th edn. 2017).

6 Mark Seidenfeld, *Microeconomic Predicates to Law and Economics* 63–4 (Lexis Nexis, 1996).

7 M. Todd Henderson, *The Nanny Corporation*, 76 *Univ. Chi. L. Rev.* 1517, 1518 (2009).

8 Ibid.

9 *See* Lindsay J. Thompson, Paternalism, in *Encycl. Bus. Ethics and Soc'y* 1 (Sage Publications, Inc., Robert W. Kolb ed., 2008) (explaining that paternalism infringes on autonomy with the intention of protecting or benefiting the individual).

a cupcake or a cigarette in a given moment, she would ultimately prefer to be a thinner nonsmoker in the longer term. A paternalistic policy could outright ban cupcakes or cigarettes or it might just increase the costs of eating baked goods or smoking in such a way that alters someone's short-term preferences in the name of moving her closer to the long-term goal of weight loss or smoking cessation.[10] Not surprisingly, given the popularity of neoclassical economics, welfarists tend to be anti-paternalistic, or at least they would limit paternalism to situations in which one's preferences could harm someone else, not merely oneself.[11] That view might justify requiring a person to be immunized, even against her will, but not to require her to lose weight.[12]

In certain cases, however, paternalistic interventions can generate real social benefit, consistent with welfarism. Consider the trend of "Tobacco 21" laws, which increase the legal age for buying tobacco products from eighteen to twenty-one years of age. While a nineteen-year-old might want to light up a cigarette, these laws would prohibit her from simply walking into a convenience store and buying a pack. To the extent that they undermine the preference of some young people to smoke, Tobacco 21 laws are paternalistic. Importantly, however, they do not make underage smoking *illegal*; they merely make it harder for anyone under the age of twenty-one to obtain cigarettes. Tobacco 21 laws are one example where the costs may be well worth the benefits. To start, we as a society do not value smoking highly, let alone underage smoking, and evidence shows that increasing the smoking age can reduce the smoking rate and the purchasing of cigarettes.[13] The long-term health benefits at both the individual and population levels would appear to outweigh any concerns about paternalism or short-term welfare loss experienced by the eighteen- to twenty-year olds who can no longer purchase tobacco products. In short, Tobacco 21 laws appear to increase net social welfare. In addition, such laws are potentially in the smoker's long-term best interest, even if against her short-term individual preferences.

But the devil is in the details. Simple predictions about how policies might affect individual behavior and social welfare may not play out as predicted. Take one particularly provocative study on the impact of cigarette taxes on

[10] *See generally* I. Glenn Cohen et al., *Nudging Health: Health Law and Behavioral Economics* (Johns Hopkins University Press, 2016).

[11] Richard A. Epstein, *In Defense of the "Old" Public Health: The Legal Framework for the Regulation of Public Health*, 69 *Brooklyn L. Rev.* 1421 (2004).

[12] For a well-stated contrary view, *see generally* Lindsay F. Wiley et al., *Who's Your Nanny? Choice, Paternalism and Public Health in the Age of Personal Responsibility*, 41 *J.L. Med. & Ethics* 88 (2013), www.aslme.org/media/downloadable/files/links/j/l/jlme-41_1-wiley-supp.pdf.

[13] Stephanie R. Morain, et al., *Have Tobacco 21 Laws Come of Age?*, 374 *N. Engl. J. Med.* 1601–4 (2016).

the federal budget. It found that cigarette taxes would reduce federal spending in the short term due to increased population health. In the long term, however, as people live longer, the tax might increase spending because the government will spend resources – in the form of federal retirement benefits and government health-care programs – on people who otherwise would have died prematurely from smoking-related issues.[14] If this study is correct and we adopt an economic definition of welfare, a cigarette tax might actually, over time, *decrease* social welfare. To put it in harsh cost-benefit terms, it could actually be more efficient for would-be smokers to conserve resources by dying as quickly and as cheaply as possible. A cigarette tax designed to discourage smoking might be paternalistic in the sense of being in an individual's best interest but not welfare-enhancing – at least in purely economic terms – for society as a whole. Of course, that is a bleak way to look at the world. Under a nonmonetary view of welfare, the cigarette tax could be considered welfare-enhancing because the individuals who do not die prematurely from smoking clearly obtain an individual benefit from living longer.

We can also consider two other notorious paternalistic policies, the Snooki tax and the Big Gulp ban.[15] The Snooki tax got its name when reality television star Nicole "Snooki" Polizzi asserted that the Affordable Care Act's 10 percent tax on indoor tanning was aimed at her personally.[16] The Big Gulp ban referred to a short-lived New York City law, enacted under Mayor Michael Bloomberg, which capped the sale of certain sugary beverages to sixteen-ounce servings.[17] Much as Tobacco 21 laws do not outright bar underage smoking, neither the tanning tax nor the portion control law actually removes a person's ability to patronize tanning salons or buy sugary drinks – they just make these activities more costly. The indoor tanning tax merely makes the activity more

[14] James R. Baumgardner et al., *Cigarette Taxes and the Federal Budget – Report from the CBO*, 367 *N. Engl. J. Med.* 2068–70 (2012).

[15] *See generally*, Jessica L. Roberts and Elizabeth Weeks Leonard, *What Is (And Isn't) Healthism*, 50 *Ga. L. Rev.* 833, 892–3, 903–6 (2016) (concluding that the Snooki tax "seems unlikely to affect the ability to make healthy choices, worsen health outcomes, or create health disparities," and that the Big Gulp ban does not clearly produce positive effects).

[16] 26 U.S. Code § 5000B; Robert Farley, *Snooki Says Obama Put a 10 Percent Tax on Tanning*, *Politifact* (June 21, 2010), www.politifact.com/truth-o-meter/statements/2010/jun/21/snooki/snooki-says-obama-put-10-percent-tax-tannning/; IRS, *Excise Tax on Indoor Tanning Services Frequently Asked Questions*, www.irs.gov/businesses/small-businesses-self-employed/excise-tax-on-indoor-tanning-services-frequently-asked-questions (last visited July 27, 2017).

[17] The New York Court of Appeals ultimately struck down the rule on administrative law grounds. *N.Y. Statewide Coal. of Hispanic Chambers of Commerce* v. *N.Y. City Dep't of Health and Mental Hygiene* (N.Y. June 26, 2014), www.nycourts.gov/ctapps/Decisions/2014/Jun14/134opn14-Decision.pdf; Haley Draznin, *NYC Loses Appeal to Ban Large Sugary Drinks*, *CNN* (June 26, 2014), www.cnn.com/2014/06/26/justice/ny-sugary-drink-rulling/index.html.

expensive, thus possibly nudging individuals away from engaging in it. Likewise, the New York law also did not ban consumption of larger amounts of sugary drinks, but it did make them more expensive and more difficult to obtain (e.g., one would have to buy two smaller drinks instead of one large one). In other words, these laws raise the costs of the unhealthy behavior, which could at some point price out certain individuals. It is worth noting that the effectiveness of these laws is far from clear.[18] But if we as a society do not view tanning or drinking sugary drinks as socially valuable activities, just a modest chance of improving health might be enough to justify the policy.

The Tobacco 21 laws, the Snooki tax, and the Big Gulp are relatively "soft" forms of paternalism, encouraging healthier choices while falling short of outright prohibiting unhealthy ones. And even though they might violate some individual preferences, there still may be a net welfare gain. Nevertheless, these policies may not be efficient long-term interventions. Tobacco 21 laws, the Snooki tax, and the Big Gulp ban do not educate the public about the health risks of nicotine use, UV exposure, and refined sugar.[19] Thus, while individuals could end up making healthier choices, those decisions may not translate into better decisions when confronted with opportunities to smoke electronic cigarettes, sun bathe at the beach, or eat an ice cream sundae.

Those three laws are government interventions. But private actors, including employers and businesses, may also adopt welfarist policies.[20] To be sure, they do not have the same coercive power as the state. Mainly, they cannot prosecute and incarcerate a person. Regardless, private actors can be powerful nannies. Employment in particular serves as a strong incentive. For example, the nicotine hiring bans from Chapter 1 encourage prospective employees to quit smoking. Additionally, as key providers of health insurance in the United States, employers can use their employee benefits to encourage certain behaviors or to discourage others.[21] Consider employer-provided wellness programs, which reward employees for things like agreeing to biometric testing, lowering cholesterol, losing weight, or quitting smoking. Although an employee can opt out, she arguably does so at a loss–first, because she will not receive the offered benefit and, second, because her employer may spend money on

[18] Jennifer Calfas, *Study: Fewer Adults Use Indoor Tanning Beds*, *USA Today*, (July 2, 2015), www.usatoday.com/story/news/nation/2015/07/01/indoor-tanning-decline-us-adults/29519255; Robert King, *Tanning Troubles: Fewer People Head Indoors to Seek Rays*, *Wash. Examiner* (July 28, 2015), www.washingtonexaminer.com/tanning-troubles-fewer-people-head-indoors-to-seek-rays/article/2569064.

[19] Roberts and Leonard, note 15, at 903–6.

[20] Ibid. at 892–3.

[21] Ibid. at 893.

those programs instead of raises or other amenities. Certainly, a worker who wants to avoid a wellness program could always look for another job. But as anyone who has been on a prolonged job hunt knows, it is often not that easy. Consequently, employers can be very effective regulators, especially when alternative, desirable employment is not easy to come by.[22]

In the past, welfarism has frequently rested on three key assumptions about how people behave. First, welfarists believe that people want to maximize utility through their actions.[23] Second, welfarists maintain that people respond rationally and predictably to incentives.[24] And third, welfarists view individuals as independent, rational actors who make decisions based on relevant, comprehensive information.[25] Yet these assumptions only get us so far. For one thing, behavioral economics acknowledges that people do not always act rationally but, rather, are influenced by implicit bias and other judgment errors.[26]

Moreover, restrictions on individual choice also undermine the rational actor model's theoretical foundations. A variety of factors – including but not limited to where a person lives, her income, education, work schedule, amount of leisure time, relationship status, caregiving responsibilities, ease of mobility or transportation, network of social support, and current health status – may impede the ability to make healthier choices.[27] Efforts to encourage healthy decision-making will inevitably fail if a person lacks meaningful choices. The literature on social determinants of health explains that interventions focused on individual lifestyle changes can backfire if the targeted populations are unable, for the reasons noted above, to make the desired changes. For example, charging smokers more for their health insurance is designed to create an incentive to quit, while potentially offsetting the costs of smoking-related health conditions. But at least one study showed that tobacco surcharges had little effect on smoking cessation but rather resulted in lower insurance uptake by smokers.[28] While it may be rational to quit smoking (for reasons including but not limited to health insurance premiums), people did not respond favorably to the insurance surcharge.

[22] Ibid.

[23] E. Roy Weintraub, *Neoclassical Economics, in The Concise Encyclopedia of Economics* (The Library of Economics and Liberty, 2007).

[24] Ibid.

[25] Ibid.

[26] *See generally Behavioral Law & Economics* (Cass R. Sunstein, ed., 2000).

[27] Wendy K. Mariner, *Beyond Lifestyle Governing the Social Determinants of Health*, 42 *Am. J. L. & Med.* 284 (2016), http://journals.sagepub.com/doi/pdf/10.1177/0098858816658268.

[28] Abigail S. Friedman et al., *Evidence Suggests That the ACA's Tobacco Surcharges Reduced Insurance Take-Up and Did Not Increase Smoking Cessation*, 35 *Health Affs.* 1176 (2016).

Additionally, incentives do not always work the way that law- and policymakers want. When the French colonized Vietnam, they discovered a serious rat infestation in Hanoi.[29] Thinking that they could get the villagers to do the work for them, the French colonial government decided to offer a bounty for every rattail that a person turned in. That is, they designed an incentive system to encourage the trapping and killing of rats. Or so they thought. Instead of leading the villagers to exterminate the pesky vermin, it led the villagers to farm them. The bounty created an unexpected market for rattails, which people filled by raising rats. When an incentive for one thing – like killing rats – has an unanticipated or undesirable effect – like farming rats – economists call that a perverse incentive. Perverse incentives can also occur when law- and policymakers attempt to encourage healthy behavior. We can return to the tobacco surcharge in health insurance. The idea behind the tobacco surcharge was to encourage people to quit smoking by imposing an additional financial burden. For some people, however, the added costs created a perverse incentive. Instead of forgoing *tobacco*, people who were faced with significant financial penalties decided to forgo *health insurance*.[30] Perverse incentives could then undermine even well-intentioned health-status differentiations.

Finally, intervening values like equality, autonomy, privacy, and social justice may render even welfare-generating distinctions based on health status problematic. Imagine that the tobacco surcharge saves insurance companies significant sums of money, resulting in a large net welfare gain, despite a markedly negative effect on the less than 17 percent of Americans who still smoke. Demographically, smokers have lower education and lower income and are disproportionately either multiracial or Native American.[31] They also face widespread social stigma.[32] The law, while improving overall societal welfare, would significantly reduce the welfare of already-disadvantaged populations. Importantly, looking only to net welfare does not tell us whom a policy might harm. In other words, welfarism notoriously neglects distributional concerns.[33]

[29] Robert Peckham, *Epidemics in Modern Asia* 114 (Cambridge University Press 2016); Michael G. Vann, *Of Rats, Rice, and Race: The Great Hanoi Rat Massacre, an Episode in French Colonial History*, 4 *French Colonial History* 191 (2003).

[30] Abigail S. Friedman et al., *Evidence Suggests That the ACA's Tobacco Surcharges Reduced Insurance Take-Up and Did Not Increase Smoking Cessation*, 35(7) *Health Affs.* 1176, 1181 (2016).

[31] Brady Dennis, *Who Still Smokes in the United States – In Seven Simple Charts*, *Washington Post* (Nov. 12, 2015), www.washingtonpost.com/news/to-your-health/wp/2015/11/12/smoking-among-u-s-adults-has-fallen-to-historic-lows-these-7-charts-show-who-still-lights-up-the-most/?utm_term=.ac7981009d8e.

[32] Jessica L. Roberts and Elizabeth Weeks Leonard, *Stigmatizing the Unhealthy*, 45 *J.L. Med. & Ethics* 484 (2017).

[33] *See* Martha C. Nussbaum, *Capabilities & Human Rights*, 66 *Fordham L. Rev.* 273, 281 (1997) (explaining that utilitarianism does not tell us "who has got the money, and whether any of it is mine").

If you care about equality, in particular, you might not want policies to single out certain populations based on animus or negative stereotyping. Alternatively, if you care about liberty, you may not want the government coming in and policing your private conduct regardless of whether that policing is for your – or society's – good. Finally, if you care about justice, you may not want economically or socially disadvantaged populations to bear the brunt of the burden of a welfare-generating initiative. Even the most well-intentioned, rational health-status differentiations can also be harmful if they intrude too deeply into our private lives (health liberty), create or perpetuate stigma (health equality), or exacerbate health disparities (health justice). Because of these complexities and contradictions, understanding and regulating healthism demands a broader theoretical framework. We therefore cannot rely on welfare alone, including in cases where it promotes other important values.

2.2.2. *Health Liberty*

The effect that differentiation based on health status has on liberty is another important consideration when determining whether the law or policy is healthist. Health is highly personal. Too much oversight, whether from public or private entities, could limit choices in a way that infringes on our much-treasured personal freedoms. The United States has enshrined this core liberty value in the Constitution. The first ten Amendments, constituting the Bill of Rights, were added to the Constitution in response to states' calls for greater protection for individual liberties. Notably, the Amendments limit governmental power. The Bill of Rights is a charter of "negative" rights, specifying what the government cannot do to us; it does not include "positive" rights, requiring any particular benefits or services that the government must bestow upon us.[34]

The notion that third parties – particularly the government – should not impede our choices invokes John Stuart Mill's liberty principle, also known as the "harm principle." It holds that impeding liberty is only appropriate to prevent harm to others.[35] According to that reasoning, regulators can tell me not to hurt my neighbor, but I should be free to engage in self-destructive behavior

[34] *See* Elizabeth Weeks Leonard, *State Constitutionalism and the Right to Health Care*, 12 *U. Pa. J. Const. L.* 1325, 1331–2 (2010).

[35] John Stuart Mill, *On Liberty and Utilitarianism* 12 (Alfred A. Knopf, Inc., 1992) (1859); *see also* Jessica L. Roberts, *Rethinking Employment Discrimination Harms*, 91 *Ind. L.J.* 393, 417 (2016). Modern libertarians include Friedrich Hayek and Robert Nozick. *See* Friedrich Hayek, *Law Legislation and Liberty* (University of Chicago Press 1976); Robert Nozick, *Anarchy, State, and Utopia* (Basic Books, Inc. 1974).

if I wish.[36] For example, the government can infringe on my liberty to prevent my spreading a contagious disease, but it cannot prevent me from getting the disease myself. Strong libertarianism rejects paternalism of any kind.

Liberty also includes notions of privacy and autonomy. Privacy connotes a "right to be left alone."[37] It allows us to make choices free from public scrutiny.[38] While counterintuitive, privacy is also essential to our relationships.[39] You probably share things with your romantic partner that you would not want to tell your employer. It is privacy that allows you to draw those lines between the secrets you share and the secrets you guard closely. Autonomy describes the ability to make free and independent choices.[40] Autonomy is what gives individuals the ability to live the kind of lives they want. Exercising autonomy, then, requires personal liberty. To make unencumbered choices, we must have the freedom to act.

Privacy and autonomy are, thus, related concepts. Both involve maintaining a certain degree of control over our lives. Policies that differentiate on the basis of health status could threaten both of these core American values. Decisions about how to treat our bodies – including what foods we eat, how much we sleep, the people with whom we have sex, whether we practice yoga or go to CrossFit – are all incredibly intimate.[41] Efforts to change those behaviors both intrude into our private lives and limit our access to free choices.

A law or policy might violate liberty in a variety of ways. It could punish people for private conduct that has no harmful effect on others. It could also cut off resources or otherwise reduce the ability of people to make healthy choices. Healthism could then encroach too deeply into our private lives or could jeopardize our personal freedom.

Consider the bans on hiring nicotine users. Employers are free to adopt tobacco-free workplaces. That is, they can forbid their employees from using tobacco products on the job. A ban on nicotine use is more expansive. It bans more conduct (tobacco versus nicotine) and extends beyond working hours. A person who might want to smoke a pipe (or even use a nicotine patch) in the privacy of her own house during off hours would violate the policy. The nicotine ban at once intrudes on privacy, by following the employee home,

36 Roberts, note 35, at 417.
37 Samuel D. Warren and Louis D. Brandeis, *The Right to Privacy*, 4 *Harv. L. Rev.* 193, 193 (1890).
38 David Orentlicher, *Genetic Privacy in the Patient-Physician Relationship*, in *Genetic Secrets: Protecting Privacy and Confidentiality in the Genetic Era* 77, 78 (Mark Rothstein, ed., Yale University Press 1997).
39 Charles Fried, *Privacy*, 77 *Yale L. J.* 475, 477 (1968).
40 Gerald Dworkin, *The Theory and Practice of Autonomy* 3–5 (Cambridge University Press 1988).
41 Roberts and Leonard, note 15, at 891.

and restricts her liberty, by forcing her to choose between using nicotine and having employment. One might then object to certain healthist policies on libertarian grounds by asserting that they both intrude into the private sphere and limit personal freedom. The lifestyle discrimination statutes described more fully in Chapter 3 purport to protect against "discrimination." However, they are libertarian legislation masquerading as egalitarian.

Yet not all health-status differentiations violate liberty. In fact, some distinctions might actually *promote* liberty by empowering individuals with opportunities and resources to make healthier choices. For example, some employers offer a range of amenities, including on-site health clinics and services, fitness centers, and prescription drugs at little to no cost.[42] These policies give people more options related to their health than they would otherwise have. Although smoking cessation programs explicitly target people based on a health-related factor, namely, smoking status, they offer an opportunity to quit that a smoker might not otherwise have. Distinctions that actually increase personal freedom are not healthist.

Before moving on to the next governing principle – health equality – a quick note about autonomy. Both health welfare and health liberty seem to proceed from the assumption that individuals possess full autonomy. In other words, welfarists and libertarians tend to assume that people are capable of making independent, autonomous decisions. At first blush, those assumptions may make laws or policies that are actually healthist seem unobjectionable. For instance, a welfarist or a libertarian could maintain that if I do not want employers to reject my job application because I am a smoker, I should either respond to the incentive or decide to quit. Of course, anyone who has actually tried to adopt healthier behaviors can attest to the difficulty of breaking a bad habit.[43]

Moreover, the ability to successfully achieve a desired health outcome may not rely solely on individual behavior. Our DNA, which is largely determined before birth and outside of our immediate control, affects personal health in numerous ways. Research has linked genetics to a person's propensity to gain weight.[44] Additionally, body chemistry and other physiological conditions,

[42] Jessica L. Roberts and Leah Fowler, *How Assuming Autonomy Undermines Wellness Programs*, 27 *Health Matrix* 101, 121–23, (2017).

[43] Jessica L. Roberts, *Healthism and the Law of Employment Discrimination*, 99 *Iowa L. Rev.* 571, 615 (2014) (citing Wendy K. Mariner, *The Affordable Care Act and Health Promotion: The Role of Insurance in Defining Responsibility for Health Risks and Costs*, 50 *Duq. L. Rev.* 271, 301 (2012); Harald Schmidt et al., *Carrots, Sticks, and Health Care Reform – Problems with Wellness Incentives*, 362 *New Eng. J. Med.* e3(1), e3(1) (2010) [citing the failure of diets to achieve long-term weight loss even though dieters want, and try, to lose weight]).

[44] *See* Anthony P. Goldstone and Philip L. Beales, *Genetic Obesity Syndromes*, 36 *Obesity and Metabolism* 37 (2008).

genetic or not, may impact a person's weight.[45] Thus, tempting as it may be to blame someone for being overweight, what she weighs may not be totally within her control.[46] Similarly, individuals may be genetically or psychologically predisposed to addictions of various types. Genetics clearly play a role in the incidence of heart disease, diabetes, cancer, and a host of other conditions, regardless of how much a person controls her diet, exercise, stress, and living conditions.

Beyond our genetics and physiology, all kinds of external factors also affect the decisions we make. What very well may have started as a purely voluntary decision could balloon into an undesirable and difficult-to-change situation. Life is inevitably path-dependent. While I might have thought smoking made me look cool and grown-up at age fifteen, by the time I am thirty years old, and seriously addicted, the decision to light up may feel less voluntary.[47] The physiological effects of addiction are now well-known and certainly belie any suggestion that smoking is entirely voluntary. In fact, most smokers would like to quit.[48] And, as many of us know too well, a person may fail to lose weight despite her genuine intent and best efforts. Making matters worse, the more weight a person gains, the more effort it requires to reach a healthy body mass index (BMI), leaving more opportunities for stumbling blocks and challenges.[49] How accountable do we want people to be for unhealthy decisions made at different times, or under different circumstances, in their lives? Is it fair to continue to punish people for something that they sincerely wish they had never done in the first place?

Those questions point to a broader tension regarding what we deem "voluntary." Surely, someone who refrains from certain activity when a gun is held to her head is not acting voluntarily. But there are varying degrees of duress. In the narrowest sense, we could say that a person is acting under duress when responding to a threat created by someone else. But what if the person is put to a hard choice because of conditions or circumstances of her own making? In a classic torts case, an employee who painted the wooden handles of hatchets notified his employer that the drying racks for the tools tend to vibrate because

45 *What Causes Overweight and Obesity?*, National Heart, Lung, and Blood Institute, www.nhlbi.nih.gov/health/health-topics/topics-obe-causes (last visited May 28, 2016).

46 Roberts and Leonard, note 15, at 843.

47 Roberts, note 43, at 614–15.

48 Ibid. at 615 (citing Ann Malarcher et al., *Quitting Smoking among Adults – United States 2001–2010*, 60 *Morbidity & Mortality Wkly. Rep.* 1513, 1513 (2011), www.cdc.gov/mmwr/pdf/wk/mm6044.pdf).

49 Jennifer Bennett Shinall, *Intersectional Complications of Healthism*, 18 *Marquette Benefits & Social Welfare L. Rev.* 255–77 (2017).

of their proximity to other mechanical equipment in the shop.[50] The vibration caused hatchets to fall off the racks onto the employee's workspace, threatening to cut off his fingers. The employer essentially responded: "Use the racks or leave." The case, which took place before workers compensation laws and the modern doctrine of assumption of risk, held that the employee's decision to stay on the job was voluntary. Therefore, he could not sue if he ended up losing a finger. But should it matter whether the employee had a family to support and no other possible employment? Or if he lacked reliable transportation to another, more remote employer? What if all hatchet factories had a similar arrangement, as a matter of industry custom?

Not having access to certain resources can also impair autonomy. For example, poverty or proximity to grocery stores, parks, and urban violence may limit a person's ability to eat fresh fruits and vegetables, to exercise regularly, or to get adequate sleep.[51] Imagine a single parent who is the sole breadwinner for a family with several children. She must work two jobs to make ends meet, leaving her little time for rest or relaxation. Because of limited housing options, she lives in a low-income neighborhood in the inner city. Her neighborhood – while full of fast food restaurants and convenience stores – lacks traditional grocery stores that sell fresh produce. Imagine it is also poorly lit in the evening and has no green spaces where she can take her children to play for free. Gunshots and other crimes are prevalent, thus, further limiting her willingness to venture out of the house. If one of her employers offered her a break on her health insurance premium for losing weight or for lowering her blood pressure, no matter how enticing the incentive, the single parent still would have substantially more difficulty meeting those goals than a married person in a two-income household with no children who lives on a quiet, suburban, residential street or in an urban high-rise with a workout facility and Whole Foods down the block. In short, a person's unhealthy "choices" may in fact be largely outside of her individual control.

Because we recognize that autonomy is not a given but rather aspirational,[52] when we consider health welfare and health liberty we are conscious that some individuals may not have access to the full complement of healthful choices. As such, we support laws and policies that create the opportunity for making healthy choices and recognize that poor health may be the result of myriad factors beyond a person's immediate control.

50 *Lamson* v. *Amer. Axe and Tool Co.*, 58 N.E. 585 (Mass. 1900).

51 Roberts and Leonard, note 15, at 893; *see also* Martha Albertson Fineman, *The Autonomy Myth: A Theory of Dependency* 10, 30 (The New Press 2004); Roberts and Fowler, note 42, at 116–21.

52 Fineman, note 51.

2.2.3. *Health Equality*

Health equality is another important consideration when determining whether a law or policy is healthist. This governing principle provides that all Americans are entitled to equitable, nondiscriminatory treatment with respect to their health. To be sure, there are several reasons why an employer might choose not to hire smokers that have nothing to do with animus or social stereotyping, like increased costs or a desire to encourage people to be healthy.[53] But an employer also might choose not to hire smokers simply because its management does not *like* smokers or believes that smokers are lazy or would undermine the company culture.[54] To single out a person based on her health status, because of an aversion to people perceived as unhealthy, or because of their lowered social value, offends health equality.

The norms underlying health equality are equitable treatment and dignity. Scholars and philosophers have long asserted that human beings have inherent value and deserve to be treated with dignity. Immanuel Kant was clear that people are not a means to an end, but rather an end unto themselves.[55] Therefore, you cannot put a price on human existence. Kant explains, "the sole condition under which anything can be an end in itself has not mere relative worth, i.e., a price, but an inner worth, i.e., dignity."[56] While a welfarist might define value in economic terms, Kant is clear that you cannot put a price on dignity, nor compare it to other values.[57] That is not to say that our approach to healthism will always rank equality above other concerns, but rather that it acknowledges the significance of dignity and the potential for equality to conflict with other guiding principles.

Thus, underlying the health equality principle are the premises that human beings possess dignity and that dignity is priceless. We deserve to be treated equally because we are all equally valuable. Treating a person or group of people worse than their peers offends their dignity by ignoring their inherent value. Thus, acting based on animus or stigma denies our human dignity and is un-egalitarian.

53 Roberts, note 43, at 579–80.

54 Ibid. at 584–6.

55 Immanuel Kant, *Groundwork of the Metaphysic of Morals*, H. J. Paton, trans., 28–29 (Harper Textbooks, 1958) ("[Persons] are objective ends, i.e., things whose existence is an end itself. It is indeed an *irreplaceable* end: you can't substitute for it something else to which it would be merely a means.")

56 Immanuel Kant, *Groundwork of the Metaphysics of Morals*, in *Justice: A Reader* 183–4 (Oxford University Press, Michael. J. Sandel, ed., 2007).

57 Ibid. ("[D]ignity is, infinitively above all price, with which it cannot be brought into comparison or computation without, as it were, violating its holiness.")

Egalitarian concerns are most readily associated with antidiscrimination law. Prohibiting discrimination on the basis of race, sex, age, disability, and genetic information certainly seeks to promote equality. The egalitarian impulse, however, arguably goes beyond the traditional kinds of civil rights laws outlined in Chapter 3 to include insurance law and even torts and contracts. The notion is that similarly situated people should be treated similarly. A woman should not be denied the ability to enter a binding contract or receive a lower tort award than a man simply because of her sex. Perhaps someone who uses tobacco should not pay more for health care than someone who races motorcycles. It is worth being attuned to the possibility that law and policy are animated by underlying animus or stigma. Federal health insurance laws single out tobacco users, allowing insurance companies to charge them up to 150 percent higher premiums than nonusers, but disallow similar discrimination against others with poor health histories, risks, or habits. Is that because the public and law-makers harbor animus toward or stigma against smokers but not motorcyclists?

Human cognitive functions – the same kind of functions that undermine the rational actor model – may lead people to disfavor certain groups or individuals, even when they do not intend to discriminate. While the rat farmers of Hanoi might have been a little too rational for their colonial overlords' good, we know that people do not always act rationally. Far from calculating each of our actions from a blank slate, human cognitive function relies on any number of shortcuts.[58] For instance, human beings appear hardwired to categorize – our brains tend to group like things together.[59] Simplifying the world through categorization allows us to function. The first time you saw a dog, you probably thought: "What is that?" But once you got used to seeing dogs, you figured out that whether you were looking at a Great Dane or a Chihuahua, you were looking at a dog. That means that, even if you have never seen an Alaskan Klee Kai, if you ever meet one, you will not think: "What is that?" You will think: "Oh look, a kind of dog that I have never seen before." Our brains' ability to categorize protects us from information overload. Life would be exhausting and unmanageable if every time

[58] *See, e.g.*, Cass R. Sunstein, *Introduction in Behavioral Law and Economics* 3–7 (Cass R. Sunstein, ed., 2000) (describing various cognitive biases that qualify for strict rational actor model).

[59] Jessica L. Roberts, *Protecting Privacy to Prevent Discrimination*, 56 *Wm. & Mary L. Rev.* 2097, 2116 (citing Linda Hamilton Krieger, *The Content of Our Categories: A Cognitive Bias Approach to Discrimination and Equal Employment Opportunity*, 47 *Stan. L. Rev.* 1161, 1164 (1995); Martha Minow, *Making All the Difference: Inclusion, Exclusion, and American Law* 7 [1990]).

we encountered something new we had to start from scratch. Like the word "discrimination," the word "stereotyping" has both neutral and pejorative connotations.[60] In the neutral sense, stereotyping simply means grouping like things together and making generalizations about their similar or dissimilar attributes. Used in this way, stereotyping makes our brains more efficient and protects us from getting overwhelmed by all the cognitive stimuli we all encounter on a daily basis.

From an equality perspective, however, problems arise because once we categorize things, we may develop preferences and beliefs surrounding those categories. Those stereotypes can be accurate or inaccurate, positive or negative, or value-neutral. Regardless, they can affect our cognitive functioning in both conscious and unconscious ways. For example, if I know I prefer cats to dogs, when I go to an animal shelter I will intentionally select a cat. Even if I do not consciously prefer cats to dogs, I may have beliefs about pet ownership, perhaps that dogs are more work than cats and require more space. Thus, when confronted with equally adorable kittens and puppies, I might select a kitten based on my belief that cats are lower maintenance than dogs, and not based on my preference for cats over dogs. The belief that dogs are higher maintenance than cats is a stereotype, even if it is true. Stereotypes can shape cognitive processes at the unconscious level.[61]

Now consider a more socially problematic example. Imagine the stereotype that men are more assertive than women. A person who holds that stereotypic belief might be more likely to put men in positions of power. A supervisor might then consciously promote Dave over Regina based solely on the stereotype. That decision would be an example of a *conscious* bias. Now assume that the supervisor wants to promote based on merit. Dave and Regina make equal contributions at team meetings. Yet the supervisor might be more inclined to notice and remember Dave's contributions – because they confirm the preexisting belief that men are assertive – than to notice and remember Regina's. Because the supervisor is more cognitively aware of Dave's contributions, the supervisor may then genuinely believe that the decision to promote Dave over Regina is based on merit and not on a stereotype about male assertiveness.

These hypotheticals raise an important point. While some discrimination occurs intentionally, people may unconsciously rely on stereotypes. This

[60] Ibid. at 2117 (citing Linda Hamilton Krieger, *The Content of Our Categories: A Cognitive Bias Approach to Discrimination and Equal Employment Opportunity*, 47 *Stan. L. Rev.* 1161, 1164 [1995]).

[61] Ibid. at 2142 (2015) (citing Linda Hamilton Krieger, *The Content of Our Categories: A Cognitive Bias Approach to Discrimination and Equal Employment Opportunity*, 47 *Stan. L. Rev.* 1161, 1164 [1995]).

cognitive phenomenon is called *unconscious* or *implicit* bias.[62] People are frequently surprised to learn of their own implicit biases.[63] Implicit bias tests are widely available[64] and have appeared in social and popular media.[65]

A significant amount of discrimination follows a common process. To discriminate – either consciously or subconsciously – a person must first recognize some kind of meaningful difference.[66] When we meet our new best friend's pet, we access all kinds of previously obtained information and past experiences that help us distinguish dogs from cats.

Yet for differentiation to move to discrimination (at least the pejorative, or "bad," kind of discrimination), the discriminator must attach a value to the difference.[67] It is one thing for me to say that cats are different from dogs. Imagine, however, that I identify as a cat person. Once a preference emerges, I move from acknowledging difference to attaching value. Instead of just merely saying that cats and dogs are different, I now express the position that cats are somehow – at least in my opinion – better than dogs. Value assignment is typically the second step in the process of discrimination. When I act on that preference, I am discriminating. Therefore, we can think of many kinds of discrimination as occurring in three identifiable steps: (1) differentiation, (2) value assignment, and (3) discriminatory acts (Figure 2.1).[68]

This three-part process captures both intentional and unintentional discrimination. As noted, if I believe that cats are superior animals, I have quite clearly differentiated between dogs and cats (step 1) and consciously assigned a value (step 2 – conscious). And even if I have no preference for cats over dogs, I might unconsciously believe the stereotype that dogs require more time and space, making cats preferable if I live in a small apartment and have a full-time

62 Linda Hamilton Krieger, *The Content of Our Categories: A Cognitive Bias Approach to Discrimination and Equal Employment Opportunity*, 47 *Stan. L. Rev.* 1161, 1165, 1188 (1995); *see also* Tristin Green, *Discrimination in Workplace Dynamics: Toward a Structural Account of Disparate Treatment Theory*, 38 *Harv. C.R.-C.L. L. Rev.* 91, 95 (2003); Melissa Hart, *Subjective Decisionmaking and Unconscious Discrimination*, 56 *Ala. L. Rev.* 741, 745 (2005); Christine Jolls and Cass R. Sunstein, *The Law of Implicit Bias*, 94 *Calif. L. Rev.* 969, 975 (2006); Jerry Kang and Kristin Lane, *Seeing Through Colorblindness: Implicit Bias and the Law*, 58 *UCLA L. Rev.* 465, 467 (2010); Susan Sturm, *Second Generation Employment Discrimination: A Structural Approach*, 101 *Colum. L. Rev.* 458, 460 (2001).

63 *See* Christine Jolls and Cass R. Sunstein, *The Law of Implicit Bias*, 94 *Cal. L. Rev.* 969, 975 (2006).

64 *See*, e.g., Project Implicit, https://implicit.harvard.edu/implicit/takeatest.html (last visited Aug. 1, 2017).

65 American Psychological Association, *Adoption of Implicit Bias Tests Is "Hasty,"* www.apa.org/monitor/2016/12/policing-sidebar.aspx; www.bbc.com/news/magazine-40124781.

66 Roberts, note 59, at 2116.

67 Ibid. at 2117.

68 Roberts, note 59, at 2118.

Differentiation (Categorization) →→ Value Assignment →→ Discriminatory Act(s)

FIGURE 2.1. *Process of discrimination*

job (step 2 – unconscious). While not based on a clear preference, I am valuing cats over dogs given my circumstances. When I select a cat for either conscious or unconscious reasons I am making a discriminatory choice (step 3).

While the three-part process of discrimination applies to both conscious and unconscious bias, it does not capture certain types of unintentional discrimination. Specifically, it does not apply to disparities that result from structural factors rather than individual decision-making. For example, an airline that requires pets in carry-on cases to be under a certain weight would favor cats – which tend to weigh less than most dogs – but not because of any explicit or implicit value judgment about the desirability of cats versus dogs. By the same token, a job that has minimum height or lifting requirements might tend to favor male applicants over females, but not because of any value judgment about women. While certain laws – like the Americans with Disabilities Act – may prohibit structural discrimination, policies that have a disparate impact would not be clearly anti-egalitarian, at least by our definition. They might, however, raise justice-related concerns.

We shift now from pets and gender to health. People also have stereotypic beliefs related to health status. Americans tend to put a premium on health and wellness. People who are considered healthy benefit from any number of positive stereotypes. They are regarded as more attractive, more competent, and more worthy of trust.[69] With respect to poor health, our culture emphasizes the role of personal responsibility over socioeconomic or biological factors.[70] It is not uncommon, then, to blame the sick person for her lot in life[71] – the view that Representative Mo Brooks expressed in the quote that

[69] Roberts, note 43, at 585.

[70] Robert Steinbrook, *Imposing Personal Responsibility for Health*, 355 N. Engl. J. Med. 753 (2006) (defining the concept of personal responsibility and recognizing that the United States government promotes personal responsibility for health); D. B. Resnik, *Responsibility for Health: Personal, Social, and Environmental*, 33(8) *J. Med. Ethics* 444 (2007) ("Although individuals should play an important role in maintaining their own health, they should not be held entirely responsible for it . . . . [There] are many other ways in which societies can promote health, such as through sanitation, pollution control, food and drug safety, health education, disease surveillance, urban planning and occupational health.")

[71] Steinbrook, note 70, at 753 (citing a national survey in which 53 percent of Americans thought it was "fair" to ask people with unhealthy lifestyles to pay higher insurance premiums and higher deductibles or copayments for their medical care than people with healthy lifestyles).

opens Chapter 1. Not surprisingly, individuals who are perceived as unhealthy, like smokers and overweight people, must deal with stereotypes that they are unattractive, incompetent, and without self-control.[72] Notoriously, President Donald Trump repeatedly has revealed stereotypes about weight, for example, disparaging former employee and Miss Universe for gaining weight after being crowned, charging that she "is somebody that likes to eat" and was a "real problem" for contest officials.[73] Even physicians are not immune from these biases. Research shows that doctors tend to undertreat chronic pain, in part due to stereotypes about pain-management patients being addicts.[74] Physicians may also fire patients, believing them to be noncompliant, when the failure to follow the doctor's orders may be due to a lack of understanding or resources.[75]

Stereotypes about health status can lead to animus and stigma. Animus typically means a deeply held – and often irrational – prejudice.[76] Antidiscrimination scholar Elizabeth Emens has explained that "[a] person discriminates based on animus if she treats someone differently because of dislike or hostility towards the protected class of which that person is a member."[77] An employer might adopt a nicotine ban for paternalistic reasons because she wants to provide an incentive for people to quit smoking. Yet an employer could adopt the same policy simply because she despises smokers and thinks they are bad people. Animus therefore speaks to motivation, not to outcome. Courts have been willing to outlaw even rational discrimination based on animus.[78]

Similarly, stigma connotes strong disapproval at a social level. Stigmatization occurs in four steps: (1) acknowledging difference, (2) associating that difference with negative characteristics, (3) classifying people based on

[72] Roberts, note 43, at 585; *see also* Jessica L. Roberts and Elizabeth Weeks Leonard, *Stigmatizing the Unhealthy*, 45 *J.L. Med. & Ethics* 484 (2017).

[73] Jenna Johnson, *Trump Attacks Former Miss Universe Who "Gained a Massive Amount of Weight" and Had "Attitude," Washington Post*, Sept. 27, 2016, www.washingtonpost.com/news/post-politics/wp/2016/09/27/trump-attacks-former-miss-universe-who-gained-a-massive-amount-of-weight-and-had-attitude/?utm_term=.07c1c0a1139e.

[74] *See* Kelly K. Dineen, *Moral Disengagement of Medical Providers: Another Clue to the Continued Neglect of Treatable Pain?* 13 *Hous. J. Health L. & Policy*, 163, 189–198 (2013).

[75] Jessica Mantel, *Refusing to Treat Noncompliant Patients Is Bad Medicine*, 39 *Cardozo* Law Rev. 127 (2018).

[76] *See generally*, Susannah W. Pollvogt, *Unconstitutional Animus*, 81 *Fordham Law Rev.* 887 (2012) (describing the jurisprudential development regarding the meaning of the term "animus").

[77] Elizabeth Emens, *The Sympathetic Discriminator: Mental Illness, Hedonic Costs, and the ADA*, 94 *Georgetown L.J.* 399, 409 (2006).

[78] *Cleburne v. Cleburne Living Ctr.*, 473 U.S. 432, 433, 450 (1985).

that difference, and (4) devaluing people based on the classification.[79] When society devalues the object of stigma, it can lead to exclusion and lowered social status. While animus is personal, stigma is social. Because of the widespread negative stereotypes associated with smoking and obesity, people who use tobacco or are overweight face social stigma.[80] Thus, even if a person does not have animus toward smokers or overweight people, she might still choose not to associate with them because of their inferior social status.

Programs – both public and private – that differentiate on the basis of health status may condone animus and perpetuate stigma.[81] Returning to examples from Chapter 1, when Dr. Bragdon refused to fill Sidney Abbott's cavity, that decision could have well been based in animus or stigma, as people who have HIV have faced ridicule and social exclusion. Turning away HIV-positive patients could perpetuate negative beliefs about that group, mainly that they are risky or dangerous. Perpetuating stigma is especially unfortunate when the stereotypic belief is unfounded. In fact, there is no evidence that HIV can be spread through routine dental care.[82] Social stigma may not only be harmful, but also misinformed.

Policies might not even need to specifically target a particular group or behavior to be healthist. When Mayor Michael R. Bloomberg adopted the Big Gulp ban, the tax applied equally to everyone, making it deceptively facially neutral. But the people of New York knew all too well that the policy was designed to decrease the consumption of sugary drinks because of their health impacts, which include weight gain and diabetes. One objection to bans on unhealthy foods and drinks holds that the law should not punish people who can eat and drink in moderation just because some people lack willpower.[83] Of course this argument is based in inaccurate, disparaging stereotypes about health and weight. Policies like the Big Gulp ban also may lead to animus and perpetuate stigma. If New Yorkers resent having to buy two smaller mochas at Starbucks, rather than one "Trenta" (thirty-one-ounce drink), they may blame overweight people for the cost and inconvenience. Moreover, the law serves

79 Bruce G. Link and Jo C. Phelan, *Conceptualizing Stigma*, 27 *Ann. Rev. Socio.* 363, 367–75 (2001).

80 Jessica L. Roberts and Elizabeth Weeks Leonard, *Stigmatizing the Unhealthy*, 45 *J.L. Med. & Ethics* 484 (2017); *see also* Lindsay F. Wiley, *Shame, Blame, and the Emerging Law of Obesity Control*, 47 *U.C. Davis L. Rev.* 121, 123–28 (2013) (noting public health campaigns aimed at stigmatizing obesity and smoking).

81 Roberts and Leonard, note 15, at 850–1.

82 Oregon Department of Education, *HIV-AIDS Questions and Answers* (2017), www.ode.state.or.us/search/page/?=1107.

83 Wiley, note 79, at 125–6.

an expressive function,[84] signaling that law-makers view a lack of self-control as the reason behind obesity.

Because stereotypes play such a crucial role in human cognition, people may act on their negative beliefs despite their best efforts not to.[85] Consider the ACA's tobacco surcharge. Purportedly, Congress wanted people to quit smoking in an effort to improve public health and reduce health-care costs. Yet, why target tobacco use and not any number of other unhealthy and potentially costly behaviors? Why not drinking alcohol? Eating red meat? Getting inadequate sleep? Failing to exercise? Not using sunscreen? Failing to get the flu shot? Considering how much of our behavior affects our health, the decision to target tobacco use and not other kinds of risky conduct might say more about the social disdain for smokers than the desire to promote health or lower costs.[86] One solution to this thorny dilemma is to ensure that laws and policies designed to facilitate health or curb spending are actually based in evidence and do not target one behavior – or class of people –without a sound empirical justification. Looking to verifiable evidence can help ensure that law- and policy-makers are not acting based on animus or stigma. The ACA includes provisions supporting evidence-based medicine, dubbed "comparative effectiveness research" (CER), at least with respect to medical interventions and treatments.[87] Similar evidence could be further developed with respect to various health-promotion laws and policies. Studying the relative effectiveness of various approaches would also further welfare, ensuring that resources are put to efficient use.

2.2.4. *Health Justice*

The last guiding principle is health justice. Health justice draws from welfarist, egalitarian, and libertarian concerns related to people's access to care and health outcomes. Lindsay Wiley has described health justice as "emphasiz[ing] the need for more probing inquiry into the effects of class, racial, and other forms of social and cultural bias on the design and

[84] Cass R. Sunstein, *On the Expressive Function of Law*, 144 *U. Penn. L. Rev.* 2021 (1996), http://scholarship.law.upenn.edu/cgi/viewcontent.cgi?article=3526&context=penn_law_review.

[85] Roberts and Leonard, note 15, at 886–7.

[86] Ibid. at 887.

[87] *See* Riaz Ali, Morgan Hanger, and Tanisha Carino, *Comparative Effectiveness Research in the United States: A Catalyst for Innovation*, 4(2) *Am. Health & Drug Benefits* 68–72 (2011), www.ncbi.nlm.nih.gov/pmc/articles/PMC4106578/. *Also see* Richard S. Saver, *Health Care Reform's Wild Card: The Uncertain Effectiveness of Comparative Effectiveness Research*, 159 *U. Penn. L. Rev.* 2147 (2011), https://papers.ssrn.com/sol3/papers.cfm?abstract_id=1690684 (identifying limits to the ACA's approach to comparative effectiveness research).

implementation of measures to reduce health disparities."[88] Health justice builds on other social justice movements grounded in human rights, equal opportunity, and fair treatment. Wiley has outlined similar trends in environmental justice, reproductive justice, and food justice.[89] Food justice, for example, focuses on the "disproportionate burden of environmental barriers to healthy food experienced by low-income communities and communities of color."[90] Similarly, health justice recognizes that various factors beyond individual choice affect health, including institutional policies and practices (e.g., where to dump pollutants, build state-of-the-art medical centers, locate walking trails or bike paths, allow liquor or cigarette advertising) as well as social determinants of health. But health justice's unique insight is that those factors are the result of existing bias and privilege and, accordingly, that reforms must address those underlying causes.[91]

Health justice overlaps with other guiding principles that we have discussed, but it also presents a unique set of concerns, values, and directives. From a welfarist perspective, health disparities and a lack of health-care access can reduce both short- and long-term welfare. From a libertarian perspective, limiting people's choices related to their health undermines personal freedom. From an egalitarian perspective, practices that classify and disadvantage certain groups or individuals are potentially animus-driven or stigmatizing. Although related to health welfare, health liberty, and health equality, health justice is distinct. In particular, health justice addresses distributive concerns at a systemic, society-wide level, focusing on underlying institutional structures and biases that have led to the maldistribution of health-care resources and opportunities.[92]

For one illustration of health justice concerns, consider the highly criticized disability law case, *Alexander* v. *Choate*.[93] In *Choate*, a group of people with disabilities challenged Tennessee's decision to reduce the number of Medicaid-covered hospital days from twenty to fourteen. The plaintiffs alleged that the change would disproportionately harm people with disabilities, who as a group tend to need more hospital care. Unconvinced by these

88 Lindsay F. Wiley, *Tobacco Denormalization, Anti-Healthism, and Health Justice*, 18 *Marquette Benefits & Social Welfare L. Rev.* 203–53 (2017).

89 Lindsay F. Wiley, *Health Law as Social Justice*, 24 *Cornell J.L. & Pub. Pol'y* 47(2014).

90 *See* Cassidy R. Hayes and Elena T. Carbone, *Food Justice: What Is It? Where Has It Been? Where Is It Going?*, 5(4) *J. Nutritional Disorders & Therapy* 1–5 (2015), www.omicsonline.org/open-access/food-justice-what-is-it-where-has-it-been-where-is-it-going-2161-0509-1000179.php?aid=64783.

91 Wiley, note 88, at 84–5.

92 Wiley, note 88.

93 *Alexander v. Choate*, 469 U.S. 287, 105 S. Ct. 712 (1985).

arguments, the US Supreme Court upheld the fourteen-day limit, finding that Tennessee did not *intend* to discriminate against people with disabilities when reducing the number of covered hospital days. Moreover, people with disabilities had access to the exact same benefit – fourteen hospital days – as people without disabilities. While the Rehabilitation Act requires giving people with disabilities meaningful access to the Medicaid program, it does not guarantee them "adequate health care." The *Choate* court explicitly noted that Tennessee had no legal obligation to favor people with disabilities in its distributive decisions.

The *Choate* case certainly sounds in the register of healthism: The Tennessee Medicaid policy affects individuals differently based on a health-related factor. Despite its veneer of health-neutrality – the limit applied with equal force to all Medicaid beneficiaries – the *Choate* decision could have a devastating impact based on health status. Many people with disabilities depend on Medicaid as their source of health insurance.[94] They may require more regular and more intensive medical treatment than nondisabled persons. Because health care in the United States is so expensive, people could forgo needed treatment when their insurance fails to cover it. Hence, Medicaid beneficiaries in Tennessee who require longer stays might end up attempting to manage serious medical conditions on an outpatient basis. Or, if they are admitted, patients may find the hospital pushing them out the door because of the billing department's reimbursement concerns. Or they may receive all of the care that is medically appropriate but then face staggering bills for the days not covered by Medicaid. Given that Medicaid is a means-tested health-care program, the chances of the hospital actually collecting the additional charges are quite low. Nevertheless, the hassles of attempted debt collection and bad-debt write-off will add to the cost of doing business with Medicaid. Institutional and individual care providers, accordingly, may be even more reluctant to treat Medicaid patients because of the myriad challenges in getting paid for the care. (Medicaid already reimburses lower than Medicare and commercial insurance, creating a baseline disincentive to treat those patients.) In short, the change to the program would affect people with disabilities more acutely than nondisabled Medicaid beneficiaries. The reduction could limit their access to needed health care and, as a result, lower their relative health, thereby increasing existing health disparities.

Yet what principle of healthism does *Choate* violate? The decision is not clearly welfare-reducing. It could be that the overall benefit of reallocating

[94] *See* David S. Mandell and Colleen L. Barry, *Care for Autism and Other Disabilities – A Future in Jeopardy*, 376 *New Engl. J. Med.* e15 (2017) (describing Medicaid as "the single largest health-care payer for people with autism or developmental disabilities").

limited state funds away from Medicaid (or away from inpatient Medicaid coverage to other Medicaid benefits) outweighed any added burden that people with disabilities felt from fewer hospital days. The policy does not offend health equality because it does not single out people with disabilities based on animus or stereotype. Nor does it clearly violate health liberty. The policy limits, but does not deny, Medicaid beneficiaries' ability to stay in the hospital beyond fourteen days. The Court was careful to point out that people with disabilities have access to exactly the same set of choices as people without disabilities. Moreover, nothing actually forbids people from staying a fifteenth day in the hospital, assuming that they are willing to accept the charges. We might dispute just how voluntary that choice is, but theoretically both healthy and unhealthy individuals enrolled in Medicaid have the same option. Since the decision does not clearly violate health welfare, health liberty, or health equality, we must look to another governing principle to understand why *Choate* may be construed as healthist. Health justice provides such an explanation.

A law or policy transgresses health justice when it impedes health-care access, worsens health outcomes, or creates or perpetuates health disparities. Moreover, health justice acknowledges the underlying biases that influence institutional design choices. Although explicit bias like animus and stereotyping falls more properly under health equality, bias can also have collateral and structural effects. Recall that our definition of health equality does not readily include disparate impact. Instead we focused on individual decision-makers. To be sure, Tennessee cut its Medicaid inpatient hospital benefit not because of – but rather in spite of – its potentially devastating impact on people with disabilities. But why wasn't the state more attuned to the needs of disabled citizenry? Health justice recognizes that biases – including implicit ones – can get baked into a given system in such a way that makes them hard to identify as instances of discrimination. Perhaps ironically, the *Choate* court itself noted that "[d]iscrimination against the handicapped was . . . most often the product, not of invidious animus, but rather of thoughtlessness and indifference – of benign neglect." Yet when the state of Tennessee made Medicaid cuts that would have a disproportionately devastating impact on Tennesseans with disabilities, the state was arguably acting with a bias in favor of the needs of its nondisabled citizens while neglecting people with disabilities.

The effects of this example of benign neglect have clear implications for health justice. The decision in *Choate* impedes health-care access for people with disabilities, who tend to require more covered hospital days. Limiting access to needed care could lead to worse health outcomes. As a group, people with disabilities experience lower levels of relative health and poorer health outcomes than people without disabilities.[95] Taking away six potentially medically necessary hospital days threatens to exacerbate those existing health disparities. In other words, the marginal utility of those additional inpatient days is greater for someone with a disability than for someone whose health status does not rely so heavily on the availability of that type of care.

Health justice then captures important concerns left untouched by the other three guiding principles, particularly the norm of distributive fairness. Because health is so tied up in other important social values, health law and policy should ensure that all Americans can access decent health care and can achieve baseline levels of health. Justice requires allocating society's benefits and burdens fairly across citizens.

John Rawls's concepts of the original position and the veil of ignorance provide a well-known account of justice. The original position is a hypothetical state of affairs in which a group of people convene to structure their society .[96] Behind the veil of ignorance, the framers do not know their race, sex, age, religion, intelligence, skills, level of education, or wealth. Because no one knows where they would stand in a social hierarchy, these hypothetical citizens adopt principles of justice that secure not only basic liberties but also the fair distribution of social resources, thereby creating a moral, just society. For example, imagine that you and I are charged with cutting a delicious cake. If one of us gets to cut the cake and the other gets to choose the first slice, then each of us should get our fair share.[97] Instead of cutting a variety of slices of different sizes and hoping we each get a bigger piece, we would instead cut all of the slices evenly. That result is what Rawls would call perfect procedural justice. In Rawls's hypothetical world everyone starts with certain basic liberties. In reality, of course, all people do not have access to the same set of choices.

Importantly, health justice, as we define it, is distinct from health equality. As a result, formal equal treatment can lead to unjust outcomes. Take the Aesop's fable of the stork and the fox.[98] When the crafty fox invites the stork over for dinner, the fox serves the stork milk (or, according to some versions of the fable, soup) in a shallow bowl. The fox can effortlessly lap up his meal from this container, while the stork – with his long beak – cannot. The stork

[95] Roberts and Leonard, note 15, at 897 (noting that people with disabilities are more likely to use nicotine or be overweight).

[96] Samuel Freeman, *Original Position*, in *The Stanford Encyclopedia of Philosophy* (2016), https://plato.stanford.edu/entries/original-position/#toc.

[97] John Rawls, *A Theory of Justice* (Harvard University Press, 1973).

[98] The US Supreme Court famously relied on this fable in *Griggs* v. *Duke Power Co.*, 401 U.S. 424 (1971), to explain why the law must reach even facially neutral, unintentional forms of exclusion to provide true equality of opportunity.

responds in kind by inviting the fox over for dinner and serving the liquid meal in a long, tall vessel. This time the stork's beak allows him to eat from the narrow jar with ease, and it is the fox that goes home with an empty stomach. Although both the stork and the fox may have been given equal quantities of milk, it would be a stretch to say that a world filled only with shallow bowls or narrow jars would be just for storks or for foxes, respectively.

So what does this discussion mean for our healthism project? Our version of distributive justice requires more than simply equal slices of cake or equal servings of milk. It likewise requires that people will be able to reach the table or will have access to utensils. And of course some citizens will come to the table hungry, while others already have had plenty of cake at home. Of course, applying the notion of distributive justice to real-world examples, such as health care, is a good deal more complicated.

Health justice recognizes that certain policies or laws may disproportionately harm particularly vulnerable groups,[99] including people labeled as unhealthy. For example, certain populations may be more likely to use tobacco or to be overweight. Specifically, people of certain races and ethnicities, people with disabilities, and those with lower incomes are more likely to smoke and to be heavier than their white, able-bodied, more affluent counterparts.[100] Laws and policies that penalize tobacco use and high BMIs, accordingly, will disparately impact these groups. Moreover, those populations already tend to experience lower levels of relative health.[101] Denying them certain privileges, such as reduced premiums or employer-subsidized wellness programs, exacerbates existing disparities and reinforces existing social stratifications.

Efforts to discourage or to punish unhealthy behavior may just pile onto these existing disadvantages. Recall the single parent living in poverty. She already faces significant obstacles to adopting healthy behaviors. Charging her more for health insurance because she does not hit her targeted BMI could simply add insult to injury. It is money diverted away from being able to buy healthier foods (which tend to be more expensive), obtain childcare (so she can exercise, sleep, or de-stress), or even pay for needed health care. Instead of improving her health and wellness, the policy could end up making her worse off. Thus, even well-intentioned differentiations based on health can exacerbate existing health disparities and make the lives of particularly vulnerable people even more challenging. As such, those policies raise distributive justice concerns even if they generate net welfare

[99] Roberts, note 43, at 607; *see also* Roberts and Leonard, note 15, at 905.
[100] Roberts, note 43, at 616–17.
[101] Ibid. at 617–18.

by improving some people's lives or by saving the employer or the health insurer money. In other words, a policy may serve health welfare yet still undermine health justice.

Imagine an employer decides not to hire women of reproductive age. The policy may be, from the employer's perspective, welfare-enhancing. Women of childbearing age, unlike their male counterparts, bear the physical and financial burdens of pregnancy and childbirth. Even if the child is adopted or born by a surrogate, in a heterosexual couple, the woman is more likely to be the primary caregiver for a newborn.[102] A pregnant employee may be costlier than a nonpregnant employee in terms of health insurance and productivity. Arguably, then, it would be economically rational for an employer to adopt a blanket policy against hiring women of childbearing age, say, under fifty. Even if a prospective female employee of that age has no interest in becoming a parent, a blanket policy is cheaper and easier to administer than trying to make individualized determinations regarding which applicants or employees might end up having children. Assuming a steady supply of capable workers that are men or women over fifty, an employer might decide the cost of the ban is worth the benefit.

However, the law restricts an employer's ability to adopt such a policy. Specifically, federal employment discrimination law prohibits discrimination based on age, pregnancy, and family leave.[103] Likewise, the ACA largely prohibits health insurers from making decisions about whom to insure and how much to charge in premiums based on individual health status. With respect to health status in other contexts, however, legal protections remain incomplete. For example, employers generally may refuse to hire tobacco users, obese workers, or other individuals deemed unhealthy or risky. Moreover, although the ACA's Essential Health Benefits (EHB) package includes preconception and prenatal care as "preventive services," the EHB requirement does not apply to employers, and preventive services do not include labor and delivery costs.

While the law would prohibit employers from screening out women of reproductive age, employers can still legally obtain information about their employees' reproductive choices. Companies like Castlight Health have created services to help employers mine their employees' health data, including workers' compensation claims, pharmaceutical records, doctor's appointments,

[102] Josh Levs, *"Primary" Caregiver Benefits Sound Gender-Neutral but Aren't*, *Atlantic*, Oct. 1, 2015, www.theatlantic.com/business/archive/2015/10/primary-caregiver-equality/404266/.

[103] *See* Age Discrimination in Employment Act of 1967, Pub. L. No. 90-202, 81 Stat. 602. (prohibiting discrimination against individuals 40 and over); Family and Medical Leave Act of 1993, Pub. L. No. 103-3, 107 Stat. 6; Pregnancy Discrimination Act, Pub. L. No. 95-555, 92 Stat. 2076.

and search queries on the companies' website.[104] Ostensibly, these companies aim to reduce employers' health-care costs by providing employees with information to make informed choices about their health and wellness. But the data miners can also predict whether employees are trying to get pregnant, are in need of major surgery, or are at risk for diabetes or other health conditions. For example, if an employee stops filling her prescription for birth control pills and searches the health plan website for covered obstetricians, she may be flagged as trying to get pregnant. So long as the data are not identified with a particular employee, the company could share it with the employer and stay clear of the Health Insurance Portability and Accountability Act (HIPAA). Nevertheless, that information may influence hiring decisions, either explicitly or implicitly.

Health justice also does work where health liberty might fail. As noted, people are not equally situated to make autonomous decisions. We can again go back to the single parent with limited resources. Offering an incentive to lose weight does not limit her choices or intrude on her privacy and, thus, does not offend health liberty. But the deck may be disproportionately stacked against her in terms of her ability to respond to the wellness incentive because of various socioeconomic, environmental, and other barriers to healthy eating and exercising. Therefore, it is entirely possible that a seemingly innocuous workplace wellness program might violate the principle of health justice by neglecting people who already face disadvantage.

While health equality certainly addresses some justice-oriented concerns, it would also leave some potentially healthist conduct unregulated. When animus or stereotype is driving discrimination, treating people equally is frequently enough to solve the problem.[105] For instance, if an employer does not want to hire women of reproductive age, eliminating discrimination is as easy as forbidding the employer from considering gender or age. It is enough to force the employer to treat men and women, and people of all ages, the *same*. In some cases, however, formal equal treatment can actually create or perpetuate disparities. Disability offers a helpful example. Frequently, treating people with disabilities the same as their nondisabled counterparts results not in

104 Rachel Emma Silverman, *Bosses Tap Outside Firms to Predict Which Workers Might Get Sick*, *Wall Street Journal*, Feb. 17, 2016, www.wsj.com/articles/bosses-harness-big-data-to-predict-which-workers-might-get-sick-1455664940; Valentina Zarya, *Employers Are Quietly Using Big Data to Track Employee Pregnancies*, *Fortune*, Feb. 17, 2016, http://fortune.com/2016/02/17/castlight-pregnancy-data/.

105 Susan Sturm, *Equality and Inequality: Legal Aspects*, *in International Encyclopedia of Social and Behavioral Sciences* 894 – 902 (James D. Wright, ed., 2nd edn., Elsevier 2015).

their inclusion but their exclusion.[106] To keep out people who use wheelchairs, an employer need not adopt a hiring ban. It can simply operate in a building with no ramps or elevators. Targeting discrimination may then require taking positive actions to make both facilities more accessible. We can think of our single parent in terms of access as well. She may have difficulty losing weight because her income and work hours limit her access to healthy foods or the time and other resources necessary to exercise. Health justice might call for accommodating her by providing healthy snack options at work or allowing exercise while on the clock.

In sum, a principle of health justice is necessary to understand healthism because it encompasses distributive justice concerns not captured by health welfare, health liberty, or health equality.

2.3. IDENTIFYING HEALTHISM

From these four guiding principles, we can create two sets of factors for law- and policy-makers, as well as private actors, to consider in evaluating the potential for healthism. The top section of Table 2.1 outlines the defining characteristics of desirable health-status differentiations, and the bottom section outlines the defining characteristics of healthism.

Identifying healthism requires a theoretically sound rubric. Not all health-based classifications are troubling. In fact, some can do a lot of good. Yet it is about more than just intent. Even well-intentioned classifications can have undesirable results, such as punishing people for things outside of their control, perpetuating stigma, exacerbating health disparities, invading privacy, or infringing on personal liberty. We therefore adopt four principles to guide our analysis of whether a law or policy is healthist: health welfare, health liberty, health equality, and health justice. From these four principles, we can formulate a framework to allow law- and policy-makers to think through these potentially thorny problems.

We apply this rubric in Chapter 6 by working though specific examples. This nuanced approach is necessary because health impacts people in so many different ways and raises so many competing concerns. Moreover, social norms, health-policy priorities, and empirical data change and develop over time. Our overarching goal is not to provide cookie-cutter answers to questions of healthism, but rather to heighten awareness of the pervasiveness of

[106] Jessica L. Roberts, *Health Law as Disability Rights Law*, 97 *Minn. L. R.* 1963, 2014 (2013).

TABLE 2.1. *Healthism Rubric*

Characteristics of socially desirable health-status differentiation
Promotes healthy decision-making*
Facilitates individual choices regarding health#
Lowers health risks*
Lowers health-care costs*
Facilitates better health care and better health-care access°
Characteristics of healthism
Is driven by animus†
Stigmatizes individuals unfairly†
Punishes people for their private conduct#
Impedes access to health care°
Cuts off resources or otherwise limits the ability to adopt healthy life choices#
Produces worse health outcomes°
Maintains or increases existing health disparities†

*Health welfare
#Health liberty
†Health equality
°Health justice

health-status discrimination and the need for closer attention to both its causes and its effects (Table 2.1). Our rubric is not an algorithm to apply mechanically. Instead, we seek to create a vocabulary and a platform for discussion to enrich the debates surrounding health policy.

3

Limits of Antidiscrimination and Privacy Law

3.1. INTRODUCTION

In Chapters 1 and 2 we introduced the concept of healthism and its theoretical underpinnings. In the following chapters, we assess how healthism plays out within various areas of law, mainly antidiscrimination and privacy law (Chapter 3), insurance law (Chapter 4), and private law (Chapter 5). We consider where the law addresses healthism and where the law leaves substantial pockets of discrimination unprotected. We also note how some laws and legal doctrines could inadvertently lead to healthism. These three chapters are mostly descriptive, providing a comprehensive view of the current legal protections related to healthism.

This chapter focuses on civil rights and privacy law. Healthism is, after all, a form of discrimination. Antidiscrimination or civil rights law communicates that society does not want to allocate its benefits and burdens based on certain attributes.[1] Returning to our guiding principles from Chapter 2, antidiscrimination law responds to egalitarian and justice-related concerns by eliminating certain kinds of disadvantage.[2] It should then come as no surprise that some antidiscrimination laws may already apply to healthism. However, while existing laws prohibit discrimination based on disability, genetic information, and even appearance, they do not offer comprehensive protection against healthism.

Another possible candidate for combatting healthism is privacy law. Although American privacy law is vast, encompassing protections ranging from the Fourth Amendment's guarantees against government surveillance to the constitutional

[1] Jessica L. Roberts, *Protecting Privacy to Prevent Discrimination*, 56 *Wm. & Mary L. Rev.* 2097, 2110 (2015).

[2] Ibid., 2097, 2126.

right to reproductive choice,[3] we focus here on the legal protections designed to avoid unwanted health-related inquiries or medical exams.[4] Like civil rights law, privacy law also furthers core American values. As we noted in Chapter 2, privacy – the right to be left alone – assumes the ability to make choices about our lives. Accordingly, privacy law is most readily associated with liberty. Yet privacy can also serve equality and justice. Keeping health information private could stop would-be discriminators in their tracks by preventing them from accessing the very information that they could use to discriminate.[5] Consider data-mining firms like Castlight. If employers cannot access health-related data about their employees' prescription histories and search queries, they cannot discriminate against employees for trying to get pregnant. Like antidiscrimination law, however, privacy protections do not reach all potential forms of healthism.

This chapter examines dedicated antidiscrimination and privacy laws. We leave health insurance laws, which also include certain privacy and antidiscrimination protections, to Chapter 4.

3.2. HEALTHISM UNDER EXISTING ANTIDISCRIMINATION AND PRIVACY LAWS

Several statutes – at both the state and federal levels – target certain kinds of healthism. We focus our discussion here on four major areas of protection: disability, genetic information, lifestyle and appearance, and employee benefits.

3.2.1. *Disability and Healthism*

While not explicitly targeting *health status*, the law already prohibits discrimination on the basis of legally recognized *disabilities*. Health and disability are not synonymous, but they are surely connected.[6] Acquiring a disability can

3 *See* Daniel J. Solove, *A Taxonomy of Privacy*, 154 *U. Pa. L. Rev.* 477 (2006) [hereinafter Solove, *Taxonomy of Privacy*]; Daniel J. Solove, *Conceptualizing Privacy*, 90 *Calif. L. Rev.* 1087 (2002).

4 Alan Westin, *Privacy and Freedom* 7 (Antheneum, 1967); *see also* Elizabeth L. Beardsley, *Privacy: Autonomy and Selective Disclosure*, in *Privacy* 56, 65 (J. Roland Pennock and John W. Chapman eds., 1971; Charles Fried, *Privacy*, 77 *Yale L.J.* 475, 483 (1968); Hyman Gross, *Privacy and Autonomy, in Privacy* 169, 171 (J. Roland Pennock and John W. Chapman eds., 1971); Andrei Marmor, *What Is the Right to Privacy? USC Gould Sch. of Law Ctr. for Law & Soc. Sci., Legal Studies Research Papers Series* No. 14–13, 2014, available at http://perma.cc/QJ39-N5KK.

5 Roberts, note 1, at 2097, 2142.

6 Jessica L. Roberts, *Healthism and the Law of Employment Discrimination*, 99 *Iowa L. Rev.* 571, 594 (2014) ("While 'health' and 'disability' are not identical concepts, they are nonetheless related."); Jessica L. Roberts, *Health Law as Disability Rights Law*, 97 *Minn. L. Rev.* 1963, 1977 (2013) ("The concepts of 'health' and 'disability' have a complicated, long-standing relationship.").

certainly impact health status. For example, paralysis following a car accident will make exercising more difficult. Likewise, health status may lead to disability. Smoking increases the risk of developing any number of disabilities, including diabetes and lung cancer.

The point that health and disability are related but not synonymous is worth emphasizing. Drawing on our Chapter 1 definitions, a person may be considered "unhealthy" when she suffers from a sufficiently severe condition that she or society deems undesirable. To the extent that someone with paralysis has a mobility-limiting impairment, she may be considered "unhealthy." Elite para-athletes, however, clearly challenge the notion that health and disability are incompatible. Although health and disability are not the same, there is enough overlap in these categories that some disability laws could simultaneously safeguard against healthism.

Antidiscrimination

At the federal level, two statutes provide relatively comprehensive protection against discrimination on the basis of disability: the Rehabilitation Act and the Americans with Disabilities Act (ADA). The Rehabilitation Act, a law that catalyzed the disability rights movement in the United States, outlaws discrimination against qualified individuals with disabilities in federally funded programs.[7] The ADA, signed into law almost two decades later, forbids private employers, state and local governments, and commercial entities from discriminating on the basis of disability.[8] Thus, Americans with disabilities now enjoy legal protection in both the public and private sectors. Unfortunately, the path to equality via these laws has not been smooth. After a series of limiting decisions by the US Supreme Court, Congress amended the ADA to restore the intended breadth of its protections.[9] But more on that later.

Federal law also prohibits discrimination on the basis of disability in certain specific contexts. For instance, the Fair Housing Act (FHA) provides that people who are selling or renting homes, as well as mortgage brokers, cannot consider race, color, national origin, religion, sex, family status, or disability in their decisions. Consequently, a person cannot refuse to sell her house to a prospective buyer because she is HIV-positive, and a lender cannot deny an applicant a loan because the applicant has cancer. Similarly, the Air Carriers Access Act (ACAA) prohibits discrimination on the basis of disability by both American

7 The Rehabilitation Act of 1973, 29 U.S.C. §§ 701–96.

8 Americans with Disabilities Act of 1990, 42 U.S.C. §§ 12101–213 (2013) (amended 2008).

9 Americans with Disabilities Amendments Act, 110 Pub. Law No. 325 (enacted 2008) (codified as 42 U.S.C. §§ 12103, 12205(a)); Roberts, *Health Law as Disability*, note 6, at 1963, 1976.

and foreign air carriers.[10] A person cannot be removed from a plane or asked to pay extra because she has a legally recognized disability. However, despite its clear prohibition, the ACAA does not provide equally clear remedies.[11]

These federal protections share a common definition of disability, which covers current, past, and perceived impairments.[12] A current impairment must substantially limit the ability to perform at least one major life activity.[13] Major life activities include things like walking, standing, breathing, hearing, speaking, seeing, communicating, and being able to take care of oneself.[14] If a person's impairment is episodic or in remission, a court will assess how limiting it is when the condition is active.[15] The past disability provision prohibits discrimination based on a record of an impairment.[16] In other words, if an individual at some point had a substantially limiting impairment, she cannot face discrimination on the basis of her previous disability, even if the impairment completely went away. And finally, these laws forbid discrimination based on a perceived impairment. Even if the individual has no actual or past disability, the law still covers her if a discriminator regards her as disabled.[17] The ADA also covers associational discrimination.[18] That is, a covered entity cannot discriminate against a person without a disability because of her relationship with a person with a disability.

This broad definition of disability covers certain instances of healthism. In fact, one of the ADA's first and most infamous cases is an example of healthism from Chapter 1.[19] Remember the story of Sidney Abbott? She was the

[10] 49 U.S.C. § 41705(a).

[11] Courts have split on whether the statute may be enforced by judicial cause of action, as opposed to an internal grievance process. *See Lopez* v. *Jet Blue Airways*, 662 F.3d 593, 596 (2nd Cir. 2011) (denying private right of action for violation of the ACAA, but noting that the statutory administrative enforcement scheme was "[d]esigned to vindicate fully the rights of disabled passengers)"; *Boswell* v. *Skywest Airlines*, Inc., 361 F.3d 1263, 1268 (10th Cir. 2004). *But see Shinault* v. *Am. Airlines, Inc.*, 936 F.2d 796, 800 (5th Cir. 1991); *Tallarico* v. *Trans World Airlines, Inc.*, 881 F.2d 556, 570 (8th Cir. 1989).

[12] 42 U.S.C. § 12102(1); 29 U.S.C. § 705(9)(B).

[13] 42 U.S.C. § 12102(1)(A); 29 U.S.C. § 705(9).

[14] 42 U.S.C. § 12102(2)(A); 29 U.S.C. § 705(20)(B).

[15] 42 U.S.C. § 12102(4)(D); 29 U.S.C. § 705(9)(B).

[16] 42 U.S.C. § 12102(1)(B); 29 U.S.C. § 705(9)(B).

[17] 42 U.S.C. § 12102(1)(C); 29 U.S.C. § 705(9)(B). Under the ADA's definition of "disability," a person is "regarded as disabled" if his employer mistakenly believes that he has a physical impairment that substantially limits one or more major life activities, or mistakenly believes that an actual, nonlimiting impairment substantially limits one or more major life activities. *Haynes* v. *Williams*, 392 F.3d 478, 481–2 (D.C. Cir. 2004).

[18] 2 Amer. Disab.: Pract. & Compliance Manual § 7:194 (explaining Title I associational claims); 1 Amer. Disab.: Pract. & Compliance Manual § 2:86 (explaining Title II associational claims); ibid. § 4:62 (explaining Title III associational claims).

[19] *Bragdon* v. *Abbott*, 524 U.S. 624 (1998).

HIV-positive woman whose cavity Dr. Bragdon refused to fill outside a hospital. Abbott sued under the ADA. The Supreme Court held that even though she remained asymptomatic, Abbott was nonetheless disabled within the meaning of the statute. Disability discrimination laws seem to clearly apply when healthism is based on a diagnosis. But what about other kinds of health statuses?

The most developed line of those cases pertains to weight discrimination. In 1993, Bonnie Cook made legal history by successfully claiming that obesity constitutes a legally recognized disability.[20] Cook weighed over 320 pounds and stood at 5′2″ tall. She worked as an attendant at the Ladd Center, a residential program for people with intellectual and cognitive disabilities, run by the Rhode Island Department of Mental Health, Retardation, and Hospitals. She had been employed at the Center on two different occasions, once from 1978 to 1980 and again from 1981 to 1986. Cook ended her job voluntarily both times and, according to the court, "[left] behind a spotless work record." Yet, in 1988, when she decided to return a third time, the department refused to have her back, alleging that Cook's weight impeded her ability to help residents evacuate during an emergency and made her more likely to develop conditions that could lead to absenteeism and workers' compensation claims.

Cook sued the department under the Rehabilitation Act and won, securing a $100,000 verdict. When the department appealed, the reviewing court affirmed. Rejecting the argument that Cook's obesity should not qualify as a disability because it was the result of her voluntary conduct, the court opined: "the Act indisputably applies to numerous conditions that may be caused or exacerbated by voluntary conduct, such as alcoholism, AIDS, diabetes, cancer resulting from cigarette smoking, heart disease resulting from excesses of various types, and the like."[21] It concluded that Cook had established herself as a person with a disability under both the actual and the perceived definitions. Cook was a trailblazer under the Rehabilitation Act. Around the same time, other plaintiffs also brought successful weight discrimination claims using state laws.[22]

[20] *Cook* v. *State of R.I., Dept. of Mental Health, Retardation, and Hosps.*, 10 F.3d 17 (1st Cir. 1993).

[21] *Cook* v. *State of R.I., Dept. of Mental Health, Retardation, and Hosps.*, 10 F.3d 17, 24 (1st Cir. 1993).

[22] *See Gimello* v. *Agency Rent-A-Car-Systems, Inc.*, 594 A.2d 264, 275 (N.J. Super. Ct. App. Div. 1991) (holding that an obese person may be considered handicapped for purposes of New Jersey laws against discrimination); *Greene* v. *Seminole Elec. Co-op., Inc.*, 701 So. 2d 646, 647–8 (Fla. Dist. Ct. App. 1997) (holding that allegations of morbidly obese employee that his employer conditioned a probationary period of his entry-level employment on his losing

Almost two decades later, in 2011, another court decided that obesity was a disability under the ADA.[23] When Lisa Harrison started working at a residential house for people with chemical dependencies, she weighed 400 pounds. When she was fired almost eight years later, she weighed 527 pounds. She filed a complaint with the Equal Employment Opportunity Commission (EEOC), the agency responsible for enforcing federal employment discrimination laws, alleging that she was fired because of her weight. Although Harrison died two years later, the EEOC filed suit on behalf of her estate. The court hearing the case found that the ADA covers severe obesity. In April 2012, the agency settled her claim for $125,000.[24] Only three months later, the EEOC secured $55,000 in yet another obesity case. Material handler Ronald Kratz II alleged that his employer, a company that develops combat and tactical vehicles, fired him based on his obesity and for regarding him as disabled.[25]

Despite these encouraging developments, legal protections based on weight remain limited. To qualify as a disability, weight must either substantially limit a major life activity – like walking, standing, or breathing – or must be perceived as disabling. Thus, while being significantly overweight may qualify under certain circumstances, simply carrying a few extra pounds will not. Additionally, as we explain below, a number of other health statuses that relate to conduct are not recognized under the ADA, leaving large swaths of potential healthism unregulated.

Privacy

In addition to its civil rights protections, the ADA also safeguards privacy.[26] It limits an employer's ability to ask disability-related questions and to conduct medical examinations.[27] Although a number of states – California,

---

substantial weight and subsequent refusal to promote him to more than one position was sufficient to state a disability claim under the Florida Civil Rights Act). *But see Morrison* v. *Pinkerton*, 7 S.W.3d 851, 855 (Tex. App. – Houston [1st Dist.] 1999, no pet.) (holding that a former employee seeking to recover for disability discrimination under the Texas Commission on Human Rights Act could not prove that he was disabled within the meaning of the statute even assuming that he was morbidly obese and suffered from respiratory impairment because of his weight).

23 EEOC v. *Res. for Human Dev., Inc.*, 827 F. Supp. 2d 688 (E.D. La. 2011).

24 EEOC, *Press Release, Resources for Human Development Settles EEOC Disability Suit for* $125,000, at www.eeoc.gov/eeoc/newsroom/release/4-10-12a.cfm.

25 EEOC, *Press Release, BAE Systems Subsidiary to Pay $55,000 to Settle EEOC Disability Discrimination Suit*, at www.eeoc.gov/eeoc/newsroom/release/7-24-12c.cfm.

26 Roberts, note 1, at 2097, 2100.

27 42 U.S.C. § 12112(d)(1) ("The prohibition against discrimination as referred to in subsection (a) of this section shall include medical examinations and inquiries.").

Maryland, Michigan, New Jersey, New York, Ohio, and Washington – explicitly prohibit preemployment medical examinations, we focus on the federal protections.

Under the ADA, before an applicant has an offer, a covered employer can only ask whether the person can perform the job. The employer cannot ask whether the applicant has a disability or order a medical exam. After extending an offer, however, the employer can make the job contingent on passing a medical examination, as long as the exam is standard and its results are kept confidential and not used to discriminate.[28] Even after hiring, an employer can only inquire about disability or require a medical examination if the question or the exam relates to the person's job and is necessary for business reasons.[29] Since the definition of disability includes both physical and mental impairments, the ADA also applies to inquiries and exams related to psychological health. However, these privacy protections apply to *all* applicants and employees regardless of disability.[30] That means that even if the applicant or employee does not have a legally recognized disability, she can still challenge an unlawful medical exam under the ADA. As we explore later in this chapter, however, applicants who have tried to invoke this provision in conjunction with wellness programs generally have not been successful.

[28] 42 U.S.C. § 12112(d)(3). This provision allows an employer to condition an offer of employment on the results of a medical examination if (1) all entering employees are subjected to such an examination regardless of disability, (2) the information obtained regarding the medical condition of history of the applicant is confidential, and (3) the results of the examination are used only in accordance with the ADA. Ibid.

[29] 42 U.S.C. § 12112(d)(4)(A). The employer shoulders the burden of proving the job-relatedness and business necessity justifying a medical examination or disability-related inquiry. *Bates* v. *Dura Auto. Sys., Inc.*, 767 F.3d 566, 581 (6th Cir. 2014). Whether the employer's medical examination is job-related or a matter of business necessity is a question of fact to be determined by a jury. Ibid. The EEOC instructs that a disability-related inquiry or medical examination of an employee may be job-related and consistent with business necessity when an employer has reasonable belief, based on objective evidence, that: (1) an employee's ability to perform essential job functions will be impaired by a medical condition; or (2) an employee will pose a direct threat due to a medical condition. Ibid.

[30] Michelle Travis, *Lashing Back at the ADA Backlash: How the Americans with Disabilities Act Benefits Americans Without Disabilities*, 76 *Tenn. L. Rev.* 311, 337, n. 151 (2009) (listing cases where courts have held that, because the ADA establishes a "process barrier" to help prevent disability discrimination, all job applicants may enforce pre-offer medical inquiry provisions, regardless of their disabled or nondisabled status, as long as they can demonstrate a cognizable injury from the violation); *see also* 1 Disability Discrimination Workplace § 6:9 (2016) (explaining that an employee who does not have a disability has standing to challenge an inquiry or medical examination that allegedly violates the ADA).

3.2.2. *Genetics and Healthism*

Laws governing genetic information also protect against certain types of healthism. When Congress passed the Genetic Information Nondiscrimination Act (GINA) in 2008,[31] it was arguably reacting to a specific variety of healthism – discrimination on the basis of genetic information. Despite state laws prohibiting genetic-information discrimination,[32] people reported concerns about the use of their data, prompting Congress to act.

Antidiscrimination

In 2004, the Secretary's Advisory Commission on Genetics, Health, and Society (SACGHS) held a public forum and compiled a report. GINA's proponents cited several anecdotal examples of discrimination based on genetic information. A letter from congresswoman and GINA advocate Representative Louise Slaughter to SACGHS told the story of a woman in North Carolina who was fired after a genetic test indicated that she was at risk for developing a lung disorder.[33]

Similarly, an email from a genetic counselor told the story of a patient who was fired after testing positive for a genetic variant correlated highly with breast and ovarian cancer.[34] Her benefits covered the testing and the patient was forthright with her employer, explaining exactly why she would be missing work. On the day of her blood draw, her boss asked when she would get her results. She told him it would take about a month. A day or two later, he called her into his office and told her that he was firing her because she was going to raise the office's insurance rates. When she requested formal, written notice of her termination, the part of the form that should have listed the reason for firing her was left blank.

Finally, comments from the Council for Responsible Genetics (CRG) to SACGHS recounted the story of a social worker named Kim who was fired from a large human services agency, despite her outstanding performance

[31] Genetic Information Nondiscrimination Act of 2008, Pub. L. No. 110–233, 122 Stat. 881 (codified as 42 U.S.C. § 2000ff–2000ff–11).

[32] *See* Jessica L. Roberts, *Preempting Discrimination: Lessons from the Genetic Information Nondiscrimination Act*, 63 *Vand. L. Rev.* 439, 446–7 (2010) (describing pre-GINA state laws).

[33] Secretary's Advisory Committee on Genetics, Health, and Society, Public Perspectives on Genetic Discrimination, 57 (Sept. 2004–Nov. 2004), at http://osp.od.nih.gov/sites/default/files/Public_Perspectives_GenDiscrim_0.pdf

[34] Secretary's Advisory Committee on Genetics, Health, and Society, Public Perspectives on Genetic Discrimination, 89 (Sept. 2004–Nov. 2004) (statement of Eric Fowler), at http://osp.od.nih.gov/sites/default/files/Public_Perspectives_GenDiscrim_0.pdf

reviews. The agency terminated her one week after she mentioned during a staff meeting that she had been the primary caregiver for her mother, who died of Huntington's disease (HD) and that she herself had a 50 percent chance of developing the condition.[35]

In addition to written comments, SACGHS heard live testimony. Heidi Williams spoke about how an insurer initially denied her children health insurance because they were carriers of the gene for alpha-1 antitrypsin deficiency.[36] Phaedra Malatek discussed her family history of hemochromatosis and how she did not seek genetic testing for her two young sons because she feared discrimination by insurers.[37] Rebecca Fisher told the committee about hiding her BRCA1 (the breast cancer gene) mutation from health-care providers.[38] Tonia Phillips explained that when she tested positive for BRCA1 and underwent a preventive hysterectomy and a preventive mastectomy, her boss confronted her about the insurance costs and offered to pay her to switch to her husband's plan.[39] Paula Funk recounted how – because of her strong family history of breast cancer – she paid for her own genetic test instead of going through insurance and, after a positive BRCA1 result, was still waiting for approval from her insurance company for her preventive mastectomy.[40] Carolina Hinestrosa, a breast cancer survivor and executive vice president of National Breast Cancer Coalition, explained to SACGHS that she did not undergo genetic testing out of concern that the results could negatively impact her daughter.[41] Lastly, Phil Hardt, diagnosed with both hemophilia B and HD,

[35] Secretary's Advisory Committee on Genetics, Health, and Society, Public Perspectives on Genetic Discrimination, 155 (Sept. 2004–Nov. 2004) (statement from the Counsel for Responsible Genetics), at http://osp.od.nih.gov/sites/default/files/Public_Perspectives_GenDiscrim_0.pdf.

[36] Secretary's Advisory Committee on Genetics, Health, and Society, Public Perspectives on Genetic Discrimination, 2–4 (Sept. 2004–Nov. 2004) (statement of Heidi Williams), at http://osp.od.nih.gov/sites/default/files/Public_Perspectives_GenDiscrim_0.pdf.

[37] Secretary's Advisory Committee on Genetics, Health, and Society, Public Perspectives on Genetic Discrimination, 5–8 (Sept. 2004–Nov. 2004) (statement of Phaedra Malatek), at http://osp.od.nih.gov/sites/default/files/Public_Perspectives_GenDiscrim_0.pdf.

[38] Secretary's Advisory Committee on Genetics, Health, and Society, Public Perspectives on Genetic Discrimination, 9–13 (Sept. 2004–Nov. 2004) (statement of Rebecca Fisher), at http://osp.od.nih.gov/sites/default/files/Public_Perspectives_GenDiscrim_0.pdf.

[39] Secretary's Advisory Committee on Genetics, Health, and Society, Public Perspectives on Genetic Discrimination, 14–15 (Sept. 2004–Nov. 2004) (statement of Tonia Phillips), at http://osp.od.nih.gov/sites/default/files/Public_Perspectives_GenDiscrim_0.pdf.

[40] Secretary's Advisory Committee on Genetics, Health, and Society, Public Perspectives on Genetic Discrimination, 16–19 (Sept. 2004–Nov. 2004) (statement of Paula Funk), at http://osp.od.nih.gov/sites/default/files/Public_Perspectives_GenDiscrim_0.pdf.

[41] Secretary's Advisory Committee on Genetics, Health, and Society, Public Perspectives on Genetic Discrimination, 20–2 (Sept. 2004–Nov. 2004) (statement of Carolina Hinestrosa), at http://osp.od.nih.gov/sites/default/files/Public_Perspectives_GenDiscrim_0.pdf.

relayed how he hid his hemophilia from his boss, was denied credit insurance and long-term care insurance because of his HD, had a daughter who was told that she had to test negatively for HD to get life insurance, and regretted that his grandson could not obtain health insurance because of the child's inherited hemophilia.[42] He also told the committee that his two children paid out-of-pocket for HD tests and that he had helped set up anonymous testing.

Moved by these stories, Congress opted to prohibit genetic information discrimination in two contexts: health insurance and employment. This chapter covers GINA's employment section. As Chapter 4 explains, federal law now also broadly prohibits discrimination in health insurance based on health status, including genetic information.[43] Insurers may not refuse to sell, nor charge more for, a policy based on genetic information. Several states also have genetic-information discrimination and genetic privacy laws, including many that predate GINA. California's state law, dubbed CalGINA and passed after the federal law, offers particularly expansive protection. It goes beyond health insurance and employment to protect against discrimination in a variety of other contexts, including commercial transactions, housing, mortgage lending, and emergency services.[44] Given the diversity of state protections, we look primarily to the federal statute.

GINA's definition of genetic information covers a person's genetic test results, the genetic test results of her family members, and her family medical history.[45] Interestingly, nothing in the text of the law explicitly limits family medical history to hereditary conditions. Regardless, some courts have chosen to restrict the definition to family medical history that communicates genetic risk.[46] Notably, while GINA forbids employers from making employment-related decisions based on a family member's health condition, employers *can* make decisions based on the employee's *own* manifested condition.[47]

[42] Secretary's Advisory Committee on Genetics, Health, and Society, Public Perspectives on Genetic Discrimination, 23–5 (Sept. 2004–Nov. 2004) (statement of Phil Hardt), at http://osp.od.nih.gov/sites/default/files/Public_Perspectives_GenDiscrim_0.pdf.

[43] 42 U.S. Code § 300gg–4(a)(6).

[44] California Genetic Information Nondiscrimination Act, 2011 Cal. Legis. Serv. ch. 261 (West); *see also* Roberts, note 32, at 439, 446–47 (describing pre-GINA state laws).

[45] 42 U.S.C. §§ 2000ff(4)(A)(i)–(iii). The definition of genetic information excludes any information about sex or age. Ibid. § 2000ff(4)(C).

[46] *See, e.g., Poore* v. *Peterbilt of Bristol, LLC*, 852 F. Supp. 2d 727 (W.D. Va. 2012); *see also Maxwell* v. *Verde Valley Ambulance Co.*, CV-13–08044-PCT-BSB, 2014 WL 4470512, at *16 (D. Ariz. Sept. 11, 2014) (citing *Poore*); *Allen* v. *Verizon Wireless*, No. 3:12-cv-482 (JCH), 2013 U.S. Dist. LEXIS 80228, at *74 (D. Conn. 2013) (citing *Poore*).

[47] GINA defines "genetic information" as (1) an individual's genetic tests; (2) the genetic tests of an individual's family members; (3) the manifestation of a disease or disorder of the individual's family members. *See* 42 U.S.C. § 2000ff(4)(A); *see also* 29 C.F.R. § 1635(c). Discrimination

Therefore, under GINA, your employer cannot fire you because your sister has breast cancer but could fire you because you yourself have breast cancer. Congress' primary concern in passing GINA was pre-symptomatic genetic risk.[48] This state of affairs may seem shocking until you consider that the ADA offers protection against employment discrimination on the basis of disability. Put simply, the ADA seems to pick up where GINA leaves off. Yet, as we establish in our discussion of the law's limitations, that might not always be the case.

Privacy

Like the ADA, GINA includes both antidiscrimination and privacy protections.[49] GINA's privacy provision, however, is even more robust than the ADA's. It prohibits employers from requesting, requiring, or purchasing their employees' genetic information. Accordingly, an employer can violate GINA by simply *asking* for genetic information, even if the employer never receives – let alone acts on – it.[50] The prohibition on requests for genetic information applies with equal force to medical exams that are acceptable under the ADA.[51] Thus, even if an employer is conducting a lawful, post-offer medical examination or a medical examination that is job-related and consistent with business necessity, GINA still forbids the employer from requesting genetic test results or family medical histories.

Because GINA is relatively new and its protections are relatively narrow, there have not been many court decisions interpreting it.[52] In the limited examples to date, GINA plaintiffs have had the most success challenging their employer's attempts to acquire family medical history. The first two GINA

based on a condition, as opposed to "genetic information," is not covered by GINA. *See Jacobs v. Donnelly Communications*, 1:13-CV-980-WSD, 2013 WL 5436682, at *2 (N.D. Ga. Sept. 27, 2013); *see also* Roberts, note 32, at 439, 454.

48 Jessica L. Roberts, *The Genetic Information Nondiscrimination Act as an Antidiscrimination Law*, 86 *Notre Dame L. Rev.* 597, 637 (2011); Mark A. Rothstein, *GINA, the ADA, and Genetic Discrimination in Employment*, 36 *J.L. Med. & Ethics* 837, 839 (2008).

49 42 U.S.C.A. § 2000ff–1; *see also* Roberts, note 1, at 2097, 2101.

50 Roberts, note 1, at 2097, 2128.

51 *See* 29 C.F.R. § 1635.8(d). ("The prohibition on acquisition of genetic information, including family medical history, applies to medical examinations related to employment. A covered entity must tell health care providers not to collect genetic information, including family medical history, as part of a medical examination intended to determine the ability to perform a job, and must take additional reasonable measures within its control if it learns that genetic information is being requested or required.")

52 Mark A. Rothstein, Jessica Roberts, and Tee L. Guidotti, *Limiting Occupational Medical Evaluations Under the Americans with Disabilities Act and the Genetic Information Nondiscrimination Act*, 41 *Amer. J.L. & Med.* 523, 552 (2015).

cases filed by the EEOC dealt with requests for family medical history. Rhonda Jones worked for Fabricut for ninety days as a temporary clerk.[53] When she applied for a permanent job, Fabricut extended her an offer contingent on the results of a medical exam. As part of her physical, Jones was asked to fill out a medical questionnaire that included questions about her family medical history. The exam concluded that she either had, or was predisposed to, carpel tunnel syndrome. Fabricut then withdrew its offer, leading Jones to file a complaint with the EEOC. The EEOC sued Fabricut under both the ADA and GINA, and the company settled for $50,000. Importantly, despite providing compensation to the injured party, settlement agreements do not establish legal precedent. Thus, Jones's case provides no authority for similarly postured job applicants.

The EEOC's second GINA lawsuit raised similar claims. The agency filed a class action claim against Founders Pavilion, alleging that the company violated GINA by requesting family medical history during its medical examinations, as well as other federal employment statutes, including the ADA.[54] Again the EEOC settled the case, this time for $370,000. Following those initial victories, the EEOC has continued to sue employers who ask their applicants and employees to provide family medical history.[55] In addition to the EEOC, people have also filed their own claims challenging their employers' requests for family medical history, but, as we will see, they have not met with as much success.

Perhaps the most notorious GINA case dealt with a request not for family medical history, but for genetic testing.[56] And it is a real stinker. The powers that be at Atlas Logistics were none too pleased when someone started defecating in the company's warehouse. They decided to take matters into their own hands and enlist a forensic genetic testing firm to ferret out the culprit. Based on schedules and access to the warehouse, Atlas Logistics narrowed its search to two suspects, Jack Lowe and Dennis Reynolds, and insisted that the men submit to genetic testing to compare their DNA to the DNA in the fecal matter. While the testing ruled both men out, they were nonetheless outraged and sued under GINA. The judge dubbed it the "case of the devious defecator."

53 EEOC, Press Release, *Fabricut to Pay $50,000 to Settle EEOC Disability and Genetic Information Discrimination Lawsuit*, May 7, 2013, at www.eeoc.gov/eeoc/newsroom/release/5-7-13b.cfm.

54 EEOC, Press Release, *Founders Pavilion Will Pay $370,000 to Settle EEOC Genetic Information Discrimination Lawsuit*, Jan. 13, 2014, at www.eeoc.gov/eeoc/newsroom/release/1-13-14.cfm

55 Rothstein et al., note 52, at 523, 555.

56 *Lowe* v. *Atlas Logistics Group Retail Services* (Atlanta), LLC, 102 F. Supp. 3d 1360, 1361 (N.D. Ga. 2015).

Despite the clever moniker, Lowe and Reynolds's lawsuit was no laughing matter. The jury came back with a whopping $2.25 million verdict, which the judge reduced to $600,000, $300,000 to each employee, the maximum amount the statute allows.[57]

To sum up, GINA and similar state laws address a particular form of health-status discrimination primarily based on asymptomatic genetic conditions or predispositions. California's version of the law is exceptional in its breadth, but federal protection extends only to insurance and employment. Moreover, GINA does not protect against discrimination based on manifested health conditions. The ADA may step in if the condition meets that statute's definition of disability. And, as we explain in Chapter 4, insurance law may also prohibit discrimination based on diagnosed or manifested health conditions. But GINA still leaves significant room for healthism.

3.2.3. *Lifestyle, Appearance, and Healthism*

A third category of legal protections that could apply to healthism – lifestyle discrimination legislation – blends privacy and antidiscrimination. They are civil rights laws that protect against discrimination based on private conduct outside of work.[58] Conduct that may interest employers could include anything from alcohol consumption to moonlighting at other jobs, from political organizing to recreational sports. To date, more than half of states have adopted these kinds of protections.[59] The laws vary substantially from state to state, both in terms of the protected individuals – applicants and current employees or current employees only – and the protected behavior – any legal, off-duty conduct or the off-duty use of certain lawful products.[60] State lifestyle discrimination statutes became prominent in the late 1990s and early 2000s as a means to protect smokers from being fired for smoking while not at work. In recent years, health-care reform has ushered in a new era of interest in employee health.[61] State legislators, however, have less sympathy toward employee privacy. As of early 2014, at least one state proposed a bill *revoking*

57 Carolina Bolado, *Warehouse Co. Ends Appeal of Devious Defecator Verdict*, *Law360.Com*, Oct. 18, 2016, at www.law360.com/articles/852874/warehouse-co-ends-appeal-of-defecator-dna-test-verdict.

58 Roberts, *Healthism and the Law*, note 6, at 571, 608–10.

59 Ibid., 571, 608.

60 Ibid., 571, 608–610.

61 More than half of states have statutes that prohibit employers from not hiring smokers. Harald Schmidt et al., *The Ethics of Not Hiring Smokers*, 368 *N. Eng. J. Med.* 1369, 1369, Apr. 11, 2013. For a description of the modern trend, *see* Roberts, *Healthism and the Law*, note 6, at 571, 582–3.

its lifestyle discrimination law with the specific goal of allowing employers to screen for tobacco use.[62] Regardless of the potential backlash, these state laws may still offer some protection against discrimination on the basis of conduct perceived as unhealthy.

Just as lifestyle discrimination statutes broaden civil rights law to cover what a person does off the clock, appearance discrimination laws extend antidiscrimination protection to cover what a person looks like. Appearance discrimination has been colloquially called "lookism." The ADA's regulations include cosmetic disfigurement on the list of covered impairments.[63] Some states and municipalities go further and prohibit discrimination based on physical appearance, apart from disability. Michigan has a law that prohibits discrimination in employment, housing, public accommodations, public programs, and education on several bases, including weight as an explicit category (opposed to construing weight as a disability).[64] Howard County in Maryland outlawed discrimination based on personal appearance in housing, employment, law enforcement, public accommodations, financing, and "any other facets of the lives of its citizens where such practices may be found to exist."[65] Among the municipalities that prohibit lookism are San Francisco, California, which added height and weight to the prohibited bases for discrimination in its administrative and police code in 2000;[66] Washington, DC, which prohibits discrimination based on personal appearance in employment, housing, public accommodations, and education;[67] Santa Cruz, California, which bans discrimination based on height, weight, or physical characteristics also in employment, housing, public accommodations, and education;[68] Madison, Wisconsin, which forbids discrimination based on physical appearance in employment, housing, and public accommodations;[69] Urbana, Illinois, which

62 *See* Barb Berggoetz, *Indiana Chamber Back Employers Not Hiring Smokers*, *USA Today*, Jan. 9, 2014, at www.usatoday.com/story/news/politics/2014/01/09/indiana-smokers-bill-of-rights/4389149/.

63 29 C.F.R. § 1630.2(h)(1).

64 Mich. Comp. Laws Ann. § 37.2101 (West 2016).

65 Howard, Md., Code of Ordinances § 12.200(III)(6), subtitle 2, at www.municode.com/library/md/howard_county/codes/code_of_ordinances?nodeId=14680.

66 San Francisco, Cal., Admin. Code ch. 12A, 12B, and 12C (2000), at http://sf-hrc.org/sites/default/files/Documents/LBE_EBO/EBO/Height_and_Weight.pdf; San Francisco, Cal., Mun./Police Code, art. 33 (2000), at http://sf-hrc.org/sites/default/files/Documents/LBE_EBO/EBO/Height_and_Weight.pdf.

67 D.C. Code Ann. § 2–1401.02(22) (2010).

68 Santa Monica, Cal., Mun. Code ch. 9.83 (1995), at www.codepublishing.com/CA/SantaCruz/html/SantaCruz09/SantaCruz0983.html.

69 Madison, Wis., Code of Ordinances ch. 39.02(9)(b), at www.municode.com/library/wi/madison/codes/code_of_ordinances?nodeId=Chapter%2039%20Department%20of%20Civil%20Rights.

again bans discrimination on the basis of personal appearance in employment, housing, and public accommodations;[70] and finally Binghamton, New York, which adopted a law prohibiting discrimination in employment, housing, public accommodations, and education on the basis of several factors, including height and weight.[71]

Anti-lookism laws are a particularly powerful supplement to privacy law in their ability to combat healthism. Privacy law is most valuable as a tool of antidiscrimination when the basis for discrimination is not immediately apparent. Consider smoking and obesity. A privacy protection might adequately protect a smoker who smokes at home by outlawing nicotine tests or by forbidding questions about tobacco use. By contrast, a privacy protection would do little for an overweight person. An employer does not need an applicant to take a test or fill out a questionnaire to learn about her weight. All the employer needs to do is schedule an interview.

3.2.4. *Benefits Law*

Employee benefits law may also protect against healthism in employment. For one, the Employment Retirement Income Security Act (ERISA) includes an anti-retaliation provision. ERISA is a notoriously convoluted and, at times, seemingly incoherent statutory scheme that applies to employee benefits, including health plans. The statute contains a number of detailed requirements for pension and retirement plans, but its biggest impact for health plans is that it preempts state laws that would otherwise apply to employer-sponsored health insurance. The law is something of a curse for employees, who lose various health insurance, managed care, and consumer protections otherwise available under state law, but a blessing for employers, who are freed of the challenge of complying with the myriad laws of the different states where they operate. ERISA contains an express private right of action for employees seeking to claim, or clarify, their right to benefits and imposes a fiduciary duty on plan administrators.

Congress drafted the anti-retaliation provision specifically to stop employers from preventing their current and former employees from obtaining their lawfully entitled employee benefits.[72] For instance, ERISA bars employers

[70] Urbana, Ill., Code of Ordinances § 12–39 (1997), at www.municode.com/library/il/urbana/codes/code_of_ordinances?nodeId=COOR_CH12HURI_ARTIIIDI_DIV1GE_S12-39DE.

[71] Binghampton, N.Y., Code of Ordinances ch. 45–2 (2008), at www.binghamton-ny.gov/ordinance/binghamton-human-rights-law.

[72] 29 U.S.C. § 1140; *see also Kowalski* v. *L&F Products*, 82 F. 3d 1283, 1287 (3rd Cir. 1996) (stating that Congress drafted Section 510 "[p]rimarily to prevent employers from discharging or harassing their employees in order to keep them from obtaining ERISA-provided benefits").

from firing their employees for using their employer-provided health plans, like in Yovany Gonzalez's case from Chapter 1. To succeed under this claim, the employee must prove that the employer took action explicitly to interfere with accessing her rightful benefits. Thus, any action short of intentional wrongdoing would not support a claim.

3.3. LIMITS OF ANTIDISCRIMINATION AND PRIVACY LAW

Although laws governing disability, genetic information, private conduct, appearance, and employee benefits offer some protection against healthism, even cobbled together they do not provide adequate legal safeguards against discrimination on the basis of health status. All of the laws described above suffer from notable shortfalls.

3.3.1. *Limits of Disability Rights Law*

While American disability rights law adopts a broad definition of disability, it still does not capture all the health statuses that could be subject to healthism.

Antidiscrimination

At first blush, the ADA might seem comprehensive. We can return to the foundational examples of healthism: nicotine and obesity bans. Does the ADA offer protection? Take a person who, after a lifetime of smoking, develops lung cancer. Cancer undoubtedly constitutes a disability.[73] Disability rights laws do not point the finger and ask: "Did you cause your own disability?" They protect the person with a two-pack a day habit who develops lung cancer just the same as the person with a genetic abnormality who develops lung cancer.[74] Blameworthiness is simply not part of the calculus. Likewise, the law affords an obese person who develops diabetes – another well-accepted disability – the same protection that it would give a juvenile or thinner person with that very same condition.[75] Under this analysis it would seem then that disability rights law has healthism pretty well covered. But, looks can be

[73] *See* 29 C.F.R. § 1630.2(j)(3)(iii) (2013) (explaining that cancer "substantially limits normal cell growth").

[74] Roberts, *Healthism and the Law*, note 6, at 571, 595; *see also* Jennifer L. Pomeranz and Rebecca M. Puhl, *New Developments in the Law for Obesity Discrimination Protection*, 21 *Obesity* 469, 470 (2013).

[75] 29 C.F.R. § Pt. 1630, App.

deceiving. While cancer and diabetes receive protection, nicotine use and obesity frequently do not.

Remember Bonnie Cook, the obese woman who successfully sued under the Rehabilitation Act? Despite her success, studies show that 98 percent of weight discrimination claims are decided in favor of the employer.[76] Hence, outside the context of lookism laws, weight goes largely unprotected. Whereas obesity-related illnesses, such as diabetes, would qualify as disabilities, obesity in and of itself almost invariably does not.[77] To win her case, a person must establish that her weight substantially limits her in a major life activity or that she has been regarded as being disabled. While some advocates have passionately argued that obesity is a physical impairment worthy of protection under disability rights law,[78] courts have been far more skeptical of such claims.

After Bonnie Cook won her case in 1993, the US Supreme Court began to limit the legal definition of disability.[79] For example, it defined a perceived disability as requiring a mistaken belief that the person has a substantially limiting impairment.[80] To prove a perceived disability, a person had to show that the discriminator incorrectly thought she had an actual disability. To qualify as disabled, then, it would not be enough to establish that your boss fired you because she thought you were hard of hearing. Instead, you would have to show not only that she incorrectly believed that you had a hearing impairment, but also that she incorrectly believed that the hearing impairment substantially limited you. With this narrowing came a corresponding unwillingness to apply disability rights law to obesity.[81]

[76] *Weight Discrimination Laws, Rulings, Attorneys*, The Council on Size & Weight Discrimination (2000), at www.cswd.org/docs/legalaction.html; *see also* Elizabeth Kristen, *Addressing the Problem of Weight Discrimination in Employment*, 90 *Calif. L. Rev.* 57, 61 (2002) (noting that obese plaintiffs "[h]ave had great difficulty succeeding in the courts with disability" claims and advocating for the passage of state and local laws explicitly prohibiting weight discrimination).

[77] Roberts, *Healthism and the Law*, note 6, at 571, 595–6.

[78] Camille A. Monahan, Tanya L. Goldman, & Debra Oswald, *Establishing a Physical Impairment of Weight Under the ADA/ADAAA: Problems of Bias in the Legal System*, 29 *A.B.A. J. Lab. & Emp. L.* 537, 540 (2014).

[79] *See Sutton* v. *United Air Lines, Inc.*, 527 U.S. 471, 482, 489 (1999) (requiring a claimant to show an inability to work in a "broad range of jobs," rather than one specific job); *Toyota Motor Manufacturing, Kentucky, Inc.* v. *Williams*, 534 U.S. 184, 200–01 (2002) (explaining that when addressing the major life activity factor, "[t]he central inquiry must be whether the claimant is unable to perform the variety of tasks central to most people's daily lives, not whether the claimant is unable to perform the tasks associated with her specific job.")

[80] Sutton, 527 U.S. at 474.

[81] Abigail Kozel, *Large and in Charge of Their Employment Discrimination Destiny: Whether Obese Americans Now Qualify as Disabled Under the Americans with Disability Act Amendments Act of 2008*, 31 *Hamline J. Pub. L. & Pol'y* 273, 290 (2009) ("Following a similar timeline

Consider, for example, Doretha Smaw, who began working as a Virginia state trooper in 1982.[82] Although her weight – 219 pounds – exceeded the allowable maximum under state guidelines, she was hired with the understanding that she would shed some pounds. In her nine years working as a trooper, Smaw received several warnings, and a doctor found that "no medical reason prevented her from reaching the prescribed weight." She was ordered to lose three pounds per month and then subjected to monthly weigh-ins. Regardless, Smaw's weight held steady. In 1991, she was fired from her position as a trooper and offered a job as a dispatcher. She sued under the Rehabilitation Act and the ADA, alleging that she faced discrimination on the basis of her weight. The court found that, while the reason for Smaw's demotion was undisputedly her weight, it was not clear that she had a physical impairment, as required by the statutes. Moreover, the court concluded that, even if she did have an impairment, her job as a dispatcher demonstrated that she was not substantially limited in her ability to work and that her employer did not perceive her to be so limited. Therefore, she had no claim.

In 1997, seventy-six law enforcement officers in Ohio alleged that they were perceived as disabled based on their weight and other factors.[83] The court reviewing the case held that the State of Ohio did not regard the officers as having impairments, as defined by the statute, but merely regarded them as not being a desirable weight. According to the court, an impairment must be more than "a mere physical characteristic" and that a person's weight is "a mere, indeed possibly transitory, physical characteristic" and therefore not worthy of protection as a disability. In a similar case, John Francis, a firefighter who was disciplined for failing to meet weight requirements, sued under the ADA and the Rehabilitation Act.[84] Although in a different court, the reasoning was the same: Francis was not perceived as disabled. The court concluded that failing to meet weight requirements was not sufficient to garner legal protection under disability rights laws.

The court reached a similar result in the case of Stephen Grindle, who worked for Watkins Motor Lines.[85] Over his five years there, his weight fluctuated from 345 pounds to 450 pounds. He injured his knee on the job after a rung of the ladder he was climbing broke. Grindle took leave to recover,

as general ADA claims, obesity-as-a-disability claims under the ADA began with broad coverage, but quickly limited any hope for obese plaintiffs.").

82 *Smaw* v. *Virginia Dep't of State Police*, 862 F. Supp. 1469, 1474 (E.D. Va. 1994).

83 *Andrews* v. *Ohio*, 104 F.3d 803, 810 (6th Cir. 1997).

84 *Francis* v. *City of Meriden*, 129 F.3d 281 (2nd Cir. 1997).

85 *EEOC* v. *Watkins Motor Lines, Inc.*, 463 F.3d 436, 440 (6th Cir. 2006).

but before Watkins would let him return to work, the company sent him to an industrial clinic doctor to get a work release letter. Following the exam, the doctor wrote, "the most notable item is the patient weighs 405 pounds," and concluded that Grindle could not safely perform his job. Watkins put Grindle on safety hold and eventually fired him. Grindle sued under the ADA. The court rejected the argument that Grindle was disabled. First, it held that obesity that was not caused by physiological factors did not qualify as an impairment for ADA purposes. Second, it used the narrowed version of perceived disability, which requires the discriminator to mistakenly believe that the person has a substantially limiting impairment. The court reasoned that because obesity was not a protected impairment, Watkins did not perceive Grindle as disabled.

Congress amended the ADA in 2008.[86] It explicitly rejected the interpretation that perceived disabilities require a mistaken belief. Following the amendments, a plaintiff would have to show only that the discriminator perceived her to be impaired, not that the employer also perceived the impairment to substantially limit a major life activity. Hence, plaintiffs who allege that they are regarded as disabled like Smaw, Francis, and Grindle might now have stronger claims. Additionally, the amendments instructed courts to construe the definition of disability broadly and provided an enumerated list of major life activities.[87] While a person wishing to establish an actual disability would still have to show that her weight substantially limits her, given the amended ADA's more expansive notion of perceived disability, broad rule of construction, and newly clarified definition of major life activities, some commentators hope that overweight plaintiffs will have a better shot at successfully litigating their discrimination claims.[88]

Those hopes seem to have been realized, at least in part. The EEOC managed to settle at least two post-amendments lawsuits. The agency reached settlements in both Lisa Harrison's and Ronald Kratz's cases, described earlier in this chapter, after the amendments. Yet post-amendments, courts have still been reluctant to hold that obesity satisfies the legal definition of disability. It would then seem that even the amended ADA has not offered adequate legal recourse for weight discrimination. Take the following examples.

86 ADA Amendments Act of 2008, Pub. L. No. 110–325, 122 Stat. 3553 (codified as amended at 42 U.S.C. § 12101 (West 2008)).

87 42 U.S.C. § 12102(2)(A).

88 Pomeranz and Puhl, note 74, at 469, 470 (arguing that the ADA Amendments Act (ADAAA) "will likely have a positive impact on weight-based discrimination claims in the future"); Kozel, note 81, at 273, 327 (stating that "[w]ith the passage of the ADAAA, certain claims of obesity-as-a-disability will likely be successful in the future").

In 2012, Charles Lescoe, a corrections officer trainee, lost his appeal.[89] Lescoe weighed 300 pounds and stood at 5′7″. He sued the Department of Corrections, alleging that he faced not only discrimination – he was not allowed to sit during trainings – but also harassment because of his size. He alleged that he was teased about his weight and his belly, which caused him stress and anxiety. The reviewing court held that the lower court did not err when it decided that Lescoe failed to show that his weight substantially limited him, as he passed multiple medical and physical exams during the training. The court likewise rejected Lescoe's argument that the department regarded him as disabled, finding that no evidence suggested that the department perceived Lescoe's weight to limit a major life activity or that the department treated Lescoe differently than other employees. Somewhat puzzlingly, the court found that "due to Lescoe's numerous disciplinary actions," the department had shown that it did not consider him a person with a disability. Instead of construing Lescoe's many disciplinary actions as evidence of differential treatment based on disability, the court seemed to assume that the department would not have disciplined an employee with a disability.

Sisters Nancy and Phyllis Sibilla also lost their post-amendments lawsuit in 2012. They raised a variety of employment discrimination claims, including one for disability discrimination based on their weights. Nancy weighed more than 400 pounds, and Phyllis weighed 271 pounds. The sisters worked at a campus bookstore for several years. When the bookstore changed hands, they were told to interview with the new owners to keep their jobs. Both applied for manager positions. Phyllis applied to be store manager. The new owner, instead, offered her a text manager position. But she fared better than her sister: The new owner offered Nancy a job as a full-time cashier, which paid hourly. Both jobs would have paid the sisters less than they received from the previous owner. In rejecting their ADA claims, the court reasoned similarly to Stephen Grindle's case, concluding that the employer's perceiving the women to be overweight was not equivalent to its perceiving them as having an impairment.

More recently, Melvin Morriss sued BNSF Railway Company for failing to hire him.[90] BNSF gave Morriss a conditional offer for a position as a machinist. On his intake questionnaire, Morriss indicated that he was 5′10″ tall and weighed 270 pounds. During his medical examinations, Morriss weighed in at 285 pounds and 281 pounds, thus exceeding the company's

[89] *Lescoe* v. *Pennsylvania Dep't of Corr.* – SCI Frackville, 464 F. Appx 50, 53–4 (3rd Cir. 2012).

[90] *Morriss* v. *BNSF Railway Co.*, No. 14–3858U (8th Cir. 2016) at http://media.ca8.uscourts.gov/opndir/16/04/143858P.pdf.

maximum permitted BMI of forty. BNSF emailed him that he was not qualified for the job because of his weight and revoked the offer. Morriss claimed discrimination on the basis of an actual and a perceived impairment. The court rejected his claim on the theory that for obesity to be considered an impairment under the ADA, it must result from an underlying physiological cause, despite the amendments. The court went on to explain that BNSF did not perceive Morriss' weight to be an impairment.

Employees are not the only ones who have tried – and failed – to argue that obesity qualifies as a disability. Anthony Torcasio, an inmate in Virginia state prison, sued under both the ADA and the Rehabilitation Act.[91] Torcasio, who stood at 5′7″ tall and weighed more than 460 pounds, argued that the laws required the state to modify his living conditions to accommodate his size and difficulty walking. Torcasio requested a larger cell that was closer to needed facilities, handrails by the toilet, wider entrances to the showers and his cell, non-skid matting in a common area, and alternative opportunities for recreation. Beyond expressing skepticism about whether to apply those laws to state prisons and their officials, the court held it was unclear that Torcasio's weight qualified him for protection.

People have also filed claims alleging weight discrimination in public accommodations. For example, Gary Sellick sued Denny's after an embarrassing experience there.[92] Sellick weighed more than 400 pounds at the time of the lawsuit. When a hostess escorted him to a booth, he chose not to sit there. On a previous occasion, Sellick had found himself wedged between the booth and the table. He requested a larger booth or a chair with no arms. The restaurant, however, was unable to accommodate him. In the course of the debacle, a Denny's waitress apparently pointed at Sellick and shouted, "You can't sit him in that aisle!" in front of several other patrons. Sellick sued under an Oregon disability discrimination statute and lost, with the court unceremoniously finding that the restaurant treated Sellick "exactly as it treats all other customers."

Deborah Birdwell found herself in a similar situation when she tried to go to the movies. Birdwell who was 5′4″ tall, and 360 pounds, wanted to bring her own chair to the theater.[93] When she called to ask permission, the cinema approved her request. Yet when Birdwell arrived at the movies, the manager had different ideas. He berated her in front of forty other moviegoers as she waited in line, telling her that the chair would present a fire hazard.

91 *Torcasio* v. *Murray*, 57 F.3d 1340 (4th Cir. 1995).
92 *Sellick* v. *Denny's Inc.*, 884 F. Supp. 388 (D. Or. 1995).
93 *Birdwell* v. *Carmike Cinemas, Inc.*, No. 2:94–0014 (M.D. Tenn. filed Feb. 23, 1994).

Birdwell sued under the ADA and settled, providing a remedy for her but no precedent for future moviegoers.

Christina Anderson filed an ADA claim against Macy's, alleging weight discrimination.[94] Anderson asserted that the department store discriminated by charging higher prices for plus-sized clothing, as well as by failing to sell plus-sized items alongside identical items in average or petite sizes. Anderson argued that the store effectively made a plus-sized ghetto by placing the department in the back of the store, away from cosmetics, jewelry, and fragrances, but near bedding, kitchenware, and the public restrooms. The court ultimately punted on the issue of whether obesity is a disability, instead throwing out Anderson's claim on procedural grounds.

Because all federal disability rights laws – the Rehabilitation Act, the ADA, the FHA, the ACAA, and Section 1557 – adopt the same definition of disability, these restrictive interpretations go beyond the ADA. For example, many airlines require people who cannot fit comfortably in a single seat because of their size to purchase an extra ticket.[95] This practice implies that the airlines do not view obesity as a disability under the ACAA. While Kenlie Tiggeman from Chapter 1 tried suing Southwest Airlines under the ADA (not the ACAA), her claim was never considered on the merits. Thus, it remains unresolved whether a similarly situated airline customer would have a valid discrimination claim under either statute.

The outcomes of many of these cases are unsatisfying for various reasons – specious reasoning, dodging the question, failing to abide by congressional intent, and leaving various health statuses unprotected from discriminatory treatment. Of particular concern is the distinction between obesity that results from a physiological condition as opposed to a volitional choice. Under that line of reasoning, only a person who is not personally "at fault" for her weight deserves legal protection.[96] As already noted, the distinction between voluntary, "mutable" health statuses and involuntary and unchangeable health statuses is illusory at best. Weight, like many health conditions, is a product of underlying physiology and genetics as well as habits, behaviors, and the environment. Moreover, even among the apparently voluntary conditions, such as diet and exercise, life circumstances restrict certain individuals' options. Accordingly, by recognizing only a narrow subset of individuals with

94 *Anderson* v. *Macy's Inc.*, 943 F. Supp. 2d 531 (W.D. Pa. 2013).

95 *Airline Policies for Overweight Passengers Traveling this Summer*, CheapAir.com, Jan. 20, 2015, at www.cheapair.com/blog/travel-tips/airline-policies-for-overweight-passengers-traveling-this-summer/.

96 Jessica A. Clarke, *Against Immunity*, 125 *Yale L.J.* 2, 21 (2015).

obesity, based on a false premise, disability rights laws continue to permit discrimination on the basis of health status.

Nicotine use raises similar concerns. Smoking, like obesity, coincides with health risk. As noted, a person who develops a smoking-related illness, like lung cancer, would have a disability.[97] That said, do disability laws offer independent protection for smokers and other nicotine users? To gain protection from the ADA based on smoking alone, a plaintiff would have to establish that her smoking substantially limits her in a major life activity or that she was regarded as disabled based on her smoking. Smoking, like obesity, also invites the suggestion that smokers should be denied protection for smoking-related illnesses on the basis that they "caused" their disabilities.

That reasoning carried the day in a 2001 case, brought by Daniel Brashear, a prisoner. Brashear asserted his right to smoke under the US Constitution and the ADA. He argued that the prison system had effectively banned smoking by prohibiting the sale and possession of tobacco.[98] The court dismissed his claim as frivolous yet nonetheless offered its thoughts on his claims. While the ADA quite clearly covers addiction,[99] the court found the notion that Congress intended to cover smoking "absurd." Despite the ADA's indifference to fault, the court adopted something like a personal responsibility standard, opining:

> [B]oth smoking and "nicotine addiction" are readily remediable, either by quitting smoking outright through an act of willpower (albeit easier for some than others), or by the use of such items as nicotine patches or nicotine chewing gum. If the smokers' nicotine addiction is thus remediable, neither such addiction nor smoking itself qualifies as a disability within the coverage of the ADA, under well-settled Supreme Court precedent.

The judge in Brashear's case used the pre-amendments, restrictive definition of disability, leaving open the possibility that smokers might fare better now.[100]

97 *See* Karen L. Chadwick, *Is Leisure-Time Smoking a Valid Employment Consideration?*, 70 *Alb. L. Rev.* 117, 125 ("Although smoking may lead to eventual disability, it is not, in and of itself, a disability because it does not limit major life activities as required under the ADA."); Mitchell H. Rubinstein, *Is Smoking a Disability Under the ADA as Amended?*, *Adjunct L. Prof Blog* (Nov. 23, 2009), http://lawprofessors.typepad.com/adjunctprofs/2009/11/is-smoking-a-disablity-under-the-ada-as-amended.html ("I would be surprised if smoking per se (as opposed to smoke related illnesses) are [sic] protected under the ADA.").

98 *Brashear* v. *Simms*, 138 F. Supp. 2d 693, 694 (D. Md. 2001).

99 Brashear, 138 F. Supp. 2d at 695.

100 Jon Hyman, *Smoking as a Disability Redux*, *Ohio Employer's L. Blog*, Nov. 16, 2009, www.ohioemployerlawblog.com/2009/11/smoking-as-disability-redux.html ("[T]he 'regarded as' prong of the new ADA is sufficiently broad to possibly encompass actions taken against employees pursuant to employer anti-smoking policies.") ("Employees can claim that anti-smoking

Yet, to date, plaintiffs have had zero success with such claims under the ADA. In fact, in an ironic twist for the nicotine-use-as disability line of argument, the ADA may expressly *allow* smoking bans in public accommodations because smoke allergies could qualify as disabilities.[101]

As with weight discrimination, the shared definition of disability across federal statutes means that if the ADA does not cover smoking and nicotine use, the other laws would not either. Consider housing. Grandmother Beulah Toombs had been smoking for almost eighty years, since the mid-1930s, when her subsidized, low-income senior housing went smoke-free in 2013.[102] Toombs had lived – and smoked – there for over a decade when she was told she must either quit or face potential eviction. The near-nonagenarian told reporters, "I don't think so . . . . This is my home, and I think you can do whatever you want to in your home." Unable to move in with any of her children because their homes were not accessible, Toombs began the search for new housing. Would evicting Toombs constitute discrimination? The answer is a staunch no.

The US Department of Housing and Urban Development (HUD) has outright stated that federal fair housing regulations do not apply to smokers.[103] HUD even includes a resource page on its website that offers educational materials, sample leases, and tips for enacting and enforcing smoke-free policies.[104] But it does not stop there. Effective February 2017, HUD requires every public housing agency to make its properties smoke-free within eighteen months.[105] Public housing agencies must outlaw tobacco use not only within housing units but also in hallways, offices, community centers, laundry

policies violate the ADA. Addiction is a protected disability. Diseases related to or caused by smoking [cancers, lung diseases, asthma, and other respiratory conditions, for example] are also protected disabilities. Employees will claim that an adverse action taken pursuant to an anti-smoking policy is being taken because the employer regards the employee as disabled. Adverse actions taken against employees because of smoking should now be viewed as high risk, at least until courts begin weighing in on this controversial issue."); Michael Moore, *ADA Amendments May Open the Door for Nicotine Addiction Claims, Pa. Lab. & Emp. Blog*, Oct. 29, 2008 (explaining that after the amendments "[e]mployers may well be required to reasonably accommodate nicotine-addicted employees much as they would need to do so with other addictions"), at www.palaborandemploymentblog.com/2008/10/articles/discrimination-harassment/ada-amendments-may-open-the-door-for-nicotine-addiction-claims/.

101 *See, e.g.*, *Staron* v. *McDonald's Corp.*, 51 F.3d. 353 (2nd Cir. 1995).

102 *89-Year-Old Woman Chooses Eviction Over Quitting Smoking, CBS Cleveland* (Apr. 21, 2017 2:01 PM), http://cleveland.cbslocal.com/2014/04/21/89-year-old-ohio-woman-chooses-eviction-over-quitting-smoking/.

103 2 *Real Estate Leasing Practice Manual* § 52:8 Apartments – Smoking Bans.

104 *U.S. Dep't Housing & Urban Development, Change is in the Air: An Action Guide for Establishing Smoke-Free Public Housing and Multifamily Properties*, at https://portal.hud.gov/hudportal/HUD?src=/program_offices/healthy_homes/smokefree2.

105 81 Fed. Reg. 87430 (2016).

facilities, day care providers, and even outdoors.[106] The new rule applies to "prohibited tobacco products," which it defines as "[i]tems that involve the ignition and burning of tobacco leaves, such as (but not limited to) cigarettes, cigars, and pipes," as well as hookahs.[107] Yet, even before the HUD mandate, several municipalities and a minimum of forty-seven public housing authorities had already outlawed smoking.[108] Toombs would not seem to have any legal remedy if evicted for her tobacco use.

Moreover, private property owners can also ban smoking without running afoul of the law. The American Lung Association (ALA) provides guidance for landlords who want to make their properties smoke-free.[109] Those materials encourage landlords to educate and inform tenants, post signs, and perform regular inspections. In the event of a violation, the ALA counsels landlords to follow the same procedures that they would for "any other lease violation," including verbal and written warnings and eventual eviction. The guidance specifically reassures landlords that "[t]here is no legal or constitutional right to smoke" and "[t]here is no Americans with Disabilities Act exemption for smoking."

Although the genesis of our healthism project was concern for discrimination on the basis of weight and nicotine use, we recognize that plenty of other unprotected health statuses could also be the basis of discrimination. If the health status has a corresponding medical diagnosis, like HIV, disability rights laws may reach it. But many other health statuses, however, do not rise to the legal definition of disability. In particular, health-related conduct remains outside of legal protections. We attribute this state of affairs to a trait–conduct distinction within the law, which we explore more deeply below.

In addition to the limited reach of the definition of disability, other aspects of disability rights law leave people vulnerable to healthism. For one, the ADA and the Rehabilitation Act include something called a "direct threat defense,"[110] which Dr. Bragdon tried to raise when he did not want to fill Sidney Abbott's cavity in his office. The idea behind the direct threat defense is that it is acceptable to discriminate on the basis of disability for health and safety

[106] 24 C.F.R. § 965.653(a) (banning tobacco use "in all public housing living units and interior areas [including but not limited to hallways, rental and administrative offices, community centers, day care centers, laundry centers, and similar structures], as well as in outdoor areas within 25 feet from public housing and administrative office buildings.").

[107] 24 C.F.R. § 965.653 (c).

[108] 2 *Real Estate Leasing Practice Manual* § 52:8 Apartments – Smoking Bans.

[109] American Lung Association, *Steps for Effective Enforcement of Smoke-free Policies in Multi-Unit Housing*, www.lung.org/our-initiatives/tobacco/smokefree-environments/multi-unit-housing/steps-for-effective-smokefree-policies.html.

[110] 29 U.S.C. § 705(18)(D); 42 U.S.C. § 12113(b); 29 C.F.R. § 1630.2(r).

reasons. The actual language of the direct threat defense provides an exception for when the person with a disability "pose[s] a direct threat to health and safety of *others*." The EEOC's regulatory interpretation of the statute extended it to cover the person with a disability herself. The EEOC would then permit employers to discriminate against an employee with a disability to protect the employee from herself.[111] In short, a person with a disability cannot simply roll the dice and assume the risk of possible injury, even if she wants to.

Mario Echazabal decided to challenge those regulations. Echazabal had worked at a Chevron oil refinery through an independent contractor for more than two decades. He twice applied for regular employment with the company, but it revoked his offers both times when Chevron's medical exam revealed liver damage because of hepatitis C.[112] The company's doctors feared the toxic chemicals at the refinery would further harm Echazabal's liver. After his second application, Chevron contacted the independent contractor where Echazabal technically worked and requested reassignment to a position without toxic exposures or removal from the refinery entirely. The contractor ultimately let him go. Echazabal sued Chevron, arguing it had discriminated against him based on his liver condition. Chevron raised the EEOC's version of the direct threat defense, arguing that it acted to protect Echazabal from harm. Echazabal challenged the EEOC's interpretation of direct threat. He maintained that the agency lacked the authority to extend the defense to the individual with a disability. The US Supreme Court, however, sided with Chevron. It held that the EEOC regulations could not "be fairly called unreasonable as allowing the kind of workplace paternalism the ADA was meant to outlaw." Thus, the ADA allows an employer to engage in disability discrimination so long as that discrimination is designed to protect people from risk.

Disability rights laws may also fall short with respect to combatting healthism because discriminators can allege alternative reasons for their actions. A key provision of the Rehabilitation Act prohibits discrimination "solely by reason of disability."[113] To succeed, a claimant has to show that she faced discrimination on the basis of her disability – and nothing else. When a potential discriminator has more than one reason for its actions, lawyers call it a "mixed-motive" claim. Laws related to race and sex explicitly allow victims of discrimination to raise these kinds of claims so long as the prohibited basis for discrimination was "a motivating factor."[114] In forbidding discrimination based "solely" on disability, the Rehabilitation Act appears not to cover mixed-motive

[111] 29 C.F.R. § 1630.2(r).

[112] *Chevron* v. *Echazabal*, 536 U.S. 73 (2002).

[113] Rehabilitation Act of 1973, 29 U.S.C. § 794(a).

[114] 42 U.S.C. § 1983.

claims.[115] Yet the ADA does not include the word "solely," arguably leaving the door open for claims with more than one motivating factor. While courts have not yet settled whether mixed-motive claims are viable under the ADA,[116] at least two courts have already rejected mixed-motive claims under the ADA's employment title.[117]

Proving discrimination "on the basis of" disability is particularly problematic for disability rights law's application to healthism. In cases of personal or familial illness, time away from work is frequently necessary and emotions are raw. Given the exhausting and emotionally charged nature of illness, an employee who is sick or has a close family member who is sick may very well supply an employer with a valid nondiscriminatory reason – increased absenteeism, decreased productivity, or distraction at work – that will bar recovery, even if disability is the true motivator.[118]

Consider this real-life example. Tony Dewitt, who was diagnosed with prostate cancer in 1995, lived with his wife Phyllis.[119] Phyllis worked at Proctor Hospital, which partially self-insured its employees.[120] During Tony's battle with cancer, the hospital inquired about the high cost of his cancer treatment and asked Phyllis whether her husband planned to seek hospice care. After her supervisor twice mentioned the expense of Tony's care and hospice as an option, Phyllis realized that the executives at Proctor were monitoring her spouse's health-care costs. Tony's medical bills continued to increase in the

115 *See Palmquist* v. *Shinseki*, 689 F.3d 66 (1st Cir. 2012) (discussing the but-for causation for Rehabilitation Act retaliation claims).

116 9–156 Larson on Employment Discrimination § 156.02(2)(a) (2014) (discussing the uncertainty of mixed-motive claims under the ADA); 2 Americans with Disabilities: Practice & Compliance Manual § 7:422 (2014) (noting the circuit split with respect to ADA mixed-motive claims).

117 *See* Americans with Disabilities: Practice & Compliance Manual, at § 7:422.

118 Notably, this critique applies to much of employment discrimination law: But-for causation is a significant impediment to certain employment discrimination claims. *See* e.g., 1–3 Employee Rights Litigation: Pleading and Practice § 3.03(1)(b) The Basic Legal Theories of Discrimination Based on Age (2013) (describing the absence of mixed-motive claims under the Age Discrimination in Employment Act as having a "deplorably negative impact"); *See also* Andrew Kenny, *The Meaning of "Because" in Employment Discrimination Law: Causation in Title VII Retaliation Cases After* Gross, 78 *Univ. Chi. L. Rev.* 1031 (2011); Bran Noonan, *The Impact of Gross* v. *FBL Financial Services,* Inc. and *the Meaning of the But-For Requirement*, 43 *Suffolk U. L. Rev.* 921 (2009–2010). Because none of us are perfect, employers can usually derive reasons to fire someone unrelated to the forbidden reason.

119 Judith Graham, *Fired Because of Medical Expenses? A Peoria Case, Chicago Tribune Blog*, Jan. 5, 2009, at http://newsblogs.chicagotribune.com/triage/2009/01/fired-because-0.html; Jon Hyman, *High Medical Costs as Direct Evidence of Disability Discrimination, Ohio Employer's Law Blog*, Feb. 28, 2008, at www.ohioemployerlawblog.com/2008/02/high-medical-costs-as-direct-evidence.html#.Uw_K9_1bxuY.

120 Proctor would pay the first $250,000 of annual costs and held stop-loss insurance to cover the rest. Hyman, note 119; *See also* Graham, note 119.

early 2000s. Then, during summer 2005, when the family was on vacation, Proctor called Phyllis to ask her to come in for a meeting. After she refused, allegedly raising her voice and being critical, the hospital fired her, despite Phyllis's perfect score on her annual employment evaluation. As a result of Phyllis's termination, the Dewitts found themselves without health insurance. Pursuant to federal law, the family opted to pay $900 out of pocket to keep their coverage for eighteen months. Tony died in 2006. Phyllis sued her former employer for violating the ADA and ERISA.[121] The court held that the hospital had provided evidence of "inappropriate, unprofessional, and disrespectful behavior" on Phyllis's part, which was sufficient to prove a nondiscriminatory reason for firing her.

When people are sick and tensions run high, individuals may act in a way that arguably justifies terminating them, like Phyllis Dewitt's frustrated phone call. Yet, taken in context, Dewitt's reaction to her less-than-sympathetic employer is far more understandable. Even though disability rights law offers some recourse, discriminators can simply offer an alternative nondiscriminatory reason to support their decision, thus leaving people vulnerable to healthism.

Health care is one important area where disability rights law is decidedly patchy. Although the ADA expressly applies to physicians,[122] the Rehabilitation Act has limited applicability to doctors.[123] Moreover, disability rights laws may have a limited effect on health insurance, the subject of Chapter 4. Remember *Alexander* v. *Choate*, our paradigmatic health justice case in Chapter 2? In it, a group of Medicaid recipients with disabilities sued the State of Tennessee under the Rehabilitation Act for lowering the number of covered inpatient hospital days.[124] They argued that the reduction disproportionately hurt disabled people. The US Supreme Court unanimously held that the change was acceptable because people with disabilities got "meaningful access" to exactly the same set of benefits as people without disabilities. It did not matter that disabled people would need more hospital days than nondisabled people. The *Choate* decision has cast a long shadow. When tackling issues of both public and private benefits, courts have held that disability rights laws entitle

[121] *Dewitt* v. *Proctor Hosp.*, 517 F.3d 944, 946 (7th Cir. 2008).

[122] Roberts, *Health Law as Disability*, note 6, at 1963, 1999–2002.

[123] *See* Sara Rosenbaum, David M. Frankford, Sylvia A. Law, and Rand E. Rosenblatt, *Law and the American Health Care System* 118 (explaining that Medicare Part B has been interpreted as a "contract of insurance" and thus not federal financial assistance); *see also United States* v. *Univ. Hosp.*, 729 F.2d 144, 161 (2nd Cir. 1983) (holding that medical treatment decisions are not within the scope of the Rehabilitation Act provision, prohibiting discrimination against an otherwise qualified handicapped individual).

[124] *Alexander* v. *Choate*, 469 U.S. 287 (1985).

people with disabilities to *equal access to* the programs or policies, but not to *equal benefit from* those programs or policies.[125]

For an example from the private sector, take the case of two anonymous men who challenged two of Mutual of Omaha's health insurance policies for capping lifetime benefits for AIDS, but not for other expensive conditions.[126] The insurance company effectively admitted that its policy was discriminatory, stipulating that the AIDS caps were not based on any risk calculations or actuarial principles. Instead, it argued that the content of health insurance policies is immune from the ADA. Siding with the insurers, the court noted that the insurance company would have happily sold its policies to the two men, even if those policies had less value for them personally because of the coverage caps. It held that while the ADA might guarantee access, the law does not regulate the content of the goods and services that commercial entities choose to provide.

Disability rights laws were not alone in their challenges combatting discrimination in health care. The civil rights laws governing race, sex, and age have also provided inadequate protections. These shortcomings are what prompted Congress to include an antidiscrimination right when it passed health care reform in 2010. Section 1557 of the Affordable Care Act (ACA), discussed more fully in Chapter 4, extends preexisting federal antidiscrimination laws prohibiting discrimination based on race, color, national origin, sex, age, and disability to federally funded health-care programs or activities and health insurance plans sold on the exchanges.[127] Those protections, however, are vulnerable to the political winds of change ushered in by President Donald Trump's administration and by the new members of Congress. Moreover, they suffer from the same limits that we have already identified with respect to antidiscrimination law. Therefore, the robustness of the ACA's new protection remains to be seen.

Privacy

Even the privacy protections associated with disability rights laws may not sufficiently safeguard against healthism. Privacy can help bypass healthism by keeping health-related information out of the hands of potential

[125] Samuel R. Bagenstos, *Law and the Contradictions of the Disability Rights Movement* 42–50 (2009) (describing how courts' interpretations of the "'job-related' rule" and the "access/content distinction" have effectively transformed accommodation into discrimination); Valarie K. Blake, *Restoring Civil Rights to the Disabled in Health Insurance*, 95 *Neb. L. Rev.* 1071(2016).

[126] *See Doe* v. *Mutual of Omaha Ins. Co.*, 179 F.3d 557 (1999) (challenging two insurance policies that imposed lifetime caps on AIDS coverage that were significantly lower than the caps on other conditions).

[127] 42 U.S.C. § 18116.

discriminators. People have tried to do just that and challenged the biometric screenings associated with employer-provided wellness programs. The ACA, however, *allows* employers to collect health-related data in conjunction with wellness programs, so long as they are voluntary and the results are confidential.[128] Despite the ADA's limitations on medical examinations and disability-related inquiries, the following series of cases demonstrates that wellness programs could still open the door for healthism.[129]

Bradley Seff, the named plaintiff in a class action lawsuit, sued his employer, Broward County, alleging that its wellness program violated the ADA.[130] The program consisted of a health risk assessment questionnaire and biometric screening, involving a blood draw. The administrator of the plan would then use that information to identify employees with a variety of different health conditions – including asthma, diabetes, and hypertension – and then offer those employees disease-management training. Although participating in the program was not required, nonparticipants who enrolled in the county's health insurance plan were charged $20 with each pay check. The court, relying on a provision of the ADA's employment title that carves out a safe harbor for certain kinds of insurance plans, rejected Seff's claim. The ADA does not prohibit an employer from sponsoring or administering a bona fide benefit plan that underwrites and classifies risks. The court was not compelled by Seff's asserted link between privacy and discrimination, stating that "[t]hough Plaintiff brings this claim under the ADA, it is hard to see how the wellness program relates to discrimination in any way."

Undeterred by the outcome of Seff's case, the EEOC challenged Orion Energy System's wellness program, which involved a health risk assessment that inquired about family medical history, a blood draw, and a physical exam, on behalf of Wendy Schobert.[131] Schobert did not want to participate, but opting out came at a significant price. She had to pay the full cost of her premium, plus a $50 penalty for declining to participate in the fitness evaluation. Employees who fully participated by both answering the health-related questions and undergoing the exam had their full insurance costs paid by the employer. Thus, she questioned whether the health assessments were truly voluntary, as well as whether their results would be kept confidential. Not long after she opted out, Orion fired Schobert. The EEOC alleged that the wellness program included wrongful medical exams and disability-related inquiries under the ADA. The parties eventually settled.

[128] 42 U.S.C. § 2705(j)(3)(A).

[129] Ifeoma Ajunwa et al., *Limitless Worker Surveillance*, 105 *Calif. L. Rev.* 735 (forthcoming 2017).

[130] *Seff* v. *Broward Cnty., Fla.*, 691 F.3d 1221 (11th Cir. 2012).

[131] *EEOC* v. *Orion Energy Sys.*, 145 F. Supp. 3d 841 (E.D. Wis. 2015).

Following this success, the EEOC has continued to sue employers who adopt wellness programs that involve health-risk assessments and biometric screenings. Next, the agency filed ADA and GINA claims against Honeywell International, whose wellness program required employees – and their spouses – to complete biometric testing or face a premium surcharge of $1,500 for the employee and another $1,000 for the spouse.[132] The EEOC tried to stop Honeywell from operating its program, but the court found that the agency had not met the necessary legal standard to warrant a court order. The parties later voluntarily dismissed the case.

In yet another case, the EEOC challenged Flambeau's wellness program.[133] Like Broward County and Orion Energy System, Flambeau's wellness program involved a health-risk assessment and biometric screening. Flambeau adopted particularly harsh penalties for nonparticipants. The company subsidized 75 percent of participating employees' premiums but terminated the coverage of employees who did not complete the program, requiring them to pay the entirety of their premiums out of pocket. The EEOC alleged that, given the severity of the penalty, the medical examinations and inquiries were not voluntary and thus violated the ADA. Instead of analyzing the program under the voluntariness exception, the court in *Flambeau*, like the court in *Seff*, found that the wellness program fell within the ADA's insurance safe harbor.

Not surprisingly, given the agency's aggressive attempts to apply the ADA to wellness programs, the EEOC's regulations reject the reasoning in these cases. The final rule provides that the ADA's safe harbor does *not* apply to wellness programs because the employer is not obtaining the health-related information to determine insurability or set rates.[134] The EEOC thus takes the position that both *Seff* and *Flambeau* were wrongly decided and that employers should not be allowed to collect health-related data in conjunction with workplace wellness programs. Incoherence between agency and judicial interpretation of a controlling statute is not entirely unusual but operates as another incomplete protection for potential healthism.

3.3.2. *Failure of Genetic Discrimination Law*

Like disability rights law, genetic-information discrimination law is ultimately too limited to provide adequate protection against healthism. GINA protects against discrimination on the basis of very specific health statuses – genetic

[132] *EEOC v. Honeywell Int'l*, CIV 14–4517 ADM/TNL, 2014 WL 5795481, at *1 (D. Minn. Nov. 6, 2014).

[133] *EEOC v. Flambeau, Inc.*, 131 F. Supp. 3d 849 (W.D. Wis. 2015).

[134] 29 C.F.R. § Pt. 1630, App.

test results and family medical history – and in very specific contexts – health insurance and employment.

Antidiscrimination

GINA leaves a significant amount of potentially discriminatory conduct untouched. Recall that GINA primarily targets pre-symptomatic risk and, as a result, does not cover manifested conditions. The EEOC regulations define manifested as being reasonably diagnosable by nongenetic means. A condition is not "manifested" for purposes of GINA if the diagnosis is based primarily on genetic information.[135] Yet these seemingly clean lines are far fuzzier than they first appear. In reality, physicians may rely on *both* genetic and nongenetic technologies to arrive at a conclusion. For instance, they may begin with a physical exam, have an idea of what is causing the underlying issue, and then use genetic testing to confirm.[136] Depending on the stage of the condition's progression, it may not yet qualify as a legally defined disability. The result is a gap between GINA – which excludes manifested conditions – and disability rights laws – which protect only legally recognized disabilities.[137] In other words, a condition might be manifested for purposes of GINA yet not be substantially limiting for purposes of disability rights law. It is then possible that some people might slip through the cracks between these two sets of protections.

Furthermore, the scope of GINA's protections is decidedly limited. It only covers health insurance and employment. Thus, outside California, any number of entities – banks, schools, even state-run programs – are free to discriminate on the basis of genetic information. Thus, the window for healthism remains open, despite the statute.

Privacy

GINA's privacy protection also may not do much good in combatting healthism. For example, when Mark Poore's employer asked him to fill out a health insurance questionnaire, he disclosed that his wife had multiple sclerosis.[138] His office manager then asked Poore when his wife had been diagnosed and what her prognosis was. Poore was fired three days later. He sued, raising GINA,

[135] 29 C.F.R. § 1635.3.

[136] *See* Jessica L. Roberts et al., *Evaluating NFL Player Health & Performance: Legal & Ethical Issues*, 165 *Univ. Penn. L. Rev.* 227, 287 (2017) (using Marfan syndrome as an example).

[137] Roberts, note 48, at 597, 637; Rothstein, note 48, at 837, 839.

[138] *Poore v. Peterbilt of Bristol*, 852 F. Supp. 2d 727 (W.D. Va. 2012).

ADA, ERISA, and age-discrimination claims. The court dismissed his GINA claim, finding that his wife's multiple sclerosis was not family medical history for purposes of GINA. GINA explicitly allows employers to obtain, use, and share medical information that is not genetic.[139] Of course, employers would still have to comply with the ADA's medical examination and disability-related inquiry provisions.

Also, remember that the EEOC tried to use GINA's privacy provisions to challenge the wellness program in *Honeywell*. Before the case was dismissed, Honeywell asserted that the information it was obtaining fell outside the statute's definition of genetic information. Alternatively, it maintained that the wellness program would fall under GINA's insurance provision, making it outside the EEOC's authority. And, finally, Honeywell argued that GINA provides an exception for voluntary wellness programs. Similarly, when Alfred Ortiz III, a firefighter-turned-paramedic, challenged the San Antonio Fire Department's mandatory wellness program under GINA, the court dismissed his claim, in part for conflating the statute's narrow definition of "genetic information" with medical information generally.[140] Genetic Information Nondiscrimination Act's privacy provision, then, might not combat broader forms of healthism.

3.3.3. *Failure of Lifestyle Discrimination and Anti-Lookism Law*

The laws that prohibit discrimination on the basis of disability and genetic information share a common deficiency: They protect health-related traits, but not health-related conduct.[141] We defined health status in Chapter 1 to include both health-related traits and health-related conduct. Health-related traits mean static statuses, like health records, diagnoses, and genetic information. Health-related conduct could potentially include a variety of activities and habits, including – but not limited to – tobacco use, alcohol consumption, diet, recreational activities, exercise, sleep patterns, living conditions, relationship status, and occupation. Existing laws protect health-related traits more effectively than health-related conduct.

[139] 42 U.S.C. § 2000ff-9 ("An employer . . . shall not be considered to be in violation of this chapter based on the use, acquisition, or disclosure of medical information that is not genetic information about a manifested disease, disorder, or pathological condition of an employee or member, including a manifested disease, disorder, or pathological condition that has or may have a genetic basis.").

[140] *Ortiz* v. *City of San Antonio Fire Dep't*, 806 F.3d 822 (5th Cir. 2015).

[141] Roberts, *Healthism and the Law*, note 6, at 571, 594.

Disability law is particularly instructive regarding this trait–conduct divide. Because of the protection of past disabilities, once a person has a legally defined actual disability, she is – for legal purposes – forever disabled, even if her impairment completely disappears. For example, a person with cancer has a substantially limiting impairment. Once that person becomes cancer-free, she continues to be a person with a disability because she has a record of a substantially limiting impairment. Legal disability is, therefore, relatively constant, making it a trait. Whether obesity qualifies as a disability seems to turn on the trait–conduct distinction. As explained, courts are more willing to consider obesity an impairment that could form the basis of a disability if it is the product of a physiological condition (trait), but not if it is the product of food choice (conduct). Drug addiction provides another useful example. Disability rights laws quite clearly protect addiction. The ADA, however, does not cover people who are actively partaking in illegal drugs.[142] Thus, the law protects addiction (trait), but not drug use (conduct).

Likewise, much of what GINA covers – genetic test results, the genetic test results of family members, and family medical history – would also meet our definition of a trait. (Of course, studies related to gene function, epigenetic changes, and mutations demonstrate that our genetics are not nearly as unchangeable as we might have previously thought.) Although research links genetics with weight, as well as with addiction and other behavioral tendencies,[143] it is highly unlikely that any court would interpret GINA to extend to health-related behaviors.

Lifestyle discrimination statutes would then seem to provide a solution to the trait–conduct problem presented by the other kinds of civil rights laws. Unfortunately, those laws are patchwork and offer only limited protection. First, federal law does prohibit discrimination on the basis of lawful conduct.[144] States are therefore free to develop their own idiosyncratic protections. As a result, the type of protected conduct varies significantly by state. In some places, all lawful off-duty conduct is protected, from political party affiliation to food of choice.[145] In other states, only tobacco

[142] 42 U.S.C. § 12114(a).

[143] Roberts, *Healthism and the Law*, note 6, at 571, 599–600.

[144] *See generally* Roberts, *Healthism and the Law*, note 6, at 571, 625 (arguing for a federal lifestyle discrimination statute to outlaw employer healthism).

[145] *See* Cal. Lab. Code §§ 96(k), 98.6 (West 2011); Colo. Rev. State. § 24–34–402.5 (2012); 820 Ill. Comp. Stat. Ann. 55/5 (West 2012); Minn. Stat. § 181.938 (2012); Mont. Code Ann. § 39–2–313 (2011); Nev. Rev. Stat. (2011); N.Y. Lab. Law. § 201-d (McKinney 2009); N.C. Gen. Stat. § 95–28.2 (2011); N.D. Cent. Code § 14–02.4–03 (2009 & Supp. 2012); Tenn. Code Ann. § 50–1–304 (West 2013); Wis. Stat. § 111.321 (2012).

use is protected.[146] This variation creates geographic inconsistencies. For instance, in a lawful-conduct state, an employer could not fire someone for using an indoor tanning bed, but in states without broad lifestyle discrimination protections, that decision would be perfectly legal. Moreover, lifestyle discrimination statutes tend to be employment discrimination laws, applicable only to employers. Consequently, state and local governments, recipients of federal funding, and commercial entities – think schools, hospitals, landlords, bars, restaurants, theaters, stores, law practices, and health clubs – could still discriminate on the basis of lawful conduct.

Lookism laws may also fail to fully address healthism. First of all, only a small number of jurisdictions outlaw discrimination based on physical appearance. Moreover, even when those laws are available, litigants must prove that it was their appearance, rather than some other factor, that prompted the discriminatory action. Finally, not all health statuses that provoke healthism manifest as physical characteristics, rendering laws that prohibit appearance discrimination ineffective.

3.3.4. *Failure of Benefits Law*

Employee benefits laws also fall short. ERISA applies only to current full-time employees. Its protections then do little to help individuals who are not already full-time workers.[147] People who were never hired, hired as contractors, or hired only part time therefore have no protection. Mixed-motive claims also create an issue in the ERISA context. To recover, a claimant must establish that the employer took the prohibited action "*for the purpose* of interfering with the attainment of any right to which such participant may become entitled

[146] Conn. Gen. Stat. § 31–405 (2013); D.C. Code § 7–1703-03 (2008); Ind. Code Ann. § 22–5-4–1 (West 2005 & Supp. 2012); Ky. Rev. Stat. Ann. § 344.040 (West 2011 & Supp. 2012); La. Rev. Stat. Ann. § 23:966 (2010); Me. Rev. Stat. Ann. tit. 26 § 527 (2007); N.H. Rev. Stat. Ann. § 275:37-a (2010); N.J. Stat. Ann. § 34:6B-1 (West 2011); N.M. Stat. Ann. § 50–11–3 (2007); Okla. Stat. Ann. tit. 40 § 500 (West 2013); R.I. Gen. Laws § 23–20.10–14 (2008); S.C. Code Ann. § 41–1–85 (2012); S.D. Codified Laws § 60–4-11 (2009); Va. Code Ann. § 2.2–2902 (2011); W. Va. Code Ann. § 21–3-19 (LexisNexis 2008); Wyo. Stat. Ann. § 27–9-105 (2013).

[147] Kathryn L. Moore, *Pay or Play Penalty Under the Affordable Care Act: Emerging Issues*, 47 *Creighton L. Rev.* 611 (2014); James N. Nelson, *The Patient Protection and Affordable Care Act, ERISA § 510 and the Next Generation of Benefits Litigation Concerns*, *ABA Employee Benefits Committee Newsletter* (1995) explaining that decisions to limit the number of full-time employees directly and disproportionately affects the un- and under-employed, who lack standing under ERISA), at www.americanbar.org/content/newsletter/groups/labor_law/ebc_newsletter/13_spr_ebcnews/ppaca.html.

under the plan."[148] In other words, ERISA explicitly requires intent.[149] Thus, if an employer can point to any valid alternate explanation for its conduct, it can likely escape liability.

Although some health-related traits and the workplace seem relatively well protected, antidiscrimination and privacy law do not come close to capturing all the kinds of health statuses that form the basis for discrimination, nor do they cover all the contexts where unacceptable healthism is present. To adequately serve the values of health welfare, health liberty, health equality, and health justice, we must then go beyond our current civil rights and privacy laws.

[148] 29 U.S.C. § 1002(7) (Emphasis added).
[149] Moore, note 147, at 611, 629.

4

Limits of Health Insurance Law

4.1. INTRODUCTION

This chapter examines how health insurance laws apply to healthism. The Patient Protection and Affordable Care Act (ACA) of 2010 made considerable strides at eradicating health-status discrimination in health insurance, but opportunities for healthism still remain.[1] Some of the ACA's changes sparked our healthism project, and the statute should be applauded as a landmark antidiscrimination law. In many ways, the ACA operates as a *Brown* v. *Board of Education*[2] for the unhealthy, adopting a nationwide policy that disadvantaging treatment based on health status is illegal.

For all its promise, the ACA is highly vulnerable to political tides and, even if fully realized and enforced, offers protection in a relatively narrow band of commercial health-insurance practices. Medical insurance in the United States is a fairly recent development and has evolved since the first half of the twentieth century into a patchwork of private and public programs, all of which are highly regulated. Throughout that history, the United States remains strongly committed to a private-market approach to providing and paying for health care. At several turns, proposals for a universal, government health-care program have been met with vehement objections, based on fears of "socialized medicine." At heart, Americans are free-market capitalists, even when it comes to matters as critical as health. Currently, more than half of the US population obtains coverage through employer-sponsored health plans, either as employees or dependents of employees.[3] Relying on private firms

[1] *See generally* Patient Protection and Affordable Care Act § 2001(a)(1), 42 U.S.C. § 1396 (2014).

[2] *Brown* v. *Board of Education*, 347 U.S. 483 (1954) (declaring unconstitutional "separate but equal" segregation of black and white students in public schools).

[3] *See 2016 Employer Health Benefits Survey*, Henry J. Kaiser Family Foundation, available at: http://kff.org/report-section/ehbs-2016-summary-of-findings (stating that "Employer-sponsored insurance covers over half of the non-elderly population").

to provide health insurance is a antiquated practice and an anomaly among developed countries.

For those not covered by employer plans, insurance is available in the private market on an individual or small-group basis.[4] The individual and small-group markets vary by state, are notoriously expensive, and are difficult to navigate. Commercial health-insurance markets are local, and insurance cannot be purchased across state lines. States maintain primary authority for regulating commercial health insurance, outside of the employer-sponsored market, with an expanded federal overlay under the ACA. Nevertheless, the individual and small-group markets suffer from a number of characteristic market imperfections. The ACA addresses some of those flaws, including persistent healthist practices in health insurance underwriting, ratemaking, and coverage decisions. But even under the ACA, considerable opportunities for insurers to discriminate based on health status persist.

To date, law-makers have declined to provide universal health insurance coverage for all Americans.[5] Instead, government health-care programs cover select groups and, in a few cases, specific diseases and conditions. Government coverage is generally considered a fallback, or a safety net, for those unable – usually for no fault of their own – to provide for themselves. Hewing to our capitalist values, only those "deserving" of government assistance get assistance. Traditionally, the "deserving" included the very young, elderly, disabled, pregnant, and caregivers of dependent children.[6] Accordingly, eligibility for government benefits was closely tied to health status.

As we explain, even adopting universal health care would not eliminate the potential for health-status discrimination in health insurance. A government health-care program could guarantee certain minimal benefits for all. But it seems likely that law-makers would continue to make distinctions based on health status, extending more generous benefits to some compared to others. Giving priority to those with the greatest health-care needs seems

[4] Rachel Garfield, Rachel Licata, and Katherine Young, Henry J. Kaiser *Family Foundation, The Uninsured at the Starting Line: Findings from the 2013 Kaiser Survey of Low-Income Americans and the* ACA (2014), available at: https://kaiserfamilyfoundation.files.wordpress.com/2014/02/8552-the-uninsured-at-the-starting-line7.pdf (regarding 18 percent uninsured rate); ibid. at 5 (regarding 5 percent non-group insurance purchasers).

[5] *See* Elizabeth Weeks Leonard, *The Fragility of the Affordable Care Act's Universal Coverage Strategy*, 46 *U. Tol. L. Rev.* 559 (2015) ("The United States has deliberately and repeatedly declined to establish a comprehensive national health-care system.").

[6] *See generally* Sara Rosenbaum et al., *Public Health Insurance Design for Children: The Evolution from Medicaid to SCHIP*, 1 *J. Health & Biomedical L.* 1, 7–8 (2004); Sandra J. Tanenbaum, *Medicaid Eligibility Policy in the 1980s: Medical Utilitarianism and the "Deserving" Poor*, 20 *J. Health Pol. Pol'y & L.* 933, 933–4 (1995).

perhaps eminently right and rational. Moreover, some way of allocating scarce resources would be necessary under any system. To state it more bluntly, health-care rationing – and differentiating based on health status – likely would still be tempting even under a single-payer system.[7]

4.2. HISTORY OF HEALTH INSURANCE

Before health insurance became common, most health care in the United States was paid directly by the patient or her family. For much of the long history of medicine, only limited interventions were available, and much of that care could be provided in the patient's home. If additional, professional care was warranted, patients and their family members would simply pay out of pocket, as they would for any other goods and services delivered to their doors. Sanitariums housed people with infectious diseases, and charitable hospitals or almshouses existed to treat and institutionalize the seriously ill who lacked family or financial support.[8]

As medical science and pharmacology advanced, services became more comprehensive and expensive. When paying out of pocket was no longer feasible, a private market for health insurance arose.[9] Large US automakers were one of the first industries to provide health insurance for their employees.[10] The high costs of providing treatment, assessing individual risk, and marketing health insurance policies made insuring on an individual basis difficult. Thus, group enrollment – particularly among workers who tended to be relatively healthy and thus more attractive risks for insurers to cover – was particularly viable. Moreover, marketing plans to a few large employers was cheaper than attempting to sell policies to multiple individuals, and insurers could collect premiums readily through payroll deductions. Early insurance products were quite limited, covering disability or loss of income rather than comprehensive medical expenses. Even when medical insurance was offered, the policies

7 *See* M. Gregg Bloche, *The Emergent Logic of Health Law*, 82 *S. Cal. L. Rev.* 389, 443 (2009) (discussing the possibility of single-payer or public-option approaches); Dan Eggen, *"Single-Payer" Supporters Challenge Democrats, Washington Post*, June 6, 2009 at A3, available at: www.washingtonpost.com/wp-dyn/content/article/2009/06/05/AR2009060503518.html.

8 *See* Nicole Huberfeld, Elizabeth Weeks, & Kevin Outterson, *The Law of American Healthcare* 152 (2017) (summarizing the start of private health insurance); *see also* Paul Starr, *The Social Transformation of American Medicine* 294–6 (1982) (describing the origins of private health insurance in the United States).

9 Huberfeld et al., note 8, at 45 (explaining that health insurance in the United States has typically been tied to private health insurance companies).

10 Starr, note 8, at 294 ("In the twenties, group disability insurance became more common; the major advance came in 1928, when General Motors signed a contract with Metropolitan to [provide health insurance to] cover 180,000 workers.").

typically did not cover routine, preventive care as expenses associated with those services did not present unpredictable, potentially catastrophic financial risk, like hospitalization. The notion of insuring for the cost of checkups and regular prescription drugs was akin to insuring for haircuts.

The impetus for expanding health insurance to a broader market came from hospitals. As hospitalization became more common, the cost imposed increasing burdens on middle-class families, not to mention the less affluent. Individual hospitals offered the first insurance policies on a direct-service basis, meaning that for a few dollars a year in premiums, a person could gain pretty much open-ended access to care at a particular hospital, without having to pay the actual expenses incurred during treatment. But, over time, that model became financially untenable. The Great Depression, especially, left hospitals unable to collect patients' bills and thus bearing significant financial losses.[11] Under that climate, single-hospital plans would have been even more destabilizing to the market, given the competition among hospitals.[12]

Soon thereafter, plans that resembled our current health insurance system began to take shape. First, an alternative community-wide approach, which ultimately became Blue Cross, emerged.[13] These community-wide plans were nonprofit, offered patients free choice among participating providers, and initially covered only hospital charges.[14] Blue Shield, which covered physician services, would come later and under stronger resistance from physicians who feared losing their professional autonomy.[15] Physician services also presented a different – arguably less serious – financial risk for potential subscribers, making the demand for the products not as great. States stepped in fairly quickly to regulate these new hospital-service plans as insurance products, applying state law requirements regarding reserves, rate reviews, composition of boards of directors, and tax-exempt statuses.

Health insurance solves several problems at once. Most people prefer paying an amount certain every month rather than facing the uncertainty of potentially catastrophic health-care bills.[16] Health insurance also pools risks; all subscribers pay into the pool, but some receive more care than their premiums would otherwise cover, while others end up receiving less care than

[11] Ibid. at 295 (showing that the Great Depression exposed the financial issues in the United States noting that the "average hospital deficits rose from 15.2 to 20.6 percent of disbursements").

[12] Ibid. at 295–6 ("Single-hospital plans . . . might well have brought more instability to the hospital industry because of the competition they would have promoted.").

[13] Huberfeld et al., note 8, at 155.

[14] Starr, note 8, at 296 (describing how the community-wide plans were structured).

[15] Robert Cunningham III and Robert M. Cunningham Jr., *History of the Blue Cross and Blue Shield System* 38 (1997).

[16] Ibid. at 155.

the amount that they paid into the pool.[17] Large employer groups, such as the automobile manufacturers that first offered health plans, provide a particularly attractive, readily established risk pool of relatively low-risk, healthy individuals.

As noted above, Blue Cross plans characteristically were community-rated, meaning that all subscribers within the same geographic community paid the same premium rates.[18] Under community rating, those at greater risk for hospitalization tend to pay lower premiums because those at lower risk for hospitalization subsidize them. The alternative approach, experience rating, means that subscribers pay different rates based on their individual risk profiles like with other insurance products such as life insurance, automobile insurance, and property insurance.[19] Quite naturally, the result of experience rating is that insurance is more expensive if the customer is deemed higher risk. This fact means that coverage could be cost-prohibitive for some individuals, especially those most in need of it. Over time, that potential, while arguably appropriate for other forms of insurance, struck the public and law-makers as inappropriate and perhaps even intolerable for health insurance. It bears emphasis that experience rating in health insurance explicitly discriminates against those with higher health risks and greater health-care needs.

Over time, the commercial health insurance market grew increasingly robust and competitive, with a number of for-profit companies, including formerly nonprofit Blue Cross plans that converted to for-profits status, entering the market. Under that competition, the Blues' characteristic community rating approach gave way to widespread experience rating based on the expected risks of the group or individual. Through experience rating, insurers could better align their potential exposure for claims to the individual customer and set premiums accordingly. Risk pooling operates under both community rating and experience rating, but the effect is diluted under experience rating. Group plans typically are community-rated within the group, meaning that no individual member of the group pays more based on individual risks. The entire group, however, may experience a premium rate increase based on the risk profiles of individual members.[20]

[17] Ibid. at 161.

[18] Huberfeld et al., note 8, at 155.

[19] Ibid. at 161 (describing experience rating as a process where health insurance companies gather information like age, race, and history of illness to set each individual's premium rate).

[20] Ibid. at 155 (showing an example of how the premiums of the group would increase by stating "if one employee suffered a catastrophic illness, premiums would rise dramatically for everyone the next year").

Experience rating, while advantageous for insurers, is especially problematic for certain kinds of policyholders. A small employer, for example, could be faced with a dramatic premium rate increase if one employee suffers catastrophic injury or illness in a given year.[21] That premium increase could be unsustainable, leading the employer to stop offering coverage to all of its workers. Thus, in the workplace, an employee may be highly interested in the Twinkie quotient of her coworker's lunchbox or her colleague's inability to kick a pack-a-day cigarette habit. Outside of the group market, the effect of experience rating is even more dramatic. Those who arguably need health care most, such as the elderly or people with chronic health conditions, might find themselves declared too risky to insure or might be offered prohibitively expensive coverage.[22] Moreover, as discussed in Chapter 3 regarding privacy, insurers became increasingly nosy, seeking to uncover customers' health behaviors and habits, genetic and other predispositions to disease, and a wide range of other personal information that may speak to the likelihood of illness or injury.

Group coverage, especially employer-provided plans, grew increasingly common for a variety of reasons. As noted, insurers targeted employers because they provided attractive risk pools and offered a single entry point for marketing and plan administration. For employers, it makes good business sense to offer health insurance because providing coverage helps maintain a healthy workforce, which in turn reduces absenteeism and holds down premiums. The federal government added further incentives, allowing an above-the-line deduction from gross corporate income taxes for employers' contributions paid toward employee benefits.[23] Generally it is cheaper for an employer to offer more generous benefits than to increase wages or salaries. Finally, health insurance is so common in many industries that employees and applicants have come to expect it as part of their overall compensation package. Thus, to remain competitive for good workers, in many industries, employers offer health coverage.

In summary, paying for health care in the United States evolved from a relatively modest self-pay approach into an elaborate health insurance industry,

[21] Ibid. at 155.

[22] Ibid. at 155 (stating "[I]ndividuals found coverage to be very expensive, especially if they were older or had health problems").

[23] *See* Internal Revenue Service, available at: www.irs.gov/businesses/small-businesses-self-employed/employee-benefits (last visited March 13, 2017) ("If an employer pays the cost of an accident or health insurance plan for his/her employees, including an employee's spouse and dependents, the employer's payments are not wages and are not subject to Social Security, Medicare, and FUTA taxes, or federal income tax withholding.").

dominated by employer-provided group plans and large insurance companies offering particular products in each state, subject to the state's particular insurance law. The Health Insurance Portability and Accountability Act (HIPAA) of 1996 (better known for its privacy protections, but note that the "P" actually stands for "portability") greatly reduced healthist practices in the employer-sponsored group insurance market.[24] HIPAA addressed the problem of job-lock, meaning that employees were hesitant to change jobs for fear of losing health insurance coverage, resulting in their sometimes remaining in suboptimal employment to the detriment of their personal and social welfare. The most dramatic change in health insurance came in 2014, when most of the ACA's key provisions took effect. We turn now to discuss the operation of these and other insurance laws, specifically, their bearing on health status and presenting the potential for healthism.

4.3. HEALTH STATUS UNDER EXISTING HEALTH INSURANCE LAW

As discussed above, the United States maintains a decidedly "non-system" of health-care delivery, with some groups entitled to government benefits; some privileged to have employers that provide health plans; some able to navigate and afford individual health insurance plans; and others left out in the cold with no coverage. Even though differential treatment based on health status is increasingly seen as unfair and wrong, competitive market pressures and pragmatic reasons related to resource limits have allowed law-makers and insurers to continue distinguishing among individuals based on their health status. Our objective in this chapter is similar to the discussion of antidiscrimination and privacy laws in Chapter 3: to highlight those remaining opportunities for health-status differentiation in health insurance. We leave the normative assessment of whether such laws, practices, and policies are healthist to Chapter 6.

4.3.1. *Government Health-Care Programs*

Government health-care programs traditionally have served as a backstop to the private market. Commercial health insurance, by its very nature, excludes large swaths of the population: retirees, unless their employers generously allow them to stay on group coverage; those unable to work due to disability, underage, caretaker responsibilities, or other challenges; the elderly, chronically ill, and

[24] Health Insurance Portability and Accountability Act of 1996 (HIPAA), Pub. L. No. 104–191, 110 Stat. 1936 (1996).

any other individuals who cannot afford the high premiums offered by private insurers in the individual market. As the private market was evolving under the market dynamics described earlier in this chapter, social justice, humanitarian, and other political forces came together in the 1960s to urge government health-insurance coverage for certain groups who were priced out of private insurance. For almost a century, state and federal law-makers had repeatedly, but unsuccessfully, proposed various government health insurance programs. The political stars finally aligned in 1965 under Lyndon B. Johnson's Great Society, which included the enactment of Medicare and Medicaid.[25]

Medicare eligibility is based on age (sixty-five or older) or permanent disability.[26] The program also covers individuals with end-stage renal disease (ESRD)[27] and amyotrophic lateral sclerosis (ALS, or Lou Gehrig's disease).[28] Although it would seem easy to identify other chronic health conditions warranting public benefits, Congress has not further expanded the Medicare program to disease-specific coverage due to cost-containment and other public policy concerns. Medicare eligibility for the non-elderly clearly differentiates based on health, limiting health statuses of particularly severe disabilities, a specific kidney condition, and a progressive neurodegenerative disease. People over age sixty-five are covered regardless of health status or diagnosis, but age nevertheless operates as a rough proxy for health status, given that elderly people tend to have more frequent and severe medical issues.

The other major federal health-care program, Medicaid, also makes distinctions based on health. In contrast to Medicare – which operates somewhat like a federal pension, available to all who meet the qualifying conditions, without regard to income – Medicaid is explicitly means-tested. Medicaid provides health insurance to some, but not all, low-income individuals – only those considered "deserving" of government assistance. Traditional Medicaid, as enacted in 1965 and amended several times over its five decades, limited coverage to low-income individuals who also have another qualifying condition, namely, pregnancy, disability, blindness, childhood, old age, or primary care-taking responsibility of an eligible dependent child.[29] In short, both major federal health benefit programs openly classify individuals based on health status.

[25] *See* Jonathan Zasloff, *The Secret History of the Fair Housing Act*, 53 *Harv. J. on Legis.* 247, 254 (2016) (explaining that in 1965 Congress enacted "Johnson's Great Society programs such as Medicare and Medicaid"); *see generally* Medicaid Act, 42 U.S.C. § 1396 (1965); Medicare Act, 42 U.S.C. § 1395 (1965).

[26] Huberfeld et al., note 8, at 48.

[27] Ibid.

[28] 42 U.S.C. § 426(h) (2015).

[29] Rosenbaum, note 6.

Medicaid's basic design changed, however, under the ACA. The ACA eliminated the categories of eligibility, including health-status categories, and extended coverage to all individuals and families below a certain income threshold, regardless of other "categorical" eligibility.[30] Subsequently, however, the US Supreme Court ruled that states have the option to retain the traditional categories of eligibility or expand coverage based on income alone.[31] Since that judicial decision, a majority of states elected to expand Medicaid, dropping the health-status and other categories of eligibility, while an increasing minority of states have retained the traditional eligibility rules.[32] As a result, Medicaid differentiates based on health status in some parts of the country while not making those distinctions in other locales. Since taking office in 2017, Donald Trump's administration has invited a new form of health-status discrimination to Medicaid, encouraging states to add "work or other community engagement" requirements for their non-elderly, non-pregnant, adult Medicaid beneficiaries.[33] Requiring work, or work-promotion activities, for Medicaid eligibility discriminates against those whose health statuses impede their ability to work.

Other federal programs, such as the Ryan White Comprehensive AIDS Resources Emergency (CARE) Act, cover specific conditions, in that case, HIV/AIDS.[34] The Ryan White CARE Act is a payer of last resort, meaning that coverage kicks in only when no other resources are available. Like Medicare's ESRD or ALS benefits, Ryan White differentiates based on health. Also, the National Childhood Vaccine Injury Act (NVIC) of 1986[35] provides financial compensation for vaccine-related injuries and deaths.[36] Although not health insurance per se, NVIC does represent a program that extends federal benefits related to a particular health status.

30 *See* 42 U.S.C. § 1396a(a)(10)(A)(i)(VIII) (2014) (expanding Medicaid eligibility); *see also* 42 C.F.R. § 435.603(d)(1) (2014) (specifying 5 percent income disregard, which technically brings eligibility level to 138 percent FPL).

31 *See generally NFIB* v. *Sebelius*, 567 U.S. 519 (2012).

32 *See Status of State Action on the Medicaid Expansion Decision*, Henry J. Kaiser Family Foundation, available at: www.kff.org/health-reform/state-indicator/state-activity-around-expanding-medicaid-under-the-affordable-care-act/?currentTimeframe=0&sortModel=%7B%22colId%22:%22Location%22,%22sort%22:%22asc%22%7D (last updated June 19, 2017); *Where the States Stand on Medicaid Expansion*, Advisory Board Co., available at: www.advisory.com/daily-briefing/resources/primers/medicaidmap (last updated May 19, 2017).

33 *See* Department of Health and Human Services, *Opportunities to Promote Work and Community Engagement Among Medicaid Beneficiaries*, SMD: 18–002, Jan. 11, 2018, available at: www.medicaid.gov/federal-policy-guidance/downloads/smd18002.pdf.

34 Ryan White Comprehensive AIDS Resources Emergency (CARE) Act of 1990, 42 U.S.C. § 300ff (1990).

35 42 U.S.C. §§ 300aa-1 to 300aa-34.

36 National Childhood Vaccine Injury Act of 1986, 42 U.S.C. §§ 300aa-1–300aa-34 (1986).

Evaluating health-status differentiation in government health-care programs requires particular attention. When the government – opposed to private parties – acts, that conduct triggers a host of antidiscrimination laws. One particularly relevant law is Section 1557 of the ACA, which expressly extends existing federal antidiscrimination laws to health insurance, including government health-care programs. Section 1557 prohibits discrimination on the basis of race, color, national origin, sex, age, and disability in any health program or activity that received funding from the US Department of Health and Human Services (HHS); any health program or activity that HHS administers; and health insurance exchanges and all plans offered by issuers that participate in those exchanges.[37] One of the first successful Section 1557 claims involved disability discrimination. The case was brought against four Florida insurers that priced all HIV medications – even generics – at the highest rate.[38]

Although Section 1557 prohibits various types of discrimination in government health-care programs – a salutary development – that law does not explicitly address health-status discrimination. For all the same reasons from Chapter 3, Section 1557 leaves open large remaining pockets of potential healthism. Specifically, health conditions that fall short of the legal definition of disability and conduct that has not yet manifested into a diagnosis remain unprotected. Moreover, the ACA is regularly under attack by law-makers and subject to being struck down in whole or in part at some point during the Trump presidency. The Obama administration was committed to robust enforcement and expansive interpretation of Section 1557, but the Trump administration strongly opposes those policies.[39]

The future of both Medicaid expansion and Section 1557, each promising developments in addressing health-status discrimination in government health-care programs, is very much in question. Even if they survive the repeal and replace efforts, discussed more fully below, differentiation based on health status is likely to remain a prominent feature of government health-care programs, given the need to allocate scarce resources to competing policy priorities. Former Alaska governor and vice-presidential candidate, Sarah Palin,

[37] 42 U.S.C. § 18116 (2010).

[38] For a copy of the administrative complaint, *see* Jane Perkins and Wayne Turner, *NHeLP and The AIDS Institute Complaint to HHS Re HIV/AIDS Discrimination by Florida Insurers*, National Health Law Program (Sept. 29, 2015), available at: www.healthlaw.org/publications/browse-all-publications/HHS-HIV-Complaint#.V-ohazKZPUp.

[39] *Franciscan All., Inc.* v. *Burwell*, 227 F.Supp.3d 660 (N.D. Tex. 2016) (issuing nationwide injunction of regulations implementing Section 1557, at least as far as applied to prohibit discrimination based on sexual identity and termination of pregnancy).

struck fear in the hearts of Americans by suggesting that government "death panels" would decide whether her disabled child, or anyone's elderly parent, should live or die, based on the relative value of an individual's life. Although that accusation lies far from the true content of the ACA as proposed or enacted, Palin was not wrong to suggest that some lines will have to be drawn between those who receive care and those who do not. We cannot afford to do everything for everyone. For better or worse, health status remains a tempting basis for those distinctions.

4.3.2. *Private Insurance*

Government health insurance programs are available for only a subset – roughly a quarter – of the US population. The rest of America obtains health insurance from private companies, or not at all. From the outset, one of the challenges in serving the private market has been the problem of adverse selection, that is, the tendency of those most likely to get sick to purchase health insurance. Adverse selection affects risk pooling because it means a higher quotient of high-risk individuals and lower quotient of low-risk individuals in the risk pool. Insurers have employed various strategies to guard against adverse selection, including simply refusing to sell policies to individuals with known health conditions, such as preexisting condition exclusions, and charging higher premiums based on health status or health risk, such as experience rating.

Another recognized feature of health insurance markets is moral hazard, meaning the tendency of those with insurance to use more medical care than they otherwise would. For similar reasons, in other insurance contexts, life insurance policies typically refuse to cover suicide, and liability policies typically refuse to cover intentional harm. The concern is that people might be more inclined to commit self-harm or harm to another if they know the resulting loss will be covered by insurance. Health insurers address moral hazard by imposing various out-of-pocket costs at the time of service, including deductibles, copayments, and coinsurance. The idea is that if the patient has some "skin in the game," she will think twice before making that unnecessary trip to the emergency room or showing up at her doctor's office with simply a bad cold.

As health-care costs steadily rose – and continue to rise – health insurers sought additional ways to limit their financial exposure. Traditional indemnity policies simply paid for whatever care the doctor or hospital orders. That approach, however, has an obvious inflationary incentive. Health-care providers have no reason to limit the care that they order and can suffer from their own form of moral hazard – ordering more care for insured patients, knowing that they themselves would get paid. Accordingly, insurers began requiring preapproval before covering certain treatments, or reviewing claims retroactively for medical necessity and other limits. They might also issue policies broadly only to conduct post-claims underwriting and rescissions. Insurers would, in the face of a potentially large claim or serious diagnosis, scour the patient's application for errors, omissions, or other technical grounds for canceling coverage. Insurers also commonly placed lifetime or annual limits on coverage. They simply would not cover any health-care expenditures beyond those limits. Such limits tend to discriminate against patients with serious, chronic, or particularly costly conditions. By their very design, all of these techniques disadvantage unhealthy individuals, making private insurance more expensive or, in many cases, unavailable.

Health Insurance and Risk Assessment[40]

We already briefly discussed the difference between community rating and experience rating in health insurance. We now drill down more precisely on risk assessment in health insurance and the health-status differentiation baked into that design. Broadly defined, insurance is a risk-pooling arrangement intended to indemnify the insured against a particular type of loss, including death, property damage, illness, and injury.[41] Insurers must then set premiums calibrated to their insureds' risks. Inaccurately assessing could breakdown the insurance structure because the costs paid out would exceed the premiums paid in.

A sustainable, and even profitable, insurance plan thus relies on assessing accurate, calculable risks.[42] Risk assessment is particularly difficult in the health insurance market because health is fluid and amorphous, determined by a wide range of controllable and uncontrollable, known and unknown, factors.[43] Moreover, information asymmetries are endemic to risk assessment.

40 Portions of this subsection originally appeared in Jessica L. Roberts, *"Healthism": A Critique of the Antidiscrimination Approach to Health Insurance and Health-Care Reform*, 2012 *U. Ill. L. Rev.* 1159, 1165 (2012).

41 Huberfeld et al., note 8, at 161. An insurance contract has three key elements. It (1) redistributes risk (2) across a large number of individuals (3) by a company that is in the business of professional risk distribution. Thus, health insurance is "[c]overage that provides for the payments of benefits as a result of sickness or injury. [It] [i]ncludes insurance for losses from accident, medical expense, disability, or accidental death and dismemberment." *Dictionary of Health Insurance and Managed Care* 138.

42 Ibid. ("The health insurance company selling the plan takes a calculated risk that it will collect more in monthly premiums than it will have to pay out in medical claims.").

43 H. Tristram Engelhardt, Jr., *The Foundations of Bioethics* 189–227 (2d edn. 1996) (describing the social processes of medicalization, diagnosis, and treatment).

Insureds know more about their own health than insurers. And health-care providers typically know more about available treatments and prognoses than insurers or insureds. To assess the potential health risks of a particular applicant, insurers rely not only on applicants' own reports but also opinions and diagnoses of health professionals, including medical experts working for the insurer.[44] To inform those opinions, health insurers historically have sought detailed individual and family medical histories, in addition to demographic and behavioral factors like sex, age, weight, occupation, and smoking that statistically tend to correlate with greater health risks.[45] That information gathering raises considerable privacy concerns, as discussed in Chapter 3.

Even assuming perfect information, to be financially viable (as either nonprofit or for-profit companies) insurers must maintain sustainable risk pools. Just as high-risk individuals are more likely to purchase insurance, low-risk individuals are more likely to opt out of insurance.[46] This phenomenon exacerbates the adverse selection. As more high-risk people opt in, they drive up the overall risk level in the pool and thereby drive up premiums. Increasingly, then, low-risk people opt out, deeming the higher premiums not worth it. They would rather take the gamble that they will stay well than pay out a chunk of money every month.[47] As more low-risk people leave, rates again rise, driving those lower relative risks to leave the market, and so on, until the market collapses, creating a "death spiral."[48]

Under those pressures, private insurers have adopted a number of practices that disadvantage the unhealthy. The strategies operate somewhat differently in the individual and group markets, but differential treatment based on health status occurs in both settings. Much of what we describe below captures the insurance markets pre-ACA. Later we will discuss the changes effected by

44 Ibid.

45 *See* Deborah A. Stone, *The Struggle for the Soul of Health Insurance*, 18 *J. Health Pol. Pol'y & L.* 287, 300–8 (1993) (describing the process of medical underwriting in health insurance).

46 Jessica L. Roberts, *"Healthism": A Critique of the Antidiscrimination Approach to Health Insurance and Health-Care Reform*, 2012 *U. Ill. L. Rev.* 1159, 1165 (2012).

47 Adverse selection drives up the cost of insurance. *Dictionary*, note 39. For example, "[l]ow enrollee out-of-pocket costs might lure those individuals requiring more health services into an HMO rather than an indemnity-plan because the former does not have a deductible. Therefore, the HMO would have a greater proportion of less-healthy enrollees, thereby driving up costs and increasing financial risks." Ibid. at 12.

48 For the definition of "death spiral," *see Dictionary*, note 39, at 80 (defining a "death spiral" as "[a]n insurance term that refers to a vicious spiral of high premium rates and adverse selection, generally in a free-choice environment"). This cycle has also been called a lemon pricing problem. In the used car market, pricing reflects the average used car. Thus, individuals with "good" used cars cannot get a high enough price and exit the market, leaving behind "lemons." *See* George A. Akerlof, *The Market for "Lemons": Quality Uncertainty and the Market Mechanism*, 84 *Q. J. Econ.* 488, 489–90 (1970).

that law and the remaining opportunities for health-status differentiation even under its progressive anti–health discrimination reforms.

In the individual market, health insurers historically engaged in risk selection, using health information for eligibility or underwriting decisions. Insurers evaluate applications using underwriting.[49] First an insurer assesses risk, then it will either assign the applicant to a rating class or decline to offer coverage.[50] In the individual market, the insurer might choose not to offer coverage for potentially costly conditions that predate the policy application, called preexisting condition exclusions.[51] Preexisting conditions can range from minor conditions like allergies to major ones like cancer.[52]

Health insurers also engage in ratemaking based on health status. Ratemaking follows underwriting. Once the insurer decides that a particular applicant is insurable, it then decides how much to charge in premiums to carry that individual's risk. That process includes assessment of the individual's health risks based on her current and past health conditions. Under a traditional experience-rating model, those with higher risks pay higher rates.[53] The combined result of these two practices is that those most likely to need medical services are also those least likely to be individually insurable.

Most Americans with private health insurance have group policies.[54] Group health insurance plans (most commonly, employer-sponsored health insurance) assess the risk of the group in its entirety. Because the risk is distributed more widely, group plans tend to be more affordable. Group health plans may be either large or small. The smaller the group, the larger the impact an individual health risk could have.[55] Individuals with group insurance also face

49 Roberts, note 44, at 1166.

50 Ibid.

51 Ibid. Individual insurers can accept an individual but exclude coverage for a certain disease.

52 *See* Karen Pollitz et al., *How accessible is individual health insurance for consumers in less-than-perfect health?*, The Henry J. Kaiser Family Foundation, 3–4 (2001), available at: www.kff.org/insurance/20010620a-index.cfm.

53 *See* Stone, note 43, at 306 (noting that both individual and group insurers may increase premiums, limit coverage, or do both with respect to high-risk individuals).

54 Of the privately insured, 87.2 percent hold employer-provided health insurance policies. *See* Carmen DeNavas-Walt et al., *U.S. Dep't of Commerce, U.S. Census Bureau, Income, Poverty, and Health Insurance Coverage in the United States*: 2009, at 71 tbl.C-1 (2010); *see also* The Kaiser Comm'n on Medicaid & the Uninsured, The Henry J. Kaiser Family Foundation, *The Uninsured: A Primer, Key Facts About Americans Without Health Insurance*, 31 tbl.5 (2010), available at: www.kff.org/uninsured/upload/7451-06.pdf (reporting that 58.1 percent of the non-elderly hold employer-based health insurance policies and that only 5.2 percent of the non-elderly hold private, individual health insurance policies).

55 Small-group health insurers are more likely to operate in a manner akin to the individual market. Because the small-group market encounters many of the same risk-assessment challenges as the individual market, small-group insurers have adopted similar practices. *See* Mark

discrimination on the basis of health status, albeit less directly than those in the individual market.[56].

For one, insurers in the group market may reject the group as a whole for being too risky.[57] That is to say, one bad apple may spoil the bunch. Group health insurers can offer limited coverage to the group,[58] such as not covering a specific health condition.[59] For example, an employer group plan might place a $5,000 lifetime cap on coverage for HIV/AIDS. In a small group, a single person's diagnosis can raise everyone's premiums. As a result, some employers have asked costly employees to leave the group[60] or have tried to avoid employing them in the first place.[61]

In addition to creating disadvantage based on health status via premium rates, cost-sharing obligations under health insurance plans further disadvantage the unhealthy. Requiring insureds to pay some amount at the time of service – in addition to monthly or periodic premiums – relates to adverse selection but more directly addresses the problem of moral hazard. Health insurers address moral hazard through cost sharing in at least three ways: (1) deductibles, (2) coinsurance, and (3) copayments. Deductibles are typically flat dollar amounts that the insured must pay before coverage kicks in.[62]

A. Hall, *Public Choice and Private Insurance: The Case of Small Group Market Reforms*, 1998 *U. Ill. L. Rev.* 757, 766 (arguing in favor of restoring risk-pooling mechanisms found in large-group insurance to the small-group market). Thus, small-group health insurers are more likely to engage in the kind of risk assessment and cost-minimizing behaviors associated with individual health insurance. *See* Karen A. Clifford and Russel P. Luculano, *AIDS and Insurance: The Rationale for AIDS-Related Testing*, 100 *Harv. L. Rev.* 1806, 1809 n.17 (1987). ("Underwriting standards are stricter for small groups . . . because the size of the group is insufficient to spread the risk broadly enough to absorb the effect of adverse selection.")

56 Roberts, note 44, at 1167–8

57 While an insurer can choose to reject the entire group, HIPAA prevents group insurers from discriminating against individuals on the basis of their health status with regard to eligibility, contributions, or premiums. *See* 29 U.S.C. §1182(a)(1) (2006).

58 *See* 29 C.F.R. §2590.702(d)(1) (2010). The criteria for determining which individuals are similarly situated cannot be health-related.

59 Litigants have tried and failed to challenge condition-specific limitations, such as caps on coverage for AIDS-related care, as discriminatory pursuant to the Americans with Disabilities Act. *See, e.g., Doe* v. *Mut. Omaha Ins. Co.*, 179 F.3d 557 (7th Cir. 1999).

60 *See, e.g.*, Sec'y's Advisory Comm. on Genetics, Health, & Soc'y, U.S. Dep't of Health & Human Servs., *Public Perspectives on Genetic Discrimination* 14 (2004), http://oba.od.nih.gov/oba/sacghs/reports/Public_Perspectives_ GenDiscrim.pdf (statement of Tonia Phillips) (explaining how her employer asked her to switch to her husband's health insurance while she was seeking preventive treatment for breast cancer after testing positive for a genetic mutation associated with a heightened chance of developing the disease).

61 Elizabeth Pendo, *Working Sick: Lessons of Chronic Illness for Health Care Reform*, 9 *Yale J. Health Pol'y L. & Ethics* 453, 460 (2009) (noting reports of "health discrimination" in employment as the result of chronic illness) (citation omitted).

62 Huberfeld et al., note 8, at 151.

Coinsurance splits some of the covered expenses between the insurer and the insured.[63] Copayments require insureds to pay a small dollar amount toward designated services.[64]

People that consume more health care end up paying more in cost sharing.[65] Just one chronic health condition could increase out-of-pocket expenses by over 70 percent, and a second condition could increase spending by 300 percent.[66] Although intended to deter adverse selection and over-utilization of medical care, cost-sharing obligations also tend to perpetuate health-status discrimination.[67] Moreover, the deterrent effect may have the unintended effect of decreasing individual health, as patients avoid necessary treatment (including filling prescriptions for drugs essential to managing many chronic conditions) because the out-of-pocket costs are too high. Further, as patients avoid seeking or following through with treatment, the information asymmetry increases, leaving insurers less able to accurately assess risks.

Regulation of Private Health Insurance[68]

Although insurers undeniably have legitimate, economically rational reasons for differentiating based on health status, the public increasingly objected, pushing for legal protection from practices that discriminate and otherwise undermine the benefits of health insurance. States, to varying degrees, and ultimately, the federal government, eventually responded with a number of health insurance reforms.

Managed care plans were a particular target of state regulation because they often employ a variety of cost-containment strategies, which can interfere with the treatment relationship. Under indemnity coverage, the patient pays for health-care services at the time of treatment but then files a claim with the

63 Ibid.

64 Ibid.

65 Pendo, note 59, at 457; *see also* Mary Crossley, *Discrimination against the Unhealthy in Health Insurance*, 54 *U. Kan. L. Rev.* 73, 131–33 (2005); Wenke Hwang et al., *Out-of-Pocket Medical Spending for Care of Chronic Conditions, Health Affs.*, Nov.–Dec. 2001, at 267, 275–76; Kathryn Anne Paez et al., *Rising Out-of-Pocket Spending for Chronic Conditions: A Ten-Year Trend, Health Affs.*, Jan.–Feb. 2009, at 15, 18–19.

66 Catherine Hoffman and Karyn Schwartz, *Eroding Access among Nonelderly U.S. Adults with Chronic Conditions: Ten Years of Change*, 27 *Health Affs.*, July 2008, at w340, w346, available at: www.content.healthaffairs.org/content/27/5/w340.full.pdf+html.

67 *See* Crossley, note 63, at 76. ("In this disparity of costs shifted we can discern discrimination against the unhealthy.")

68 Portions of this subsection originally appeared in Jessica L. Roberts, *"Healthism": A Critique of the Antidiscrimination Approach to Health Insurance and Health-Care Reform*, 2012 *U. Ill. L. Rev.* 1159, 1165 (2012).

insurance company after the fact. Most people no longer experience health insurance that way. Instead, they typically purchase a health plan and pay a monthly premium for access to a panel of approved providers, services, and supplies. The providers submit claims to the insurer for payment, and the insurer pays the health-care providers directly under the terms specified in the contract.

Managed care plans come in various subtypes, including health maintenance organizations (HMOs), preferred provider organizations (PPOs), and point of service (POS) plans. But they all generally operate more as a way to prepay for medical care than as a way to provide financial protection against unexpected risks. Managed care plans are in the business of keeping patients healthy to decrease the health-care costs for the risk pool. Thus, managed care plans cover not just catastrophic health-care costs, such as hospitalization, but also routine and preventive care. Medical professionals are employed as administrators who review and coordinate care on behalf of subscribers. Managed care plans use various strategies – including preapproval, gatekeeping, and utilization review – to ensure that the care for which they are paying is medically necessary, cost-justified, and appropriate.[69] That description makes the arrangement sound more altruistic than it is. By the same token, if a plan participant does become sick, managed care plans would prefer that person to "die as quickly and cheaply as possible."[70]

Managed care plans typically do not reimburse participating health-care providers on a fee-for-service basis but instead use bundled or capitated payments, requiring the providers to bear some of the financial risk.[71] The risk is in providing more medical care than the predetermined reimbursement amount covers.[72] Under bundled payments, for example, the provider receives

[69] Huberfeld et al., note 8, at 162.

[70] *See Blue Cross & Blue Shield United of Wisconsin* v. *Marshfield Clinic*, 65 F.3d 1406, 1410 (7th Cir. 1995) (Posner, J.).

[71] Timothy S. Hall, *Bargaining with Hippocrates: Managed Care and the Doctor-Patient Relationship*, 54 *S. C. L. Rev.* 689, 714 (2003) (explaining that managed care's review systems were not sufficient and that payers therefore had to thwart the unreasonable incentives of fee-for-service by giving physicians incentives to consider costs by using bundled and capitated payment plans); *see* Joan H. Krause, *Reconceptualizing Informed Consent in an Era of Health Care Cost Containment*, 85 *Iowa L. Rev.* 261, 281 (1999) (explaining how the managed care's reimbursement system put physicians at financial risk for the costs of care they give).

[72] *See* Peter Fise, *Prognosis for Synergy Between Accountable Care Organizations and Bundled Payments in Medicare*, 28 *J. Contemp. Health L. & Pol'y* 296, 300 (2012) (stating how this payment structure "simultaneously requires providers to assume financial risk for any amount by which the actual cost of care exceeds the bundled payment amount for the episode"); *see also* Medicare Payment Advisory Commission, *Report To The Congress*, 83–101 (2008), available at: www.amcp.org/WorkArea/DownloadAsset.aspx?id=11845.

a scheduled amount determined by the patient's diagnosis or spell of illness.[73] Under capitated payments, the provider agrees to treat a certain population of patients annually for a per-capita amount.[74] In both cases, the incentive is to provide medical care that is no more expensive than the agreed amount of reimbursement; otherwise, the provider risks under-compensation for the excess care.[75] In the event that the provider can treat the patient for cheaper than the predetermined amount, he, she, or it retains the excess as profit.

Managed care's financial incentives do not explicitly discriminate based on health status inasmuch as the bundled or capitated amounts are derived from actual, aggregated claims data. Those data, however, are averaged, meaning that some patients will surely require care that is more expensive than the predetermined amounts. Accordingly, providers may be inclined to avoid treating those "outlier" or "high utilization" patients, unless they receive additional, exceptional compensation, which some plans offer.

State insurance and managed care regulations address a number of the typical managed care plan features described above. With respect to the insurance industry, states regulate the business and professional licenses of companies and brokers. States also may regulate solvency or require minimum financial reserves. There may be plan description, disclosure, and other consumer protection requirements. Plan participants typically enjoy certain due process rights to appeal coverage denials through internal grievance, as well as external administrative and judicial review channels. Laws may limit the financial incentives that plans impose on providers when there is a risk of compromising quality of patient care and professional judgment. Certain services – including emergency room and obstetrical care – often must be accessible without preapproval or gatekeeping. States may also mandate coverage for certain conditions and treatments. Historically, however, states tended

[73] *See* Jessica Mantel, *Spending Medicare's Dollars Wisely: Taking Aim at Hospitals' Cultures of Overtreatment*, 49 *U. Mich. J. L. Reform* 121, 154 (2015) (describing how bundled payments are a departure from the fee-for-service model, in that bundled payments "pay providers for a defined set of services, known as an episode of care").

[74] Huberfeld et al., note 8, at 162 (stating that providers in capitated managed care plans "receive a pre-established amount per patient, rather than 'fee-for-service' payment for each service they provide").

[75] *See* Mantel, note 70, at 154 ("Providers profit when the cost of treating an episode of care falls below the bundled payment amount. Bundled payments thereby encourage more cost-conscious care."); Jessica Mantel, *A Defense of Physicians' Gatekeeping Role: Balancing Patients' Needs with Society's Interests*, 42 *Pepp. L. Rev.* 633, 639 (2015) ("The capitated provider therefore assumes the entire financial risk of treating a patient, losing money if the cost of care exceeds the capitated payment and making money if the opposite occurs.") (internal citations omitted).

to impose little to no regulation of underwriting and ratemaking practices, leaving those features to competitive market forces.

The federal government also has authority to regulate the business of insurance, but, until relatively recently, Congress did not substantively regulate private health insurance significantly. For decades, the most notable federal health insurance law was ERISA, described briefly in Chapter 3. The primary effect of ERISA for health plans (as opposed to other employee benefits, such as pensions, which ERISA regulates more precisely) was to knock out, or "preempt," state regulations and common laws bearing on employer-sponsored health plans.[76] But ERISA imposed virtually no affirmative federal regulation in place of the state laws that it preempts.[77]

The few federal substantive requirements on health plans included mandatory coverage for reconstructive surgery following mastectomy[78] and minimum hospital stays following childbirth.[79] Like Ryan White or NVIC, those coverage mandates differentiate based on health status, singling out particular conditions for more favorable coverage. Additionally, the Paul Wellstone and Pete Domenici Mental Health Parity and Addiction Equity Act (MHPAEA) of 2008 generally requires health plans to cover mental health and substance abuse treatment on at least as generous terms as medical or surgical benefits.[80] But, notably, MHPAEA's mental health parity rule applied only if the plan covered mental health and substance abuse; the plans remained free to exclude such coverage altogether. Originally applicable only to group health plans, the ACA amended MHPAEA to extend the protection to individual health insurance plans as well.[81] Moreover, the ACA includes mental health and substance abuse treatment within that law's "essential health benefits" (EHB) package, applicable to plans sold in the individual and small-group markets. The result is that most health plans cannot discriminate based on mental health or substance abuse disorders. The same is not necessarily true for other health conditions.

[76] Employee Retirement Income Security Act of 1974, 29 U.S.C. § 1000 et seq.; *see generally* 29 U.S.C. § 1144 (ERISA § 514); 29 U.S.C. § 1132 (ERISA § 502).

[77] *See* Huberfeld et al., note 8, at 177 (2017). ("ERISA's greatest impact is a sweeping preemption scheme that knocks out a host of state laws with which employers would otherwise have to comply while leaving little in the way of substantive federal regulation in their place.")

[78] 29 U.S.C. § 1185b.

[79] 29 U.S.C. § 1185(a).

[80] Paul Wellstone and Pete Domenici Mental Health Parity and Addiction Equity Act of 2008 ("MHPAEA"), Pub. L. No. 110–343, 122 Stat. 3881 (2008) (codified as amended 26 U.S.C. § 9812, 29 U.S.C. § 1185a, and 42 U.S.C. § 300gg-5).

[81] 42 U.S.C. § 18022(b) (1) (E).

In other legislation, federal law-makers addressed insurers' health-status distinctions more broadly, most notably in HIPAA.[82] HIPAA was the culmination of President Bill Clinton's (or perhaps more precisely, then-First Lady, and later US presidential candidate, Hillary Rodham Clinton's) attempt at comprehensive federal health-care reform.[83] Congress did not enact the broader Hillarycare plan, which called for establishing corporate "regional alliances" of health providers subject to a government fee schedule, among other sweeping changes that would have radically altered the private health insurance market .[84]

As something of a consolation, Congress passed a more modest piece of legislation, an amendment to ERISA, which ensured that employees could maintain coverage when they changed jobs and provided significant privacy protections for health information and standards for electronic health records.[85] HIPAA's portability provisions are particularly relevant here because they restrict health-status considerations in eligibility and individual premiums for group health plans. Group health plans include most employer-sponsored plans. These protections responded to concerns that employees with health conditions would be reluctant to change jobs for fear that they would be denied health insurance at a new employer. HIPAA was Congress' first antidiscrimination approach to health insurance legislation. Supporters cited eliminating health-status discrimination as among the legislation's most significant goals. Representative William Richardson stated that HIPAA prevents discrimination against those individuals with preexisting conditions. Senator Judd Gregg noted that HIPAA "grew out of the recognition that some basic flaws in the regulation of health care caused American families monumental problems," such as "subject[ing] [individuals] to unfair discrimination in their access to health insurance if they have a medical condition that has required treatment before they joined that health plan."

Specifically, HIPAA prohibits employers from excluding new workers from coverage for more than twelve months based on preexisting conditions.[86] A preexisting condition is defined as a physical or mental condition "for which medical advice, diagnosis, care, or treatment was recommended or received

82 Health Insurance Portability and Accountability Act of 1996, Pub. L. No. 104–191, 100 Stat. 2548 (1996), available at: www.gpo.gov/fdsys/pkg/PLAW-104publ191.

83 *See* www.govtrack.us/congress/bills/103/s1757.

84 Robert Pear, *Clinton's Health Plan: The Overview; Congress is Given Clinton Proposal For Health Care*, *N.Y. Times: U.S.* (Oct. 28, 1993), available at: www.nytimes.com/1993/10/28/us/clinton-s-health-plan-overview-congress-given-clinton-proposal-for-health-care.html?pagewanted=all.

85 29 U.S.C. § 1181.

86 29 U.S.C. § 1181(a)(2).

within the six-month period ending on enrollment date."[87] Conditions from more than six months before employment cannot be the basis to deny or delay coverage.[88] The twelve-month waiting period for relatively recent, rather than historical, preexisting conditions is designed to address adverse selection, such as an employee seeking new employment precisely to gain more generous coverage. When applicable, insurers must reduce the twelve-month waiting period by any amount of "creditable coverage," which includes another group health plan or a government health-care program.[89] Accordingly, if a worker with a preexisting condition had coverage at her previous job for at least a year, she would be eligible for immediate coverage at her new job. If she were at the previous job for eight months, she must wait no longer than four months for new coverage.

HIPAA further prohibits group health plans, or insurers offering group health plans, from basing eligibility or individual premium rates on the following list of health status–related factors: health status, medical condition (both physical and mental illnesses), claims experience, receipt of health care, medical history, genetic information, evidence of insurability (including a history of domestic violence), and disability.[90] In short, HIPAA established guaranteed issue and community rating rules for group health plans. A group plan cannot discriminate against an individual employee on the basis of health status with respect to participation in, or individual premium rates for, group coverage. Nothing in HIPAA, however, prevents employers or insurers from increasing the premiums on the group as a whole. Therefore, employers and coworkers still care about that Twinkie or cigarette habit of another participant in the group plan. Depending on the size of the group, enough employees with diabetes, cancer, hypertension, or multiple pregnancies could increase the premium rates for all. Even greater health risks within the group may make the employer group an undesirable customer, and nothing in HIPAA requires insurers to sell a plan to any particular employer.

Moreover, an insurer conceivably could offer a plan that excludes coverage across the board for a particular condition or treatment, such as infertility treatment[91] or HIV.[92] Such exclusions expressly single out certain health

87 29 U.S.C. § 1181(a)(1).

88 Ibid.

89 29 U.S.C. § 1181(c)(3).

90 29 U.S.C. § 1182.

91 Shelby Livingston, *Fertility Treatment Costs Scare off Employers*, *Business Insurance* (Jan. 17, 2016), available at: www.businessinsurance.com/article/20160117/NEWS03/160119856/Fertility-treatment-costs-scare-off-employers,-but-those-who-offer-coverage-to-e.

92 *McGann* v. *H&H Music*, 946 F.2d 401 (5th Cir. 1991).

statuses. Under ERISA's sweeping preemption provisions, state law coverage mandates may not apply to some employer-sponsored health plans, depending on whether the employer itself bears the risk or purchases insurance on behalf of its employees, transferring the risk to an insurance company.[93] ERISA provides that a health plan that is "self-insured" – meaning that the employer pays medical claims out of its own financial reserves – is not "deemed" to be an insurer for purposes of state insurance regulations. As a result, any state coverage mandates (such as mandatory coverage for mental health treatment or maternity care) would not apply.

Although focused on employer group plans, HIPAA also provides some protections from health-status discrimination in the individual and small-group markets. First, in the individual market, insurers must offer all applicants with eighteen or more months of creditable coverage, and no more than a sixty-three-day gap between losing that coverage and applying for an individual policy, a plan ("guaranteed issue"), and they must renew that plan ("guaranteed renewal").[94] In other words, insurers could not impose preexisting condition exclusions on applicants for individual coverage. For example, if an employee who had been employed for two years and covered by her employer's health plan for at least a year and a half, applied for individual coverage, the insurer would have to write a policy. HIPAA's individual market protection, however, did not restrict the amount that the insurer could charge. Guaranteed issue may be largely meaningless with no controls on premium rates. Moreover, if the state had adopted an alternate approach to covering uninsured individuals, which the vast majority of states did through high-risk pools or similar mechanisms, HIPAA's individual market rules did not apply. High-risk pools, although government-subsidized, explicitly segregate individuals with health conditions or health risks into a separate, but typically not equal, risk pool. Even where HIPAA did apply, insurers often engaged in practices to circumvent the requirements, such as refusing to pay brokers' fees for selling those policies or delaying applications long enough to cause a sixty-three-day gap.

The important thing to recognize about HIPAA is that most Americans, meaning those covered by employer-sponsored group health plans, have long enjoyed decent protection from discrimination in health insurance. Accordingly, the highly publicized and popular provisions of the ACA, which extend and expand HIPAA's protections into the individual and small-group market actually were not terribly dramatic for the health insurance market writ large. However, for the relatively small segment of the population who

93 29 U.S.C. § 1144(b)(2)(B).

94 29 U.S.C. § 1181(c)(2).

historically lacked coverage entirely or struggled to obtain and maintain coverage on the individual market, the ACA was a revolution.

During the debate that culminated in the ACA, health-care reform advocates described many accepted health insurances practices as discriminatory. Representative Louise Slaughter called preexisting condition exclusions "cruel," "capricious," and "done only to enhance the bottom line."[95] Representative Edward Perlmutter called excluding his sick daughter from health insurance coverage not only "immoral" but also "probably unconstitutional under the [Fourteenth] Amendment to the United States Constitution."[96] Representative Steven Kagen called preexisting condition exclusions discrimination on the basis of "skin chemistry."[97] Senator Patrick Leahy said bluntly: "Insurance companies can and do discriminate against sick people."[98]

Trumpeted as a "Patients' Bill of Rights," the ACA expanded HIPAA's protections to all Americans with preexisting health conditions. The ACA went further than HIPAA, prohibiting preexisting condition exclusions outright, rather than setting a maximum waiting period before coverage could begin. The ACA also bans insurers from placing lifetime or annual dollar limits on coverage, requires coverage without cost sharing for preventive care, protects patients' choice of physicians, guarantees appeal rights for coverage denials, and allows dependents under age twenty-six to stay on their parents' policies, among other protections. Specifically, insurers may not establish rules for eligibility or renewal based on the same list of factors as in HIPAA.[99] In addition, the statute grants discretion to the secretary of HHS to recognize other health status–related factors that may not be the basis of eligibility determination.[100] Also, the ACA bans post-claims underwriting, that prior practice of insurers retroactively rejecting or declining to renew coverage based on an undisclosed risk factor or later diagnosed health status, except in cases of fraud or intentional misrepresentation.[101]

95 Roberts, note 44 (quoting *Rep. Louise Slaughter Makes Remarks on Preexisting Conditions at White House Health Summit, Washington Post* (Feb. 25, 2010), available at: www.washingtonpost.com/wp-dyn/content/article/2010/02/25/AR2010022503133.html).

96 Roberts, note 44 (quoting *Congressman Ed Perlmutter: Serving the 7th District of Colorado*, available at: http://perlmutter.house.gov/news/documentsingle.aspx?DocumentID=414 [last updated Sept. 9, 2009]).

97 Roberts, note 44 (quoting 154 *Cong. Rec.* 1100 *[2008]* [statement of Congressman Kagen], available at: www.gpo.gov/fdsys/pkg/CREC-2008-05-01/pdf/CREC-2008-05-01.pdf).

98 Roberts, note 44 (quoting *Patrick Leahy Senator Report, Statement on Vermont's Contribution to Health Insurance Reform Legislation [Nov. 4, 2009]*, available at: www.leahy.senate.gov/press/statement-on-vermonts-contribution-to-health-insurance-reform-legislation).

99 42 U.S.C. §§ 300-gg-1, -4.

100 42 U.S.C. § 300gg-4(a)(9).

101 42 U.S.C. § 300gg-2; *see also* 42 U.S.C. § 300gg-3. ("Prohibition of preexisting condition exclusions or other discrimination based on health status.")

The ACA also imposes a modified form of community rating, meaning that insurers generally may not vary premium rates based on health status or other health-related habits, indicators, or profiles.[102] The ACA's modified community rating rule applies to small group and individual plans, thus restoring the historical underwriting practice of the Blues and addressing a persistent concern that many states avoided. Under community rating, insurers must offer individuals in a given geographic area (the statute and implementing regulations leave the determination of those areas to the states) the same types of plans, at the same rates, without regard for their individual risk profiles. That provision of the ACA protects against health-status discrimination somewhat less than HIPAA's analogous community rating provision by allowing at least four notable exceptions, which seem to reintroduce health-status considerations.[103]

With insurers now required to sell policies to people who are already ill, injured, or otherwise unhealthy, the potential for adverse selection became very high. If a person were not inclined to purchase insurance, she could simply wait until she needed health care and purchase a policy at that time, rather than pay premiums before needing treatment. The potential for health insurance markets collapsing in a death spiral led Congress to prevent most Americans from gambling on no, or minimal, health insurance coverage.[104] As part of a larger strategy to stabilize the insurance market for higher-risk individuals, the ACA, as enacted, mandates that most individuals maintain insurance with "minimum essential coverage" or pay a tax penalty. The so-called individual mandate was designed to enhance risk pooling by compelling low-risk individuals into the market. The ACA's modified community rating rule partially averts the death spiral by prohibiting insurers from charging differential premiums based on health status. The concern was that without the individual mandate, insurance might still become unaffordable if only higher-risk individuals purchased it. As of this writing, Congress has effectively repealed the individual mandate by suspending the tax penalty, effective 2019. Whether that change spells the death knell of the remainder of the ACA, as the ACA opponents intended, is very much an open question.[105] It is plausible that the remaining reforms and the public's desire for affordable insurance will continue to ward off the death spiral and other doomsday scenarios even without the tax penalty.

[102] 42 U.S.C. § 300gg.

[103] 42 U.S.C. § 300gg(a).

[104] 26 U.S.C. § 5000A.

[105] *See, e.g.*, J. Mario Molina, *Trump Didn't Kill Obamacare by Repealing the Individual Mandate*, *Newsweek*, Dec. 28, 2017, available at: www.newsweek.com/trump-kill-obamacare-repealing-individual-mandate-763095.

Guaranteed issue and community rating rules aside, nothing in the ACA prohibits insurers from raising rates on everyone in the community-rated risk pool, although especially large premium increases are subject to disclosure requirements and state review. With a community-rated risk pool, individuals in the private market, just like employees in employer-sponsored health plans, pay premiums based on the higher-risk individuals included. In short, we now should be concerned about the junk food consumption and sleep habits of not only our coworkers but also the person standing next to us at the bus stop.

In addition, the ACA dramatically expands substantive federal coverage mandates. Federal law specifies what counts as "essential" under the law's minimum essential coverage requirement. Under the ACA, all individual and small-group health plans (sold on or off the exchanges) must cover a core package of services, or "essential health benefits" (EHB). The EHB requirement does not explicitly apply to employer-sponsored health plans, which are presumed to offer packages that are at least as generous. By statute, the EHB package includes ten categories of services, which HHS may further define by rulemaking.[106] The ten broad categories of EHBs include ambulatory patient services; emergency services; hospitalization; mental health and substance abuse disorders/behavioral health treatment; maternity and newborn care; prescription drugs; rehabilitative and habilitative services/devices; laboratory services; preventive and wellness services and chronic disease management; and pediatric services, including oral and vision care.[107]

The EHB requirement does not directly address health-status discrimination, other than expanding protection for mental health conditions. It does, however, bolster the risk pooling effect of the ACA by requiring everyone to purchase a full range of services. Customers cannot select leaner plans that exclude services that they do not want. Accordingly, they may end up with plans covering unwanted services that they do not end up using and pay higher premiums as a result. Their premiums, however, will help cover the costs of other customers who need, and will use, the fuller range of services. Purchasers who would otherwise prefer a less comprehensive set of benefits may be healthier or more risk-favoring, or may prefer to pay for potential additional care out of pocket. The EHB requirement largely denies those options, which may seem desirable from the perspective of individual liberty. But requiring EHBs, like the individual mandate and community rating provisions of the ACA, inches

[106] For example, HHS defined preventive care to include contraception, sparking protest and legal challenges from various religious organizations and employers. *See* www.hrsa.gov/womensguidelines/; *Burwell* v. *Hobby Lobby Stores, Inc.*, 134 S.Ct. 2751 (2014); *Zubik* v. *Burwell*, 136 S.Ct. 1557 (2016).

[107] 42 U.S.C. § 18022.

us toward a different conception of health insurance. Rather than conceiving of health insurance as individual protection against financial risk, the ACA establishes a mechanism for ensuring broader access to health insurance and, thereby, health care for more Americans. That policy shift comports with the various guiding principles discussed in Chapter 2, including, most directly, health justice and health equality, and, to a lesser degree, health welfare and health liberty. Although cabining individual choices, the ACA's design promotes health liberty by keeping people healthier so that they can enjoy a fuller range of activities, vocations, and pursuits.

4.4. THE LIMITS OF EXISTING HEALTH INSURANCE LAWS

As explained in the previous section, state and federal laws have addressed health-status differentiation in health insurance to a degree. For the most part, insurers may no longer deny coverage or charge higher premiums based on health status. This regulatory trend expresses the opinion that it is wrong to deny health insurance to the unhealthy because they need it most. The ACA was billed as a civil rights triumph, a victory over healthism. Despite that promise, the ACA and other health insurance laws nevertheless contain hidden pockets of health-status differentiation.

Perhaps the clearest instances of health-status differentiation within the ACA are the broad exceptions to community rating. The ACA expressly allows insurers to vary premium rates based on a few specific factors. First, insurers may charge different rates based on the plan type (individual or family).[108] Plans also may be priced differently in different geographic areas (that is, community rates may vary by community).[109] In addition, the elderly and tobacco users may be charged more, up to a point.[110] The ACA specifies that premium rates may vary based on age, up to 3:1, and tobacco use, up to 1.5:1. Finally, a provision of the ACA allows plans to offer discounts, rebates, or reduced cost sharing for participation in health promotion programs.[111]

The most obvious avenue for healthism is the ACA's premium rate variation for tobacco users. Recall that our definition of health status includes smoking and other forms of tobacco use. Given all the other kinds of conduct that implicate health risks, it is hard to imagine any other reason for singling out tobacco use – and tobacco use alone – other than pure animus. Tobacco use enjoys little social privilege or acceptance and has been a target of various

[108] 42 U.S.C. § 300gg-1(A)(i).
[109] 42 U.S.C. § 300gg-1(A)(ii).
[110] 42 U.S.C. § 300gg.
[111] 42 U.S.C. § 300gg-4(j).

policies designed to both reduce second-hand smoking effects on nonusers and paternalistically protect users from the health effects of the behavior.[112] Hence, the provision likely offends health equality both because it appears driven by animus and because it could perpetuate stigma. Moreover, as noted, tobacco use also correlates with existing health disparities. Thus, this exception would also seem to implicate health justice.

While age in and of itself is not a health status as we define it, policies that differentiate based on age could have a disparate impact on health status. Our definition of discrimination includes not only intentional but also unintentional discrimination. As people age, their needs for health-care services tend to increase. Older individuals have a higher likelihood of developing degenerative diseases such as age-related hearing and vision loss. Similarly, age may result in compromised immune and other systems, which leads to an increased risk for other kinds of health conditions and illnesses. In short, the older a person becomes, the more likely she will be to require health-care services. Thus age-rating is a close proxy for health-status rating.

The inverse is also true. On average, younger people tend to experience fewer health-related problems. The ACA further differentiates based on age by allowing young people, specifically, individuals under age thirty, to satisfy the minimum essential coverage requirement with bare-bones, or "catastrophic," coverage.[113] Those plans have low monthly premiums but very high deductibles. They must still cover EHBs, and out-of-pocket cost-sharing requirements do not apply to preventive care. But only young, presumptively healthy people can satisfy the individual mandate with catastrophic plans.[114] The health risk associated with catastrophic coverage is the inverse of the moral hazard problem. That is, individuals opting for those plans may avoid seeking out needed health care because of the out-of-pocket financial exposure in terms of deductibles or copayments, or they may not set aside enough money to pay those costs, thus incurring substantial medical debt. With the repeal of the individual mandate, it is possible that more people will opt for leaner, or catastrophic, plans.

[112] Lindsay F. Wiley, *Tobacco Denormalization, Anti-Healthism, and Health Justice*, 18 *Marquette Benefits & Social Welfare L. Rev.* 203–53 (2017); *see* Amanda J. Dillard et al., *Perceptions of Smokers Influence Nonsmoker Attitudes and References for Interactions*, *J. Applied Soc. Psych.*, April 2013, at 43.

[113] *See* Patient Protection and Affordable Care Act § 1302(2),42 U.S.C. § 18022 (setting out the details for the catastrophic health care plan).

[114] Also, individuals over age thirty who obtain a hardship exemption from the individual mandate may purchase catastrophic plans. *Catastrophic Health Plans For People With Hardship Exemptions*, HealthCare.gov, available at: www.healthcare.gov/catastrophic-plan-information/ (last visited July 12, 2017).

Two other exceptions to the ACA's community rating rules – geographic rate variation and healthy behavior incentives – could also reintroduce health-status discrimination into ratemaking. First, consider geographic rating areas. Under HHS's regulations, states may establish one or more rating areas based on existing geographic divisions, including counties, three-digit zip codes, metropolitan and nonmetropolitan statistical areas, or urban and rural regions.[115] Some states adopted a single rating area for the entire state, effectively banning geographic ratemaking within the state. Other states adopted rating areas aligned with pre-ACA state requirements, thereby minimizing market disruption. In states where rating areas corresponded to single-county areas, there could be fifty or more per state. In other states, policy-makers had difficulty designing rating areas that reflected existing regional health-care costs without perpetuating pricing mechanisms that disadvantaged particular subpopulations. At least one state representative recognized that segmenting the market too finely could isolate communities with greater health-care needs, resulting in higher rates,[116] contrary to the ACA's core antidiscrimination objective.

On the other hand, adopting relatively few rating areas could result in premium shocks for many residents, if previously low-cost areas now share risks more broadly.[117] Insurers might exit the market in expensive regions, depressing competition and further increasing rates.[118] Indeed, a number of large insurers have exited the exchange marketplaces,[119] it is not whether state-drawn geographic rating areas were the reason.[120] For healthism purposes, geographic rating, while facially health-neutral and arguably rational, could reintroduce health status into ratemaking because people in different areas may not face equal health risks.

[115] *Geographic Rating Areas Dataset*, Robert Wood Johnson Found (Feb. 14, 2014), available at: www.rwjf.org/en/library/research/2014/02/geographic-rating-areas-dataset.html; Justin Giovannelli et al., *Implementing the Affordable Care Act: State Approaches to Premium Rate Reforms in the Individual Health Insurance Market, Commonwealth Fund* (Dec. 2014), available at: www.commonwealthfund.org/~/media/files/publications/issue-brief/2014/dec/1795_giovannelli_implementing_aca_state_premium_rate_reforms_rb_v2.pdf; *Market Rating Reforms*, Center for Consumer Information & Insurance Oversight (last updated Mar. 3, 2015), available at: www.cms.gov/cciio/programs-and-initiatives/health-insurance-market-reforms/state-gra.html.

[116] *See* Giovannelli et al., note 112, at 3.

[117] Ibid. at 8.

[118] Ibid. at 7.

[119] Amy Goldstein, *Aetna Exiting All ACA Insurance Marketplaces in 2018*, *Washington Post*, May 10, 2017, available at: www.washingtonpost.com/national/health-science/aetna-exiting-all-aca-insurance-marketplaces-in-2018/2017/05/10/9dedbeea-35d4-11e7-b373-418f6849a004_story.html?utm_term=.9885f1cb764b.

[120] Jeanne Lambrewe, *Marketplace Insurer Exits Are Not Inevitable*, *The Century Foundation* (May 23, 2017), available at: https://tcf.org/content/report/marketplace-insurer-exits-not-inevitable/.

In one sense, setting premium rates based on geography is eminently practical, given the tremendous variation in medical costs, labor costs, and other costs. Health-care costs may be higher in one locale than another. For example, high-risk populations may cluster geographically, like in rural areas or the inner city. Taking a cue from law enforcement practices, some researchers and health-care providers are taking a closer look at medical "hot spots" – geographic locations where residents consume more health care – to lower costs by giving better care to the patients who need it most.[121] Those commendable efforts aside, geographic rating areas certainly carry the potential to perpetuate existing health and other disparities, thereby implicating health justice.

In addition to the ACA's explicit exceptions for age, tobacco, and geography, another provision could lead to healthism. The section that generally prohibits discrimination against individuals based on health status[122] also expressly allows group health plans to offer incentives for participating in approved health promotion or disease prevention programs – more popularly known as workplace wellness programs.[123] Specifically, group health plans and health insurers offering group health insurance can offer premium discounts or rebates, modify otherwise applicable copayments or deductibles, or offer other "carrots" for participating.[124]

The ACA distinguishes between two types of wellness programs: participation-based and outcome-based.[125] Programs that are merely participation-based have no specific requirements, other than being available to all similarly situated individuals.[126] Examples of such programs include paying the cost of gym membership or smoking cessation classes (even if the worker does not use the membership, attend the class, or stop smoking); waiving copayments or deductibles for preventive care, such as mammograms, vaccinations, prenatal or well-baby visits; or offering incentives for participation in wellness seminars, health profiles, or screening tests. Possible rewards include discounting premiums, offering rebates, waiving cost-sharing mechanisms or surcharges, and providing other benefits not available under the plan.

[121] *See* Atul Gawande, *The Hot Spotters: Can We Lower Medical Costs by Giving the Neediest Patients Better Care?*, *New Yorker*, Jan. 24, 2011, available at: www.newyorker.com/magazine/2011/01/24/the-hot-spotters.

[122] 42 U.S.C. § 300gg-4(b)(1).

[123] 42 U.S.C. § 300gg-4(j).

[124] Ibid.

[125] Ibid.

[126] 42 U.S.C. § 300gg-4(j)(2) ("If none of the conditions for obtaining a premium discount or rebate or other reward under a wellness program . . . are based on an individual satisfying a standard that is related to a health status factor . . . the wellness program shall not violate this section if participation in the program is made available to all similarly situated individuals.").

By contrast, additional requirements apply to outcome-based programs. Outcome-based programs provide incentives for achieving a certain health-related goal, such as a target weight, body mass index, blood pressure, or cholesterol level. For those programs, employers may not offer rewards that exceed 30 percent of the cost of employee-only coverage.[127] In addition, the employer must offer reasonable alternatives for people with medical conditions that make satisfying the general standard unreasonably difficult or medically inadvisable.[128]

Despite those accommodations, workplace wellness programs could still have a disparate impact based on health status. As discussed in Chapter 2, various social determinants of health may make participating much more difficult, if not impossible, for certain people. Even with employer support, apparently "voluntary" health habits and practices may not be accessible for some, especially if participation is time-consuming or must be performed during unpaid hours, when childcare, transportation, or other obligations limit participation.[129] Related concerns arise when states introduced wellness incentive programs into Medicaid plans. Due to their limited resources, Medicaid enrollees may face serious challenges to participating in required smoking cessation, weight loss, or well-baby visits.[130] Wellness programs could therefore have a disparate impact based on health status, as certain populations will be less likely to benefit from them and could face heightened premiums as a result. Moreover, the Trump administration's enthusiasm for Medicaid work requirements raises similar concerns.[131] Such policies undermine the ACA's antidiscrimination purpose and could exacerbate existing disparities, violating health justice.

The ACA further disadvantages the unhealthy through its preventive care coverage rules. Preventive care is one of the ten categories of services in the list of EHBs.[132] Furthermore, the ACA specifies that plans

[127] 42 U.S.C. § 300gg-4(j)(3)(A).

[128] 42 U.S.C. § 300gg-4(j)(3)(D)(i)(I-II).

[129] Timothy Jost, *Implementing Health Reform: Wellness Programs and Medicaid FAQ, Health Affs. Blog* (Nov. 21, 2012), available at: http://healthaffairs.org/blog/2012/11/21/implementing-health-reform-wellness-programs-and-medicaid-faq/.

[130] Tara Mancini, *More Research Needed on Medicaid Wellness Programs, Say Ahhh! Blog* (Apr. 15, 2014), available at: https://ccf.georgetown.edu/2013/04/15/more-research-needed-on-medicaid-wellness-programs/.

[131] Glenn Thrush, *Trump Signs Order to Require Recipients of Federal Aid Programs to Work, New York Times*, (April 10, 2018), available at: www.nytimes.com/2018/04/10/us/trump-work-requirements-assistance-programs.html; Nathanial Weixel, *Trump Approves Arkansas Medicaid Work Requirements, The Hill* (March 5, 2018), available at: http://thehill.com/policy/healthcare/376775-trump-approves-arkansas-medicaid-work-requirements.

[132] *See* 29 CFR § 2590.715–2713.

must cover preventive care services "first-dollar," meaning, without regard to deductibles, copayments, or coinsurance. The straightforward rationale for this policy is the opposite of the moral hazard concern: We actually do *not* want to discourage insureds from taking steps to protect their health or detect conditions at an earlier, easier-to-treat stage. The preference for preventive care, however, does favor the healthy – people who are not yet sick – over the unhealthy – people who have already been diagnosed. Healthy people will be able to maintain their good health without paying costs out of pocket, while unhealthy people will have to pay the cost-sharing requirements before receiving care. Moreover, cost sharing falls particularly heavily on the unhealthy, who are more likely to access medical treatment. Accordingly, the ACA's requirement that health insurers cover preventive care is another way in which health insurance continues to treat the healthy differently from the unhealthy. We assess in Chapter 6 whether this or similar practices would offend any of our guiding principles.

The ACA is appropriately hailed as a landmark antidiscrimination law for the unhealthy. The statute protects individuals from being denied health insurance or charged more for coverage. Although similar protection has been available since the 1990s for (mostly employer-sponsored) group health plans, the ACA extended and expanded that protection into the individual and small-group markets. But, as we have detailed, the ACA includes a number of exceptions and other provisions that may subtly continue to disadvantage individuals on the basis of health status.

Specifically, the ACA's modified community rating exceptions may have a negative effect. First and foremost, the law allows *explicit* discrimination on the basis of tobacco use, conduct that meets our definition of health status from Chapter 1. The remaining provisions, while deceptively facially neutral could nonetheless have a disparate impact. Being elderly correlates highly with health risks. Likewise, depending on how states define geographic rating areas, they may entrench health disparities for certain populations. Employers can vary premium rates by as much as 30 percent for participating in workplace wellness programs, which, as discussed in Chapter 2, not all individuals are equally capable of doing. The preventive care mandate also favors the healthy over the unhealthy, allowing the former to access care without paying out of pocket at the time of service. These exceptions to the ACA's otherwise across-the-board community rating rule crudely approximate very health-based distinctions that the law purported to eliminate. As a result, the new health-care system still tends to disadvantage the unhealthy, albeit less obviously.

4.5. HEALTHISM UNDER FUTURE HEALTH REFORM

Despite its limits, the ACA is a very positive development for reducing healthism. It expresses a shift in public opinion and rhetoric that treating people unfavorably, especially with respect to access to health insurance, is normatively wrong.[133] Almost since the law's enactment, however, repealing and replacing the ACA has been a top agenda item for Republicans, and efforts ramped up after the November 2016 elections, which named Republican Donald Trump as president and secured Republican control of Congress.[134] Even under such pressure, the ACA's antidiscrimination provisions have enjoyed broad public support. According to a December 2016 poll, 69 percent of the public, and 63 percent of Republicans, favored prohibiting insurance companies from denying coverage because of a person's medical history.[135] At the same time, arguably discriminatory first-dollar coverage for preventive care also remained popular, favored by 83 percent of the public – including 77 percent of Republicans.[136]

Republican proposals have consistently targeted the ACA's more controversial provisions, including individual and employer health insurance mandates, Medicaid expansion, and federal subsidies to reduce low-income individuals' out-of-pocket costs. The ACA's popular ban on preexisting condition exclusions and community rating rules, at least initially, were not on the chopping block. Later bills, however, would have expanded the ACA's permitted premium rate variation based on age from 3:1 to 5:1,[137] and/or would have

[133] Alicia Adamcyzk, *These Are the Faces of People with Pre-Existing Conditions. They're Terrified of the Future*, *Time: Money* (July 26, 2017), available at: http://time.com/money/4870915/faces-of-pre-existing-conditions/ ("That tens of millions of people could lose insurance coverage sparked nationwide protests over the past seven months.").

[134] Julie Rovner, *How Fast Could GOP Congress Get Obamacare Repeal to Trump's Desk?*, *NPR.org: Shots* (December 14, 2016), available at: www.npr.org/sections/health-shots/2016/12/14/505439759/how-fast-could-gop-congress-get-obamacare-repeal-to-trump-s-desk ("Republicans in Congress are so eager to repeal the Affordable Care Act that some have vowed to get a bill to President-elect Donald Trump's desk on the day he takes the oath of office.").

[135] *After the Election, the Public Remains Sharply Divided on Future of the Affordable Care Act*, KFF.org (Dec. 1, 2016), available at: www.kff.org/health-reform/press-release/after-the-election-the-public-remains-sharply-divided-on-future-of-the-affordable-care-act/.

[136] Ibid. at (KFF.org Poll).

[137] American Health Care Act of 2017, H.R. 1628, 115th Cong. (2017); Timothy Jost, *House Passes AHCA: How It Happened, What It Would Do, and Its Uncertain Senate Future*, *Health Affs. Blog* (May 4, 2017), available at: http://healthaffairs.org/blog/2017/05/04/house-passes-ahca-how-it-happened-what-it-would-do-and-its-uncertain-senate-future/; Thomas Kaplan and Robert Pear, *House Passes Measure to Repeal and Replace the Affordable Care Act*, *New York Times* (May 4, 2017), available at: www.nytimes.com/2017/05/04/us/politics/health-care-bill-vote.html?_r=0.

allowed states broadly to reinstate experience rating. One proposal would have transformed the ACA's premium assistance subsidies from income-based to age-based, resulting in older people paying more for subsidized coverage than younger people.[138] In addition, the Trump administration eliminated another federal subsidy – cost-sharing reduction (CSR) payments – in part on the grounds that the ACA never properly appropriated federal dollars for those payments.[139] At the time of this writing, lawsuits are pending over that issue,[140] and discussions regarding future funding for CSR payments continue in Congress.[141]

The repeal and replace proposals have also generally favored eroding nationwide protections for health insurance customers in favor of state flexibility. In some versions, Republican law-makers would have allowed states to opt out of most, if not all, of the private insurance market reforms, including community rating, the EHB requirement, and the ACA's annual caps on out-of-pocket expenses.[142] The ACA similarly allows state variation from some federal requirements under the 1332 waiver provision, but states remain subject to federal approval and specific "guardrails" ensuring that states implement alternate coverage approaches that are federal budget–neutral and at least as comprehensive, affordable, and inclusive as the ACA's approach.[143] The repeal and replace bills significantly diluted those requirements.

Private insurance regulations are not the only targets of repeal and replace. Medicaid expansion remains unpopular and under fire. Some proposals

[138] Jost, note 133.

[139] Timothy Jost, *Administration's Ending of Cost-Sharing Reduction Payments Likely to Roil Individual Markets, Health Affs. Blog* (Oct. 13, 2017), available at: www.healthaffairs.org/do/10.1377/hblog20171022.459832/full/

[140] See *Commonwealth Ground Healthcare v. United States*, U.S. Court of Federal Claims (April 17, 2018) (certifying class of "All persons or entities offering Qualified Health Plans under the Patient Protection and Affordable Care Act in the 2017 or 2018 benefit year, and who made cost-sharing reductions for eligible insureds . . . but did not receive a "timely and periodic" payment from the Government . . .), available at: http://premiumtaxcredits.wikispaces.com/file/view/Common%20Ground%20class%20cert%20order.pdf/628813943/Common%20Ground%20class%20cert%20order.pdf; *House v. Azar*, U.S. Court of Appeals, D.C. Circuit (March 5, 2018) (order for supplemental briefing on proposed settlement between U.S. House of Representatives and Secretary of HHS, Alex Azar), available at: www.politico.com/f/?id=00000161-f6e8-d21f-abe5-fefd497e0001.

[141] Susan Morse, *Fate of Cost-Sharing Reduction Payments Comes into Question During Spending Bill Debate*, Healthcare Finance (March 12, 2018), available at: www.healthcarefinancenews.com/news/fate-cost-sharing-reduction-payments-comes-question-during-spending-bill-debate.

[142] Jost, note 133.

[143] Sarah Lueck and Jessica Schubel, *Understanding the Affordable Care Acts State Innovation ("1332") Waivers, Center on Budget and Policy Priorities* (Sept. 5, 2017), available at: www.cbpp.org/research/health/understanding-the-affordable-care-acts-state-innovation-1332-waivers.

would gradually roll back Medicaid expansion, reinstating categories of eligibility.[144] Other proposals include alternate approaches, such as government funding to state "high-risk pools" or other mechanisms.[145] But the efficacy of those alternatives remains very much an open question. States previously employed high-risk pools, under other incentives, to varying degrees.[146] High-risk pools typically involve government (state or federal) subsidies to private insurers for developing products for high-risk individuals, thereby segregating them from the rest of the commercial health insurance pool.[147] The subsidies are intended to keep costs down so that policies do not become prohibitively expensive. High-risk pools, however, quite obviously differentiate based on health status. Moreover, history gives good reason to question the viability of that government-subsidized option for covering the Medicaid expansion population.

Other proposals would transform Medicaid from an entitlement program to a block-grant program, meaning that states with higher Medicaid rolls would simply have to cut or deny benefits when their grant money ran out. Recall *Alexander* v. *Choate* from Chapter 2; similar instances of Medicaid cuts affecting the unhealthy either directly or indirectly would be likely under a block-grant approach. Medicaid exists as a public welfare safety net for low-income individuals. Dramatic changes to the eligibility or funding approaches for Medicaid almost certainly would disparately impact the unhealthy. President Trump's executive order requiring federal welfare programs to impose work requirements[148] also invites health-status discrimination into Medicaid.

[144] Anna Maria Barry-Jester, *The 4 Big Changes to Health Care In the Latest GOP Bill, FiveThirty-Eight* (May 2, 2017), available at: https://fivethirtyeight.com/features/the-4-big-changes-to-health-care-in-the-latest-gop-bill/; Danielle Kurtzleben, *Senate Republicans Reveal Long-Awaited Affordable Care Act Repeal Bill* (June 22, 2017), available at: www.npr.org/2017/06/22/533947844/senate-republicans-reveal-long-awaited-affordable-care-act-repeal-bill; www.cbo.gov/publication/52849; Robert Pear and Thomas Kaplan, *Senate Health Care Bill Includes Deep Cuts to Medicaid* (June 22, 2017), available at: www.nytimes.com/2017/06/22/us/politics/senate-health-care-bill.html?mcubz=1&_r=0.

[145] Karen Pollitz, *High-Risk Pools for Uninsurable Individuals, KFF*.org (Feb. 22, 2017), available at: www.kff.org/health-reform/issue-brief/high-risk-pools-for-uninsurable-individuals/.

[146] Bob Bryan, *The Republican Healthcare Bill Still Has a Massive Problem, Business Insider* (May 3, 2017), available at: www.businessinsider.com/ahca-high-risk-pools-healthcare-vote-obamacare-2017-5; Richard Popper, *Do High-Risk Pools Work? It Depends, Washington Post* (May 8, 2017), available at: www.washingtonpost.com/opinions/do-high-risk-pools-work-it-depends/2017/05/08/586b95f4-319c-11e7-8674-437ddb6e813e_story.html?utm_term=.d3cf5e9f5a8a.

[147] Pollitz, note 139.

[148] Executive Order Reducing Poverty in America by Promoting Opportunity and Economic Mobility (April 10, 2018), available at: www.whitehouse.gov/presidential-actions/executive-order-reducing-poverty-america-promoting-opportunity-economic-mobility/.

Overall, the repeal and replace agenda has significant implications for our project. First and most obviously, allowing states to waive the ACA's community rating rules and reintroduce across-the-board experience rating would allow considerable opportunity for health-status differentiation. Although the ACA's ban on preexisting conditions exclusions would not be removed, that protection would be significantly diluted. Insurers would still be required to issue a policy to anyone who applies, regardless of health status, but allowing insurers to charge higher premiums based on individual risks would likely make insurance cost-prohibitive and, therefore, unavailable to a vast number of people. State high-risk pools, reinsurance, or other mechanisms to stabilize insurance markets and redirect federal funding do not seem terribly promising, based on past history. Moreover, that approach results in relegating the unhealthy to separate, less favorable, risk pools or insurance products, contrary to the ACA's signature antidiscrimination goal.

Second, the proposals' ageist policies also implicate health status since the elderly tend to have greater health-care needs than younger people. Allowing insurers to charge elderly customers five times as much as younger customers provides ample opportunity for age-based (and, by proxy, health status–based) discrimination. Likewise, reallocating federal dollars designed to make private health insurance more affordable in the individual and small-group market reintroduces health-status differentiation. Currently under the ACA, individuals with income between 100 percent and 400 percent of the federal poverty level may qualify for federal subsidies to cover part of their premium costs.[149] The subsidies are available on a sliding scale based on income.[150] Republican proposals granting premium subsidies on a sliding scale based on age, instead of financial need, work to the obvious disadvantage of the elderly.

Two existing ACA provisions – also at risk under repeal and replace – limit individuals' out-of-pocket costs, thus benefiting the unhealthy, who are more likely to use medical care. Current federal law caps out-of-pocket costs annually, effectively assuring individuals that they will never be out more than the defined amount per year, even if they have significant health-care needs.[151] After individuals reach the cap, they can access any additional necessary medical care for "free" (subject only to premiums otherwise paid or required). The second provision is the CSR payment, currently being litigated and debated. Under the ACA, individuals with incomes between 100 percent and 250 percent of federal poverty level receive subsidies from insurers that reduce

149 42 U.S.C. § 18071(b).
150 42 U.S.C. § 18071(c).
151 42 U.S.C. § 18071(c)-(1)(A).

their deductibles, copayments, and coinsurance.[152] The Trump administration suspended payment to the insurance companies, which are currently on the hook for those subsidies. Raising or eliminating the lifetime cap and undermining the CSR subsidies have implications for the unhealthy. With no cap, people with serious health conditions will always be responsible for some amount of cost sharing and, without federal need-based subsidies, insurers could be left making up the difference. Because the ACA exempts preventive care from cost sharing under the ACA, those policy changes will not impact people who enjoy good health and require less medical treatment as severely.

In addition, repealing the individual mandate and possibly allowing states to waive otherwise applicable federal requirements, including but not limited to the EHBs, undermines the ACA's risk pooling design. Because of adverse selection, repealing the individual mandate could remove a significant number of low-risk individuals from the pool, potentially driving up overall premium rates. Allowing states to waive the EHB requirement could also leave a great number of services uninsured and, therefore, subject to self-pay. For example, if a state elects to waive mental health or maternity coverage from its EHB package, an individual in that state would either have to pay for such care herself or purchase a separate policy for those discrete services, assuming insurers even offered such a product. Erosion of the EHB requirement also has spillover effects because the ACA's ban on lifetime and annual limits applies only to those benefits. Thus, the more narrowly defined the EHB, the more opportunities for lifetime and annual limits on coverage there will be. Moreover, the EHB provisions, although not applicable to employer-sponsored health plans, tend to influence the coverage under those plans.[153] Thus, individuals and families with employer-sponsored plans may find their coverage less comprehensive as well.

The future of the ACA remains uncertain, but the Trump administration and Congress seem committed to making fundamental changes to the law, including its core antidiscrimination provisions. As noted, the individual mandate has effectively been repealed through a tax bill,[154] and the CSR payments suspended.[155] The overall direction of ACA opponents signals widespread will-

[152] 42 U.S.C. § 18071(c)-(1)(B).

[153] Rebecca Savransky, *Obamacare Repeal Bill Could Affect Employer Health Plans: Report*, *The Hill* (May 4, 2017), available at: http://thehill.com/policy/healthcare/331881-obamacare-repeal-plan-could-remove-protections-for-people-on-employer.

[154] Timothy Jost, *The Tax Bill and The Individual Mandate: What Happened, and What Does It Mean?*, *Health Affairs* (Dec. 20, 2017), available at:www.healthaffairs.org/do/10.1377/hblog20171220.323429/full/.

[155] *Compare* John E. Bies, *Cost-Sharing Reduction Payments are Not Dead*, *The Hill* (Oct. 22, 2017), available at: http://thehill.com/opinion/healthcare/356510-cost-sharing-reduction-payments-

ingness to reintroduce considerations of health status into health insurance. The Trump administration's rhetoric displays a similar distaste for diversity of various sorts, including religion, ethnicity, body type, disability, and physical attractiveness.[156] Overall, the current political climate seems to invite more, not less, potential for healthism in health insurance and beyond.

4.6. HEALTHISM UNDER UNIVERSAL HEALTH CARE

Recognizing the ACA's shortcomings as an antidiscrimination law, we briefly consider alternate approaches to address potential healthism in health insurance. One alternative would be to recognize health care as a universal right or entitlement, as many other developed countries do. That would require a fundamental paradigm shift in the United States' free-market orientation and concept of rights. Most of the rights that our Constitution recognizes are "negative," meaning rights to be *free from* governmental intrusion. "Positive" rights mean that the government has an affirmative obligation to provide certain goods or services to its citizens. We generally do not enshrine such rights in our federal or state constitutions.

To the extent that the United States does recognize positive rights, they are narrow and not constitutional. Even if we could surmount that philosophical hurdle, there are challenges in defining the content of the right. What is the minimum level of care that all Americans should be guaranteed? Does the ACA's EHB package capture the essence of a health care "right"? Would the existing coverage rules for Medicare apply if the program were expanded to all people? Even the traditional Medicaid benefits package is characterized by individual state variations and more generous benefits for some groups of enrollees, such as children under the Early and Periodic Screening, Diagnostic and Treatment (EPSDT) benefit.[157]

---

are-now-dead, *with* Bob Brian, *Trump Just Made a Huge Move That Could Blow Up Obamacare*, *Business Insider* (Oct. 12, 2017), available at: www.businessinsider.com/trump-ends-cost-sharing-reduction-csr-payments-2017-10.

[156] Irin Carmon, *Donald Trump's Worst Offense? Mocking Disabled Reporter, Poll Finds*, *NBC News* (Aug. 11, 2016), available at: www.nbcnews.com/politics/2016-election/trump-s-worst-offense-mocking-disabled-reporter-poll-finds-n627736; Jenna Johnson, *Trump Attacks Former Miss Universe Who "Gained a Massive Amount of Weight" and Had "Attitude"*, *Washington Post* (Sept. 27, 2016), available at: www.washingtonpost.com/news/post-politics/wp/2016/09/27/trump-attacks-former-miss-universe-who-gained-a-massive-amount-of-weight-and-had-attitude/?utm_term=.f2fe47e0d0fb; www.nytimes.com/2016/09/29/well/live/a-400-pound-hacker-trump-comment-ignites-fat-shaming-debate.html?_r=0; *see also* Lynn Vavreck, *Measuring Donald Trump's Supporters for Intolerance*, *New York Times: The Upshot* (Feb. 23, 2016), available at: www.nytimes.com/2016/02/25/upshot/measuring-donald-trumps-supporters-for-intolerance.html.

[157] 42 U.S. Code § 1396d(r).

These queries themselves highlight the fact that the current approach to health care is anything but universal; the health benefits guaranteed to individuals varies by eligibility, plan type, geography, and a host of other factors. Even if the United States were to embrace a single-payer, government-run, Medicare-for-all health-care program, it seems highly likely that the coverage would be more generous for some populations, and some health conditions, than for others. The scarce resources necessitate rationing. Law-makers could opt to provide a leaner, but uniform, package of benefits to all, or provide services tailored to subgroups of the population. They might also decide to exclude coverage for an entire set of services, such as infertility treatment or gender reassignment surgery. Such policies would clearly differentiate based on health status in ways that disadvantage certain populations. Countries that have adopted universal health-care systems have had to make similar kinds of choices.[158]

Moreover, given our country's deeply enshrined free-market history, even if the United States adopted a universal health-care system, individuals would likely still be allowed to purchase additional health-care services and coverage. A similar question arose under the Canadian health-care system, and the Supreme Court of Canada held that it was unconstitutional for Quebec law to prohibit private health insurance.[159] Accordingly, health justice concerns would still persist. The bottom line is that differentiation based on health status, in one form or another, would likely remain a feature of the US health-care system even with a rights-based, universal, approach.

The potential for healthism runs rampant in health insurance. Although the ACA prohibits health insurers from explicitly considering health-related factors when making their determinations, the statute allows them to weigh characteristics that closely parallel health status. Older individuals, individuals in low-income areas, tobacco users, and obese individuals all face higher health risks and are, therefore, more likely to be considered unhealthy. Moreover, first-dollar coverage for preventive care favors the healthy and disfavors the unhealthy, who are slammed with deductibles and mounting copayments for the care that they receive. Put simply, as laudable as they are, the ACA's health insurance reforms still disadvantage the unhealthy, albeit in some cases unintentionally. Moreover, the specter of "repeal and replace" looms large, threatening to widen those exceptions and possibly even eliminate a number of health-based antidiscrimination provisions.

[158] *See generally Country Profiles*, The Commonwealth Fund, available at: http://international.commonwealthfund.org/countries/ (last visited July 12, 2017).

[159] *Chaoulli* v. *Quebec (AG)* [2005] 1 S.C.R. 791, 2005 SCC 35, available at: www.canlii.org/en/ca/scc/doc/2005/2005scc35/2005scc35.html.

Universal health care, in theory, could eliminate healthism, providing uniform benefits across the board, regardless of health status. But even if lawmakers elected to cover everyone through a government program, they would almost certainly be forced to make choices about what services to cover and whether to vary the coverage for certain subgroups of the population, perhaps to the detriment of those suffering from certain lesser-known diagnoses or conditions. Thus, even recognizing a right to health care would not be a silver bullet against all possible forms of disadvantage based on health status. Whether such differentiation can be justified requires deeper analysis, which we undertake in Chapter 6.

5

Limits of Private Law

5.1. INTRODUCTION

In Chapters 3 and 4, we revealed ways that laws – federal statutes – fail to fully address healthism. This chapter considers ways that private law, namely torts and contracts, similarly may disadvantage the unhealthy. Private law refers to laws that deal with relationships between individuals and institutions, as distinguished from public law, which concerns relationships between individuals or institutions and government. Tort law, sometimes called personal injury law, provides a remedy for injuries, which may be physical, emotional, or economic. Contract law allows private parties to essentially write their own laws, crafting mutually binding agreements.

How can contract and tort law be healthist? Consider the essential notion of freedom of contract. As a general matter, individuals may refuse to contract with, or may offer discriminatory contract terms to, anyone, for any reason, including health status.[1] In other words, contract law would allow a doctor to refuse to treat a patient with HIV/AIDS, a restaurant to refuse to serve a smoker, or a movie theater to refuse to seat an overweight person. Court opinions or legislations can alter this common-law baseline by prohibiting certain agreements or invalidating contracts on public policy grounds. For example, statutes prohibit racial discrimination in certain contracts.

What about tort law? How can personal injury cases be healthist? Tort functions primarily to allocate loss and to make injured parties whole.[2] The tort law is not inherently discriminatory. The unhealthy have the same right to sue and be sued as the healthy. But various tort doctrines, rules, and justifications may invite health-status differentiation. For example, a person with an infectious

[1] 15–79 Corbin on Contracts § 79.3 (2017).

[2] Dan B. Dobbs et al., *Hornbook on Torts* §2.4, *at* 21–3 (2d edn., West Academic Publishing 2016) (2000).

disease may be held liable for transmitting it to someone else. Or a judge may reduce a person's damages for an illness or injury for failing to seek medical care. In each case, we might say that the tort defendant or plaintiff faced discrimination based on health status.

Tort and contract law principally govern private disputes and arrangements, making *systematic* disadvantage harder to identify and address through prescriptive policy reforms. With those caveats in mind, we reveal various previously unexamined features of these areas of law that create opportunities for healthism. This chapter identifies examples of differential treatment based on health status in those fields.

As with the other chapters, we leave the bulk of our prescriptive analysis to Chapter 6. This chapter begins by examining the potential for health-status discrimination in tort law. By way of context, we first note various ways that tort law categorically disadvantages people based on age, race, gender, and other statuses. Next, we turn to tort doctrine and policy that disadvantage individuals based on health status. The contracts portion of the chapter proceeds similarly. We first provide context, noting existing exceptions from the freedom of contract. We then discuss various doctrinal examples that result in differential treatment based on health status.

5.2. HEALTHISM AND TORT LAW

A number of tort law rules and decisions treat unhealthy litigants differently than healthy ones. The potential for discrimination of any sort in private, largely judge-made law, may be less obvious than in public law. Therefore, before arguing for the law to regulate healthism, we note ways that tort law disadvantages more established, protected antidiscrimination categories.

5.2.1. *Other "isms" in Tort Law*

Scholars have identified discrimination in torts on the basis of gender, race, ethnicity, age, family status, and other categories. In many cases, either by common law or statutory reform, the law has evolved to correct the unequal treatment. Other cases, however, may warrant additional reform. Because healthism in tort law is not well-recognized, we anticipate an even greater need for legal attention.

Discrimination in the Common Law

Tort law has discriminated and continues to discriminate against women in multiple ways. Historically, women had no legal identity separate from their husbands and, thus, could not be sued or sue on their own behalf.[3] Likewise, any damages a woman recovered went to her husband.[4] Even when women achieved legal standing through the Married Women's Acts of the Nineteenth Century, their claims were limited to property damage.[5] The law had to evolve further for women to recover for personal injuries. Also, historically, women could not recover for loss of consortium (in short, the value of the relationship) based on injury to their husbands even though husbands could recover for injury to their wives.[6] Modern tort law has all but eliminated those formal distinctions, demonstrating "the power of changed social attitudes to influence the law."[7] Similar attitude changes may be warranted with respect to health-status discrimination.

Historical vestiges aside, modern examples of gender discrimination still operate in tort law. For instance, rules governing damages undercompensate women by incorporating wage differentials into the calculation. Even though women have longer life and work-life expectancies, they consistently receive lower awards for lost future earnings. If the purpose of tort awards is compensation – placing the injured victim in the position that she would have occupied but for the tort – then those disparities may make sense. But if we think that law should correct historical discrimination, then the rules require adjustment. We can make similar arguments for healthist tort laws.

Additionally, tort injuries to women are typically categorized as emotional or relational harms, which are compensated at a lower rate than physical injury or property damage, the types of damages that men are more likely to receive.[8] Based on those findings, Professor Martha Chamallas concludes that, although tort rules appear facially neutral, we need to examine the "deep structures" in tort law to recognize the resulting inequality.[9] Her goal is not

3 Thomas Koenig and Michael Rustad, *His and Her Tort Reform: Gender Injustice in Disguise*, 70 *Wash. L. Rev.* 1, 2 (1995).

4 Lucinda M. Finley, A *Break in the Silence: Including Women's Issues in a Torts Course*, 1 *Yale J.L. & Feminism* 41 (1989), at 45–6 (hereinafter Finley, *Yale*); Richard A. Epstein and Catherine M. Sharkey, *Cases and Materials on Torts*, (10th edn. 2012).

5 Finley, *Yale*, note 4, at 46.

6 Finley, *Yale*, note 4, at 49; *see also* Epstein, note 4; *see also*, Phong T. Dinh, *Equal Protection Clause Mandates Judicial Expansion of Necessaries Doctrine to Impose Mutual Burden Upon Spouses-Landmark Medical Center* v. *Gauthier*, 29 Suffolk U. L. Rev. 573 (accepting equal protection challenge to Rhode Island's necessaries doctrine imposing equal burden on wives to pay the necessary expenses of their husbands).

7 Finley, *Yale*, note 4, at 47.

8 Martha Chamallas, *The Architecture of Bias: Deep Structures*, 146 *U. Pa. L. Rev.* 463 (hereinafter *Deep Structures*); *see also* Martha Chamallas, *Civil Rights in Ordinary Tort Cases: Race, Gender, and the Calculation of Economic Loss*, 38 *Loy. L.A. L. Rev.* 1435 (hereinafter *Civil Rights*); *see also* Finley, *Yale*, note 4, at 65.

9 *Deep Structures*, note 8, at 530.

to suggest specific tort reforms but rather "to develop the habit of routinely assessing the differential effects of tort rules."[10] To the extent that healthism exists in tort law, we would urge similar awareness of the issue.[11]

Racism also infects tort law. Chamallas's empirical work on damages has implications for race, revealing the devaluation of black lives and other harms.[12] Like women's wages, estimates of lost future earnings for racial minorities may be depressed by historical wage differentials. Moreover, people of color may have lower work-life expectancies, due to higher rates of unemployment and incarceration.[13] Frank McClellan critically examined race bias across the torts system, including risk assessment, jury selection, burdens of persuasion, damages calculations, and settlement negotiations.[14] He suggests that "the race problem impacts every aspect of a tort claim"[15] and urges that true tort reform should take into account race, gender, and class issues.[16] And, we might add, health.

Race and gender discrimination also appears in the tort of intentional infliction of emotional distress (IIED). IIED requires the plaintiff to prove that the defendant intentionally or recklessly engaged in outrageous or extreme conduct that caused the plaintiff to suffer severe emotional distress.[17] Scholars assert that IIED, also called the "outrage tort," fails to adequately capture both gender- or race-based animus and verbal abuse[18] because the tort turns on the factfinder's assessment of whether the comment or conduct was sufficiently outrageous or extreme. All too often, juries – and even judges – are not attuned to the particular insults, offenses, or vulnerabilities that women and minorities experience. Thus, they might conclude that the defendant's conduct, while perhaps offensive, was not sufficiently extreme or outrageous to constitute a tort.[19] When insults or abuses arise in

10 Ibid. at 531.

11 *See similarly* Wendy E. Parmet, *Populations, Public Health, and the Law* 219–38 (2009) (examining various tort law examples through her population-based approach to legal analysis).

12 *Deep Structures*, note 8, at 471–4.

13 Ibid. at 481.

14 Frank M. McClellan, *The Dark Side of Tort Reform: Searching for Racial Justice*, 48 *Rutgers L. Rev.* 761 (1996).

15 Ibid. at 772.

16 Ibid. at 791.

17 Restatement (Second) of Torts § 46 (1965).

18 Martha Chamallas, *Discrimination and Outrage: The Migration from Civil Rights to Tort Law*, 48 *Wm. & Mary L. Rev.* 2115 (2007); McClellan, note 14 (arguing similarly regarding "outrageousness" and punitive damages in products liability).

19 *See, e.g., Patterson* v. *McLean Credit Union*, 805 F.2d 1143 (4th Cir. 1986) (finding plaintiff's racial harassment allegations that her supervisor stared at her for several minutes at a time, assigned her too many tasks, made her sweep and dust [jobs not assigned to white workers] fell "far short" of North Carolina law governing workplace harassment).

the employment context, tort law largely has punted to statutory protections. Certain employment discrimination statutes, namely Title VII of the Civil Rights Act of 1964[20] and Section 1981 of the Civil Rights Reform Act of 1991,[21] provide a different remedial scheme for workplace racial and sexual harassment. Those laws may not offer adequate relief, given the additional elements of proof they require.

Discrimination in Tort Reform Statutes

As the workplace statutes demonstrate, Congress or a state legislature can provide remedies for certain injuries, which replace common law claims. Other times, statutes modify the common law specifying certain procedural or substantive rules. Tort law is largely judge-made but has a significant overlay of state statutory provisions, especially with respect to damages. Beginning around 1975, tort reform swept the country. A number of states imposed caps on noneconomic damages, often specifically for medical malpractice.[22] Other statutes limited recovery in certain contexts, for example, wrongful death cases, or capped punitive damages.[23] The laws typically capped noneconomic damages at $250,000, with no adjustment for inflation. Business interests, especially the medical and liability insurance fields, strongly support tort reform. One argument is that juries award sympathetic plaintiffs astronomical amounts, especially for "intangible" harms, such as pain and suffering. Recall the infamous McDonald's hot coffee lawsuit, in which a jury awarded $2.86 million to a plaintiff whose pelvic region was severely burned when drive-through hot coffee spilled in her lap. Medical malpractice is a focus of tort reform because torts awards are seen as a major driver of escalating insurance premiums, health-care costs, and provider shortages.[24] Over time, litigants have challenged caps, and, in many cases, judges have overturned them on various constitutional grounds.[25]

[20] 42 U.S.C. § 2000e.

[21] Pub. L. 102–166, 105 Stat. 1071.

[22] Catherine M. Sharkey, *Unintended Consequences of Medical Malpractice Damages Caps*, 80 *N.Y.U. L. Rev.* 391 (2005).

[23] *See*, e.g., Colo. Rev. Stat. § 13–21-203 (2014); Ga. Code Ann. § 51–12-5.1 (2010).

[24] Joanna M. Shepherd, *Tort Reforms' Winners and Losers: The Competing Effects of Care and Activity Levels*, 55 *UCLA L. Rev.* 905 (2008).

[25] *Conditional Challenges to Caps on Tort*, 42 Me. L Rev. at 228–33; *see also* David L. Hudson Jr. *More States See Tort Limits Challenged as Unconstitutional, National Pulse* (Oct. 9, 2014, 8:18 PM) available at: www.abajournal.com/magazine/article/more_states_see_tort_limits_challenged_as_unconstitutional/; *see also* Atra, available at: www.atra.org/issues/noneconomic-damages-reform (last visited Aug. 15, 2017).

These reform efforts injected new forms of discrimination into the torts system. Where statutory caps are in place, scholars and judges have persuasively argued that they discriminate against women, the elderly, people with disabilities, and the young. The caps also discriminate on health status, singling out victims of medical error and those with the most severe injuries.

Caps disadvantage women[26] because noneconomic damages typically represent a significantly greater portion of women's total recovery.[27] Thomas Koenig and Michael Rustad studied the disproportionate impact of noneconomic and punitive damages caps on women in products liability and medical malpractice cases.[28] Noneconomic damages caps also arguably discriminate against the elderly, the young, the poor, and others with reduced earning capacity.[29] Like women, those groups also suffer less economic loss compared to their wealthy white male counterparts because of their relatively lower earning capacity and/or lack of employment.[30] Lucinda Finley examined nursing home abuse cases in Florida and found that damages in those cases included a much higher proportion of noneconomic damages than general tort awards. She concluded that the caps disproportionately impact the elderly.[31] Caps in medical malpractice cases especially impact children who suffer a disproportionate share of noneconomic injuries and experience them over a longer life expectancy. An older person with fewer years left to live who experiences a

[26] Rebecca Korzec, *Maryland Tort Damages: A Form of Sex-Based Discrimination*, 37 *U. Balt. L. F.* 97 (2007); Lucinda M. Finley, *The Hidden Victims of Tort Reform: Women, Children, and the Elderly*, 53 *Emory L. J.* 1263 (using empirical data) (hereinafter Finley, *Emory*).

[27] Finley, *Emory*, note 26, at 1266 (observing that the impact of certain women-specific injuries, including "sexual or reproductive harm, pregnancy loss, and sexual assault injuries," are primarily emotional suffering and self-esteem, rather than economic wage earning capacity or monetary expenses); Korzec, note 26 at 100 (regarding stay-at-home parents and "soccer moms," noting undervaluation for caretakers' loss when a child dies or is disabled).

[28] Koenig and Rustad, note 3, at 46–55 (regarding proposed limitations, including proposed FDA defense to punitive damages).

[29] *See Miller* v. *Johnson*, 289 P.3d 1098, 1119 (2012) (summarizing appellant's and amici AARP's arguments regarding discrimination against women and the elderly, which the court rejected on finding no discriminatory motivation against those groups); *see also Klotz* v. *St. Anthony's Medical Center*, 311 S.W.3d 752, 782 (Mo. 2010) (Teitelman, J., concurring) (noting that the "impacts of the caps will fall disproportionately on the young and economically disadvantaged. Young people, because they will have to live with their injuries and disabilities the longest, bear the brunt of Section 538.210. Similarly, those with generally more limited economic prospects – the poverty-stricken, the physically and mentally disabled, single mothers, wounded veterans, the elderly, and others – are impacted disproportionately by the arbitrary limits on non-economic damages."); *see also* Finley, *Emory*, note 26, at 1265–6 (also noting discriminatory impact of caps on the elderly, poor, and children).

[30] Finley, *Emory*, note 26, at 1280–1.

[31] Ibid. at 1305–6.

similar injury may receive full compensation, if the award is under the cap.[32] By contrast, a child could find her actual damages award slashed by a statutory cap. Caps also undercompensate in wrongful death cases involving infants and children because damages in those cases are largely noneconomic.[33] In short, caps on noneconomic damages may be both sexist and ageist (against both young and old).

Damages caps can also discriminate based on family or parenthood status. Under some state statutes, the cap applies to all victims of a single act of medical malpractice. Medical error certainly harms the patient, but it may also result in compensable harm to the spouse and children of the patient for loss of consortium or wrongful death. Consequently, an unmarried, childless victim might receive full compensation while a case involving a married victim with three children could result in undercompensation to the family group as a whole. At least a few courts have accepted this theory to strike down caps on equal protection grounds.[34]

We envision similar plausible claims for healthism in tort law. For example, litigants have successfully argued that statutory caps discriminate against the most severely injured medical malpractice victims.[35] When a victim's noneconomic damages exceed the statutory cap (e.g., $250,000), they are comparatively undercompensated compared to less severely injured victims whose damages fall below the cap.[36] More generally, tort reform discriminates against victims of medical error as a class, compared to victims injured in other settings. For instance, a statute might not cap recovery for a person killed by a drunk driver, whereas it would cap the damages if the same victim died from medical error.

32 *Ferdon* v. *Wisconsin Patients Compensation Fund*, 701 N.W.2d 440, 462 at 466 (Wis. 2005) (concluding that Wisconsin's $350,000 cap on noneconomic medical malpractice damages violated equal protection guarantees of Wisconsin Constitution).

33 Finley, *Emory*, note 26, at 1294–5 (comparing cases involving non-fatal injury to infants and children, which may involve extensive pecuniary loss due to lifetime medical, therapeutic, and special educational services for disabilities).

34 *See* Ferdon, 701 N.W.2d 440 at 466 ("because an injured patient shares the cap with family members, the cap has a disparate effect on patients with families"); *see also* Kathryn L. Vezina, *Conditional Challenges to Caps on Tort: Is Tort Reform the Dragon Slayer or Is It the Dragon*, 42 *Me. L. Rev.* 219, 228–33 (1990).

35 *See* Ferdon, 701 N.W.2d 440 at 462 (concluding that "the cap divides the universe of injured medical malpractice victims into a class of severely injured victims and less severely injured victims."); *Miller*, 289 P.2d at 1119 ("obviously true" that "the statutory cap treats personal injury plaintiffs differently based on whether their noneconomic damages are higher or lower than $250,000); *Klotz*, 311 S.W.3d at 782 (Teitelman, J., concurring) ("The caps operate on a perverse irony – those with relatively minor injuries are permitted full recovery, while the most severely injured among us are denied").

36 Ibid.

This discussion demonstrates the widespread potential for discrimination in tort law, specifically, and private law, generally. Damages caps discriminate on the basis of health status by disadvantaging medical error victims and the most severely injured plaintiffs. We turn now to tort law's potential for healthism.

5.2.2. *Health-Status Discrimination Across the Doctrine*

Turning now to health-status discrimination in tort law, we first note that tort law favors people who are well enough to take action. We then consider a few exceptions to the reasonably prudent person standard, namely mental health, age, and weight. Finally, we consider the role of health status on both sides of the courtroom – unhealthy injurers and unhealthy victims – in various rules and doctrine.

Active Versus Passive Distinction

In a broad sense, tort law distinguishes between those healthy enough to engage in activities versus those who remain passive. Under the negligence principle that applies to most accidental injuries, a person who *acts* is liable only if she fails to exercise reasonable care.[37] Thus, the law protects a person's freedom of action so long as her conduct does not fall below that standard. As a corollary of that principle, one who remains passive but nonetheless is injured, will recover only some when the defendant who caused the injury acted unreasonably. Otherwise, the victim generally must bear the loss uncompensated.[38] That is the case even if it is clear that *but for* the other's action, the victim would not have been injured. Tort law could avoid this form of discrimination through a strict liability standard. That approach would hold the individual who causes injury liable regardless of the level of care. As a result, victims could recover any time another's conduct causes harm. United States tort law, however, largely rejects strict liability in favor of negligence for accidental injuries. Negligence affords a margin of error for those healthy enough to act, at the expense of those who do not, including people whose health statuses

[37] Restatement (Third) of Torts: Liability for Physical and Emotional Harm § 7; *see, e.g., Collins* v. *HCA Health Services of Tennessee*, 2016 WL 6426739 (Tenn. Ct. App. 2016).

[38] One exception is if a defendant non-negligently creates a risk for the plaintiff, he or she may have a duty to take steps to protect against, or warn of, the risk. *See*, e.g., *Westbrook* v. *Atlanta Gas Light Co.*, 795 S.E. 2d 320 (Ga Ct. App. 2016) ("[T]he open and obvious nature of a danger obviates the duty to warn of that danger." Quoting *White* v. *Ga. Power Co.*, 595 S.E. 2d 353 [2004]).

prevent them from engaging in conduct or action. Arguably then, in the context of accidents, tort law may favor the healthy over the unhealthy.

Another way that tort law prefers healthy individuals is through the "no-duty" rule. Tort law imposes liability when someone acts carelessly but generally does not require a person to *take action* by helping, aiding, protecting, warning, or rescuing others, including those who are helpless or incapacitated.[39] A fellow pedestrian who sees a visually impaired stranger about to step into the path of an oncoming truck has no duty, as a matter of tort law (morality aside) to try to prevent the accident. Likewise, if a pedestrian comes across an unconscious person on the sidewalk in the middle of winter, she is free to ignore the person's plight. She will not be liable unless she injures the person, for example, by kicking him or removing blankets. That baseline rule protects would-be actors at the expense of needy (and sometimes unhealthy) victims.

The rule becomes perhaps even harder to swallow when we consider professional rescuers. Although morally a physician on an airplane should try to revive another passenger who loses consciousness, tort law generally does not compel it. Under the common law of both torts and contracts, a physician is free to refuse to treat anyone, even someone in dire need. In a classic case, a court held that a doctor had no obligation and, therefore, no liability for a woman who dies in childbirth when he declined to make a house call. Although he had treated her in the past, he did not have an ongoing physician–patient relationship that would require him to respond to her family's request for help.[40] Statutes create exceptions to this baseline rule. First, a few states have Good Samaritan statutes that compel certain health-care professionals to render emergency medical assistance.[41] Even so, most Good Samaritan statutes do not affirmatively require a physician (or other volunteer rescuers) to intervene but instead provide immunity from liability for any harm that occurs during a rescue attempt.[42] This rule allows even trained rescuers to go about

[39] 13 Am. Jur. Proof of Facts 2d 709 (2017).

[40] *Hurley* v. *Eddingfield*, 59 N.E. 1058 (Ind. 1901).

[41] *See* Vt. Stat. Ann. tit. 12, § 519(a) (1967).

[42] *See* Cal. Bus. & Prof. Code § 2395 (West 1990) (stating that "[n]o licensee, who in good faith renders emergency care at the scene of an emergency, shall be liable for any civil damages as a result of any acts or omissions by such person in rendering the emergency care"); Ga. Code Ann. § 51-1-29 (1982) (stating that "[a]ny person, including any person licensed to practice medicine and surgery pursuant to Article 2 of Chapter 34 of Title 43 and any person licensed to render services ancillary thereto, who in good faith renders emergency care at the scene of an accident or emergency to the victims thereof without making any charge therefore shall not be liable for any civil damages as a result of any act or omission by such person in rendering emergency care or as a result of any act or failure to act to provide or arrange for further medical treatment or care for the injured person").

their own business, free of any obligation to help another without the fear of tort liability.[43] Accordingly, the no-duty rule also favors the healthy over the unhealthy. Healthy would-be rescuers avoid liability as long as they do not cause affirmative harm, while injured parties are denied assistance and tort recovery.

Reasonably Prudent Person-ism

Tort law, and particularly the dominant theory of negligence, centers on the hypothetical "Average Joe." To the extent that a person does not conform to the average, she may find herself deemed negligent. Roughly speaking, a negligence action requires proof that the defendant (1) owed a duty of care to the plaintiff, (2) breached that duty, and that (3) the breach caused (4) harm to the plaintiff.[44] Reasonable, or "ordinary" care is often the applicable standard. The reasonable care standard is objective, meaning that an individual's subjective perspective, experience, predilections, or limitations generally do not matter.[45] The issue is not what *this* particular person could or would have done, but what an "ordinary" or "reasonable" person could or would have done.[46] In other words, an objectively reasonable person defines non-negligent conduct.[47] Hence, tort law inherently disadvantages anyone who is out of the ordinary, and poor health is a deviation from the norm.

The ordinary care standard does not require flawless conduct or extraordinary measures, but simply performance as an average member of the community. That approach can discriminate against women, racial and ethnic minorities, the elderly, the young, and people with disabilities. If "average," "ordinary," or "reasonable" roughly translates to a white male of average

43 *See generally* Neil J. Squillante, *Expanding the Potential Tort Liability of Physicians: A Legal Portrait of "Nontraditional Patients" and Proposals for Change*, 40 UCLA L. Rev. 1617 (1993) (illustrating the obstacles for an individual seeking redress for a medical malpractice claim where the physician–patient relationship does not follow traditional characteristics, such as an individual who pays for medical services).

44 Dobbs, note 2, at §9.5.

45 Ibid. at § 10.5.

46 *See, e.g., Creasy* v. *Rusk*, 730 N.E.2d 659, 666–7 (Ind. 2000) ("We hold that a person with mental disabilities is generally held to the same standard of care as that of a reasonable person under the same circumstances without regard to the alleged tortfeasor's capacity to control or understand the consequences of his or her actions").

47 *See, e.g.*, Johnny Chriscoe and Lisa Lukasis, *Re-examining Reasonableness: Negligence Liability in Adult Defendants with Cognitive Disabilities*, 6 *Ala. C.R. & C.L. L. Rev.* 1 (2015). ("[The objective reasonableness] standard burdens adult negligence defendants who have cognitive disabilities. It does so by treating these disabilities as if they do not exist in two key places: in the minds of defendants who have them and in the awareness of most plaintiffs who do not.")

intelligence and average age, then anyone who does not match that description could have her conduct called into question.[48] Although the law allows certain adjustments for children and persons with demonstrable physical disabilities, others must act at their peril, despite their differences.

First, children are generally not held to the standard of an adult but rather to the standard of a child of like age, intelligence, and experience, thus allowing some downward adjustment in the duty of care and some subjective considerations.[49] Likewise, a visually impaired person is not expected to live up to the standard of care of someone with full sight.[50] She is, however, expected to act prudently, such as by wearing corrective lenses or using a service animal.[51] But other differences, like old age, intellectual disability, gender, and inexperience, generally do not alter the reasonable care standard.[52] Tort law's rigidity in that respect presents a number of potential opportunities for health-status discrimination. We will consider, in particular, mental healthism, ageism, and sizeism.

MENTAL HEALTHISM. Tort law systematically disadvantages people with mental health conditions. While adjusting the negligence standard for physical disabilities, tort law does not do the same for mental impairments. As discussed, individuals with physical impairments – visual, hearing, mobility – enjoy an adjusted, less-demanding standard of care, when their impairment makes it difficult or impossible to comply with the reasonably prudent person standard. Accordingly, they need not conform to the standard of care for the nondisabled population but, rather, must act as reasonable disabled persons.[53]

48 *See* Restatement (Second) of Torts §283B ("Unless the actor is a child, his [or her] insanity or other mental deficiency does not relieve the actor from liability for conduct which does not conform to the standard of a reasonable person under like circumstances."); *see also* David E. Seidelson, *Reasonable Expectations and Subjective Standards in Negligence Law: The Minor, The Mentally Impaired, and The Mentally Incompetent*, 50 *Geo. Wash. L. Rev.* 17 (1981); *see also* Finley, *Yale*, note 4 at 57–65.

49 Children, however, are held to the adult standard of care when they are engaged in adult activities, such as driving. Difficult categorization issues arise with activities like skiing and hunting, which might be considered adult or child activities depending on the relevant community and customs. *See, e.g., Dellwo* v. *Pearson*, 107 N.W.2d 859, 863 (Minn. 1961); *Goss* v. *Allen*, 360 A.2d 388, 390–1 (N.J. 1976).

50 Oliver Wendell Holmes, Jr., *The Common Law* 108 (1881).

51 *See* Restatement (Third) of Torts: Phys. & Emot. Harm §11 (2010) ("[D]epending on the circumstances, a blind actor may be found negligent for walking over such terrain without a cane or some other form of assistance."); e.g., *Poyner* v. *Loftus*, 694 A.2d 69 (D.C. 1997) (holding that a blind pedestrian that failed to use a seeing eye dog or cane, failed to use reasonable care and was barred from recovering under the doctrine of contributory negligence after being injured by an elevated walkway).

52 Seidelson, note 48, at 20.

53 Holmes, note 50, at 108.

By contrast, mentally ill, intellectually impaired, and older actors are held to the objective standard of reasonable care with no adjustment for their limitations. As a result, the law may hold some people to a standard of care that they are incapable of achieving.[54] For example, suppose the plaintiff hires a person of below-average intelligence to build a shed on the plaintiff's property, and the shed collapses due to shoddy construction, causing personal injury and property damage. The defendant cannot avoid liability on the grounds that he built the shed to the best of his own personal abilities, as long as a reasonable person would and could have constructed it differently.[55] This rule protects plaintiffs and avoids line-drawing, despite seeming inherently unfair to people with cognitive impairments.

Tort law disadvantages litigants with emotional or mental conditions in other ways. First, at least historically, tort law did not compensate plaintiffs for "pure" emotional distress – meaning emotional distress without an accompanying physical injury.[56] Reasons for the distinction included the difficulty of proving subjective injuries, the risk of fraud, the reluctance to recognize emotional harms, and narrow views on the purpose of torts compensation. The doctrine has evolved, however, and pure emotional distress damages are available in certain situations, including when a plaintiff observes a severe physical injury negligently inflicted on a close relative or family member,[57] or when a defendant intentionally and outrageously causes emotional distress. Despite those changes, tort law remains skeptical of emotional distress recovery, as evidenced by caps on noneconomic damages, which include pain, suffering, and other intangible harms.

Another example of mental health discrimination in tort law involves the "blackout defense,"[58] which is available for sudden physical – but not mental – impairments. The doctrine excuses defendants who suddenly, without warning, suffer a seizure, heart attack, or other physical impairment that renders him unable to exercise the degree of care otherwise expected. The blackout cases turn on the defendants' awareness of their impairments.[59] If the defendant could reasonably foresee that her health condition could impair her ability to operate a vehicle safely, and she failed to take reasonable precautions, including not driving, then she may be liable. By contrast, if the defendant

[54] Seidelson, note 48, at 17–18.
[55] *See similarly Vaughn* v. *Menlove*, 132 Eng. Rep. 490 (C.P. 1837).
[56] *See Mitchell* v. *Rochester Ry. Co.*, 45 N.E. 354 (N.Y. 1896); *Ward* v. *West Jersey & Seashore R.R. Co.*, 65 N.J.L. 383 (1990).
[57] *See*, e.g., *Portee* v. *Jaffee*, 417 A.2d 521, 528 (N.J. 1980).
[58] *See*, e.g., *Rogers* v. *Wilhelm-Olsen*, 748 S.W.2d 671 (Ky. Ct. App. 1988).
[59] *See*, e.g., *Hammontree* v. *Jenner*, 20 Cal. App. 3d 528 (1971).

was unaware of the impairment she may avoid liability because she could not have reasonably prevented it.[60] In those cases, although the defendants' health conditions quite clearly caused injury, they are not liable. To hold otherwise, the argument goes, would amount to strict liability.

Courts, however, have not extended the blackout defense to unanticipated mental impairments. Defendants may still be liable even if they had no idea that they might black out, "wig out," or otherwise lose touch with reality.[61] As a result, courts may hold such defendants liable (strictly) despite their inability to have reasonably avoided the accident. Standard justifications for this distinction are similar to the arguments against damages for emotional distress, including the subjectivity of mental health and the difficulty proving the role the impairment played. Torts' goal of compensating injured parties also supports the distinction: between two innocent actors, the one who caused the loss should bear it.[62] Of course, one could make the same compensation argument for the injurer who has a sudden heart attack. Moreover, the distinction leaves difficult questions, such as how to classify someone with Alzheimer's disease or dementia, which has both physical and mental symptoms.[63] Admittedly,

[60] *See*, e.g., *Kollerbohm* v. *County of Los Angeles*, 2007 WL 646244 (Cal. App. 2007) (not reported) (finding defendant failed to carry burden of proof as a matter of law on sudden incapacitation defense); *Ford* v. *Carew & English*, 200 P.2d 828 (Cal. App. 1949) (finding evidence on which jury could conclude that defendant did not anticipate loss of consciousness, despite history of dizzy spells and treatment for strained heart muscles); *Wood* v. *Jones*, 516 S.E.2d 144 (N.C. 1999) (jury question on sudden incapacitation defense, based on evidence of either sensory overload due to Alzheimer's disease, "mini-stroke," or heart arrhythmia). *Storjohn* v. *Fay*, 519 N.W.2d 521, 528 (Neb. 1994) ("The [sudden incapacitation] defense is not available where a driver was put on notice of facts sufficient to cause an ordinary and reasonable person to anticipate that his or her driving might likely lead to injury to others"); ibid. at 528–9 (concluding that defendant was well aware that he was subject to seizures that would cause loss of consciousness); *Bruenig* v. *American Family Ins. Co.*, 173 N.W.2d 619 (Wis. 1970) (holding jury question whether motorist had knowledge of her paranoid schizophrenic condition and likelihood of hallucination while driving); *Eleason* v. *Western Casualty & Surety Co.*, 35 N.W.2d 301 (Wis. 1949) (holding defendant negligent as a matter of law for driving with known history of spells that would render him unconscious, even though he was not aware of technical diagnosis of epilepsy).

[61] *See Bashi* v. *Wodarz*, 53 Cal. Rptr.2d 635 (1996) (holding that sudden, unanticipated mental disorder, which the defendant described as "wigg[ing] out," may not be asserted as defense to negligently caused automobile accident).

[62] *See Breunig* v. *American Family Insurance Co.*, 173 N.W.2d 619, 622 (1970); Seidelson, note 48, at 37.

[63] *See* Edward P. Richards, *Public Policy Implications of Liability Regimes for Injuries Caused by Persons with Alzheimer's Disease*, 35 *Ga. L. Rev.* 621, 637–9 (2001) (noting difficulties with asserting sudden incapacitation defense with diagnosis of Alzheimer's disease); Vaughn E. James, *No Help for the Helpless: How the Law Has Failed to Serve and Protect Persons Suffering from Alzheimer's Disease*, 7 *J. Health & Biomedical L.* 407, 428 (2012) (noting that "traditional tort law does not allow mental or physical impairments as defenses to liability for negligent

mental impairments are highly varied, and defining an appropriate adjusted standard of care could result in an impossibly subjective standard.[64] We do not seek to resolve this issue but merely to identify the potential for a subcategory of mental health discrimination in tort law.

AGEISM. As we discussed in Chapter 4 in the context of insurance, age operates as a proxy for health status. The same is true in tort law. First, like defendants with mental impairments, elderly defendants do not get a special, adjusted standard of care for negligence.[65] They must conform to the uniform, objective, reasonable person standard. Therefore, an elderly driver who tends to drive and respond to stimuli more slowly than a younger driver could be held liable in an accident, even though she could not perform to the objective standard. Unlike children with compromised abilities, elderly adults do not get a "break" when it comes to tort law.[66] The law gives children the opportunity to make mistakes as they learn and integrate into society. Elderly adults are already integrated and presumed to know how to drive or to perform other potentially risky adult activities. To the extent that they have actual physical impairments, such as visual or hearing impairments, the elderly person would be expected to act as a reasonable person with those impairments.[67]

Second, under traditional damages rules, courts will almost certainly award older plaintiffs less than younger plaintiffs, even for the same injury. Tort victims receive a single recovery, including both past and future damages. Courts calculate future damages – which may include economic harms (like lost earnings and medical expenses) and noneconomic harms (like pain and suffering, loss of enjoyment of life, and loss of consortium) – over the plaintiff's life expectancy. Necessarily, older people have shorter life expectancies and, thus, receive lower damages. Moreover, they may receive no future earnings if they are retired or near retirement. Medical expenses and pain and suffering also tend to be lower because elderly victims do not have to live with their injuries as long. Because economic losses are often lower for the elderly,

---

accident" and concluding, accordingly, that a person with known Alzheimer's disease would not be shielded from liability for automobile accident). *But see Word* v. *Jones ex rel. Moore*, 51 S.E.2d 144 (N.C. 1999) (allowing affirmative defense if Alzheimer's disease patient can demonstrate that the condition caused a sudden, unforeseen incapacitation, such as sensory overload).

64 Seidelson, note 48, at 29–30.

65 *See, e.g., Roberts* v. *Ramsbottom*, [1980] 1 All E.R. 7 (Q.B. 1979) (noting that elderly person who "retained some control, albeit imperfect control" is held to the objective standard of care when driving and may be held liable as a result of failing to perform up to that standard).

66 *Dellwo* v. *Pearson*, 107 N.W.2d 859, 863 (Minn. 1961).

67 *See Roberts* v. *Ramsbottom*, 1 All E.R. 7 (Q.B. 1979).

caps on noneconomic losses have an even greater impact on this age group. Thus, to the extent that age correlates with poor health, tort law disadvantages the unhealthy.

SIZEISM. Throughout the book, we have noted various examples of discrimination against overweight people. We have also explained why disability discrimination laws fail to adequately protect that group. Tort doctrine also creates the potential for sizeism. The negligence standard of care, as explained above, turns on what is average, ordinary, or reasonable. Some overweight individuals could fall outside of those norms and thus be deemed "unreasonable," leading to legal liability for their actions.

Overweight people may be the targets of cruel jokes and comments, which could foreseeably result in emotional distress. As noted above, the outrage tort of IIED may compensate those harms. But just as average jurors might not find certain racist or sexist insults sufficiently outrageous for purposes of IIED, fat jokes also might not be deemed "outrageous" in a society that stigmatizes obesity and blames people for their weight. If the judge or jury does not consider the remarks outrageous, tort law would not compensate those harms.[68] However, on occasion, tort law may recognize sizeism. Take the following case that allows an IIED claim based on mistreatment of a very overweight person.

D.J. v. Marion County Coroner's Office[69] involved a thirteen-year-old plaintiff who sued the City of Indianapolis and County Coroner's Office for the emotional distress he suffered witnessing a tow truck remove his mother's remains. The plaintiff was in the family's apartment when a police officer declared his mother dead. He watched from a neighbor's house as the authorities removed her body. The deputy coroner who came to the scene was informed (wrongly) that the mortuary service did not have equipment to transport the decedent, who weighed 750 pounds. The deputy coroner did not have the phone number of the chief coroner but instead contacted the office secretary, who recalled a previous case in which a towing service removed a very large decedent. Without further consultation, the deputy coroner called a towing service. Then they dragged the decedent's remains from the apartment on her mattress, under a sheet, because the coroner's body bags were too small. Then, in the courtyard of the apartment building, they hauled her onto the bed of the tow truck. The towing service employees covered her body with a dirty carpet and tied her to the flatbed.

[68] *Meyers* v. *Hot Bagels*, 721 N.E.2d 1068 (1999).

[69] 971 N.E.2d 151 (Ind. Ct. App. 2012).

The court found that the indelicate treatment of the remains constituted the level of extreme and outrageous conduct necessary for a claim for IIED. Rather than singling out a health status for unfavorable treatment, this case arguably treats that condition *more* favorably, allowing an IIED claim precisely because the decedent was not treated with the same respect as a person of average body weight and size. Perhaps the case indicates a shift in public mores, recognizing that people deserve to be treated with dignity and respect regardless of weight. IIED claims, however, are relatively rare and highly fact-specific. Given the unique set of facts in *D.J.*, we should be cautious citing it as evidence of an anti-sizist trend.

In summary, tort law's reasonably prudent person standard discriminates against anyone who is out of the ordinary. However, courts may make exceptions for children and people with physical – but not mental – impairments. By contrast, tort law especially disadvantages people with mental impairments and the elderly. Perhaps we will see more decisions like the coroner case just described, in which courts deem disrespectful, unequal treatment of unhealthy individuals socially unacceptable and legally cognizable.

5.2.3. *Unhealthy Plaintiffs and Defendants*

We turn now to specific tort law examples in which the litigant's health status is central to the case. In some instances, the unhealthy litigant is the defendant; her health status may contribute to the harm. In other instances, the health status of the plaintiff seeking recovery is somehow legally relevant to the case. Most of the time, perceived poor health tends to correlate with adverse outcomes for both plaintiffs and defendants, although in a few instances the unhealthy may fare better. Here we merely highlight the differences without declaring them rightly or wrongly rendered.

Unhealthy Defendants

The first category of cases concerns unhealthy defendants. In many cases, the defendant's health status itself may be the source of injury to another person. We consider cases involving defendants with contagious diseases who tortiously transmit them to victims. Other cases concern defendants impaired by substance use who cause harm to others. These cases arguably operate as health-status discrimination inasmuch as the defendants are held liable *because of* their health conditions. Someone who is not contagious or under the influence, engaged in the same action – whether it is sexual contact or invasive surgery – likely would not be held liable.

CONTAGIOUS DISEASES. Defendants have faced both civil and criminal liability for exposing others to contagious diseases. In *In re Louie*,[70] the court allowed a claim for the tort of sexual battery against the plaintiff's domestic partner for failing to disclose his HIV-positive status.[71] The plaintiff's complaint alleged the essential elements of an unwanted, harmful, or offensive sexual touching, even though the plaintiff did not end up contracting HIV. Similarly, in *B.N.* v. *K.K.*,[72] the court permitted a nurse to bring claims for negligence, fraud, and IIED against a doctor for knowingly engaging in sexual intercourse without divulging he had genital herpes.[73] First, the court recognized a general tort duty to disclose a known condition. Second, it found his failure to disclose his condition sufficiently extreme and outrageous for an IIED claim, assuming that the plaintiff could demonstrate the requisite severe emotional distress.[74]

In both examples, the plaintiffs knowingly exposed their sexual partners to contagious health diseases. *Louie* alleged battery, which requires a non-consensual physical touching. Although the plaintiff agreed to sex, she essentially did so under false pretenses, without knowing of the defendant's HIV status. *B.N.* found that the defendant owed the plaintiff an affirmative duty to disclose his infectious disease status. In both cases, the plaintiffs' health conditions resulted in tort liability. We could say, then, that the decisions disadvantage the defendants based on their health status.

Another view of the cases, however, would be that the defendants were treated the same as any other defendant, including one not suffering from a health condition, because the courts held them to the same standards of liability. Thus, one could argue that these decisions are health-neutral. However, it may not be that simple. In tort law, it is not enough that the defendant engages in unreasonable or intentionally harmful conduct and that the plaintiff suffers harm. There must also be a causal link between the conduct and the harm. In these cases, a non-infected sexual partner, although still engaged in an intentional act, would not violate their partner's consent. Likewise, without the contagious condition, there would be nothing for the defendant to disclose to his partner. The health status of the defendants is therefore central to these cases.

70 *In re Alan Louie*, 213 B.R. 754 (Bankr. N.D. Cal. 1997).

71 Ibid. (The court dismissed the plaintiff's causes of action – intentional infliction of emotional distress and fraud – on the ground that he had subsequently tested HIV-negative and, therefore, could not demonstrate a reasonable fear of infection to support those claims.)

72 538 A.2d 1175 (Md. Ct. App. 1988).

73 Ibid. at 1176.

74 Ibid. at 1180.

SUBSTANCE USE AND OTHER IMPAIRMENTS. Unhealthy defendants may also cause harm by performing activities while impaired. Recall the discussion regarding the "blackout" defense, which may be available for sudden onset *physical* conditions, but not similarly sudden *mental* conditions. Those cases involve defendants with physical illnesses or conditions that impair their ability to safely operate vehicles safely. They turn on the defendants' awareness or notice of their conditions. Defendants who continue to drive despite knowing that they may black out could have acted unreasonably. Persons with mental impairments may be liable even if they had no notice and therefore no opportunity to make a choice, reasonable or unreasonable, to continue driving. Setting aside the mental healthism particulars, those are cases in which defendants' health conditions may result in liability.

Using alcohol or other substances is another health status that could be relevant to torts cases. Because our definition of health status includes health-related conduct, substance use is a health status even if the individual is not actually diagnosed with addiction. Many of the alcohol consumption cases also involve impaired driving.[75] The issue often is not whether driving under the influence is negligent or caused the accident (those legal points may be conceded), but whether driving under the influence merits *punitive* damages. In torts cases, prevailing plaintiffs typically receive damages to compensate them for the harms they suffer. In some cases, they may also receive an additional award intended not to compensate them for their injuries but to punish the defendant for particularly reprehensible conduct – those are punitive damages. Several courts have found that drunk driving warrants punitive damages. The standards vary by jurisdiction; for example, operating a vehicle under voluntary intoxication may be "wanton,"[76] "gross, willful, and wanton,"[77] "wanton and reckless,"[78] constitutes malice,[79] or satisfies other punitive damages standards.[80]

75 *See*, e.g., *Tingle* v. *Foster*, 399 S.W.2d 475 (Ky.1966) (holding that evidence of defendant's alcoholism, pattern of alcoholic indulgence, and presence of liquor bottles in her car was admissible to show pattern of reckless or wanton driving); *Fleegel* v. *Boyles*, 61 P.3d 1267 (Alaska 2002) (automobile accident case in which defendant admitted he was driving under the influence of alcohol and Valium at the time of the accident, had a history of alcohol treatment before and after the collision, and suffered anxiety disorder, panic attacks, depression, post-traumatic stress disorder, and various gastrointestinal disorders related to alcoholism).

76 Conn. Gen. Stat. Ann. §52–240b (West 2015).

77 *Knibbs* v. *Wagner*, 14 A.D.2d 987, 987 (N.Y. App. Div. 1961).

78 Or. Rev. Stat. §31.735 (West 2015).

79 Cal. Civ. Code §3295(d) (West 2015).

80 John J. Kircher and Christine M. Wiseman, *Punitive Damages: Law and Practice* § 5:3 (2d edn. 2012).

Some legislatures have *categorically* provided punitive damages against intoxicated drivers.[81] Some statutes are zero tolerance. In those states, courts may award punitive damages without evidence that the defendant had any prior history of drunk driving or other convictions.[82] By contrast, courts would consider other kinds of conduct based on the particular facts of the case. In short, the law punishes driving under the influence of alcohol with punitive damages as a rule, unlike other impairments or conditions. To the extent that alcohol use is a health condition, these rules and decisions single out a group that engages in a particular form of unhealthy behavior.

Another line of cases concerns defendants who are doctors impaired by substance use or other conditions. For example, in *Baker* v. *Connolly*,[83] the plaintiff alleged several claims, including negligent misdiagnosis and lack of informed consent, related to a colonoscopy. The informed consent claim alleged that the physician was impaired in sight, coordination, and thought processes, and that a reasonable patient would want to know of those impairments before consenting to the procedure. The patient asserted that the physician was aware of his condition and had discontinued other activities, including bridge and tennis, because of his impairments. The physician did not, however, stop performing delicate medical procedures. Nor did he inform the patient of his impairments. The plaintiff sued for battery, arguing that while she might have consented to the procedure, she did not consent to a procedure by an impaired physician. The court held that there was an issue for the jury on the battery claim.

Similarly, in *R.K.* v. *Ramirez*,[84] the Texas Supreme Court allowed limited discovery of a physician's medical and mental health records in medical malpractice case for the delivery of a baby with cerebral palsy, mental retardation, and quadriplegia. However, in *Schwaller* v. *Maguire*, a case involving liposuction and breast lift, the court found evidence of a physician's addiction to prescription painkillers inadmissible[85] because the patient could not establish that he was impaired while treating her, or that his use of painkillers proximately caused any of her injuries. *Schwaller* demonstrates that merely having an addiction will not necessarily result in liability. Across contexts, courts tend to be highly protective of physicians' privacy. Accordingly, the impaired

[81] La. Civ. Code Ann. art. 2315.4 (2014); Nev. Rev. Stat. § 42.010 (2015); Va. Code Ann. § 8.01–44.5 (West 2017).

[82] *See Taylor* v. *Superior Court*, 598 P.2d 854, 859 (Cal. 1979); *Franz* v. *Brennan*, 431 N.W.2d 711, 713 (Ct. App. 1988).

[83] 1988 WL 105958 (E.D. Penn. 1988).

[84] 887 S.W.2d 836 (Tex. 1994).

[85] 2003 WL 22976339 (Ohio 2003).

physician cases actually tend to disadvantage plaintiffs more than defendants.[86] As *Schwaller* illustrates, the plaintiff may not even be able to admit evidence of the physician's health condition, including substance abuse. Similarly situated unhealthy but *nonphysician* defendants might not receive the same solicitude.

Widlowski v. *Durkee Foods* is a rather unusual nonphysician case.[87] An employee of Durkee Foods entered an industrial tank that contained nitrogen gas, among other substances, and inadequate oxygen for breathing. The worker failed to take steps to clear the tank of hazardous gases or wear protective gear. The exposure to nitrogen gas rendered him restless, incoherent, and delirious. While still in a state of delirium and being treated for his condition at the hospital, the defendant bit off a part of a nurse's finger. The nurse sued the worker and his employer. The court held that the defendants owed no duty of care to the plaintiff because of the low likelihood of such an injury and the high burden, especially on Durkee, of guarding against potential injury. The court concluded that "liability must stop somewhere short of the freakish and the fantastic." Arguably, this defendant was "unhealthy" at the time of the incident, in the same way as other defendants acting under the influence of drugs or alcohol.[88] But, like the obese decedent case above, the unusual facts explain the court's rejection of the claim, not a desire to counteract healthism. Given the singular, unforeseeable sequence of events that brought about the nurse's injury, the court declined to hold the employee or employer liable. Thus, it seems that the defendant-employee's temporarily impaired health status did not drive the decision.

Setting aside exceptional examples like *Durkee Foods*, the cases involving impaired actors arguably disadvantage the unhealthy by holding them liable when their conditions cause harm to another person. On the other hand, decisions involving unhealthy defendants do not necessarily systematically disadvantage litigants based on health status. They are held to the same legal

86 *See, e.g.*, Schwaller, 2003 WL 22976339 (Ohio 2003) (expressing particular concern, "due to societal mores concerning abuse of drugs and [the doctor's] role as physician, [that] the jury might be incited to find liability due to his drug abuse rather than his breach of the applicable duty of care") (quoting *Blakemore* v. *Blakemore*, 450 N.E.2d 1140 [Ohio 1983]). *But see R.K., M.D. Relator* v. *Ramirez*, 887 S.W.2d 836, 840–1 (Tex. 1994) (allowing "offensive use" of patient-litigant exception to physician–patient privilege for discovery of communications or records relating to physician's physical, mental, or emotional condition).

87 562 N.E.2d 967 (Ill. 1990).

88 Ibid. (The facts in *Widlowski* do not discuss whether the defendant was aware of the hazardous gases and voluntarily proceeded into the tank anyway, which facts would suggest an assumption of risk defense. The court did not need to reach issues of affirmative defenses because it resolved the case on the threshold question that the defendants owed plaintiff no duty).

standards, whether negligence, battery, fraud, or other claims. If unhealthy defendants conform their conduct in such a way as to avoid intentionally or carelessly causing injury to others, they will avoid liability. The same is true for healthy persons. The actor simply must avoid performing a medical procedure, driving a vehicle, or having sexual contact.

Despite those valid counterarguments, the specter of healthism in tort cases involving unhealthy defendants is noteworthy. The drunk driving cases, for example, demonstrate the potential for across-the-board intolerance for injuries resulting from certain health conditions, thus disfavoring the unhealthy. Tort law's longstanding skeptical view of emotional harms and mental conditions also presents the real possibility of healthism in tort law. This book aims to raise the salience of these issues in the public's – and court's – minds, just as other scholars have suggested regarding sexism and racism in tort law.

Unhealthy Plaintiffs

The next set of cases concerns unhealthy plaintiffs, or victims of personal injury. The objective, reasonably prudent standard operates on both sides of the case. Tort victims are also expected to act reasonably with respect to their *own* safety. Failure to do so can reduce or eliminate recovery under the contributory negligence or assumption of risk doctrines. Courts also may consider plaintiffs' conduct when calculating damages. Tort law treats unhealthy victims differently than healthy victims with respect to affirmative defenses and damages. Generally, the rules disfavor unhealthy plaintiffs but, sometimes, unhealthy plaintiffs actually fare better than their healthier counterparts.

CONTRIBUTORY NEGLIGENCE. First consider *Ostrowski* v. *Azzara*, a medical malpractice case involving the plaintiff's big toenail. The plaintiff had a number of long-standing, preexisting health conditions, including insulin-dependent diabetes, hypertension, and heavy cigarette smoking. She consulted the defendant, a podiatrist, about discomfort in her feet and legs. Over the course of treatment, the defendant diagnosed the plaintiff with vascular disease and poor circulation. He eventually recommended removing her entire big toenail. Due to the poor circulation and preexisting vascular disease, exacerbated by smoking and diabetes, the wound did not heal properly. The plaintiff required multiple bypass surgeries to save the toe and to prevent gangrene and amputating the leg.

At trial, defense counsel presented evidence of the plaintiff's poor self-care, in terms of smoking, weight management, and blood sugar control both *before* her consultation with the defendant and *after* the toenail removal and subsequent bypass operations. The evidence established that her pre-injury conduct might have been as much as 50 percent responsible for the vascular disease. The jury also was permitted to consider the plaintiff's post-injury conduct. The jury found the plaintiff to be 51 percent at fault and the defendant 49 percent at fault for removing her toenail without adequately considering her vascular condition. Because the plaintiff's fault exceeded the defendant's, she received no recovery.[89]

On appeal, the court took great pains to untangle the issues. With respect to the pre-injury conduct, the court first noted the eggshell plaintiff doctrine, which provides that the defendant "takes his victim as he finds him." That rule bars the jury from considering the plaintiff's pretreatment health habits as evidence of fault. Physicians must treat their patients' health conditions, regardless of how they were acquired. In other words, a person with a heightened risk of lung cancer is entitled to a basic level of care, irrespective of whether that risk comes from smoking or genetics. Moreover, as a matter of damages, the eggshell plaintiff rule allows the plaintiff to recover from the defendant's conduct, even if the plaintiff's injury is more severe than it would have been for a healthier or less fragile plaintiff. Accordingly, the eggshell plaintiff rule actually advantages – rather than disadvantages – unhealthy plaintiffs by allowing them to recover greater damages than someone *without* that preexisting illness or condition.

Setting aside the eggshell plaintiff rule, the plaintiff's health status can play into the case in other ways. As noted, a defendant is liable only for the harm that she, in fact, causes. Therefore, if a plaintiff is already sick when the defendant negligently treats her, the defendant will not be liable for the preexisting sickness. The defendant, however, may be liable for exacerbating the underlying condition, if the defendant acts negligently or worsens the condition. In *Ostrowski*, the doctor did not cause the plaintiff's preexisting conditions. Nevertheless, the court held that evidence of the plaintiff's vascular disease was relevant to whether the defendant was negligent in recommending an appropriate course of treatment.

The court held that the plaintiff's post-injury conduct was relevant for two reasons. First, as a matter of contributory negligence, the jury could consider whether the plaintiff's conduct caused the contraindicated toe surgery and resulting bypass surgeries. Second, post-injury conduct also relates to the doctrine of avoidable consequences. That doctrine bars recovery for injuries occurring after the defendant's negligent conduct that the plaintiff could

89 *Ostrowski* v. *Azzara*, 545 A.2d. 148 (N.J. 1988).

have reasonably avoided.[90] The plaintiff thus has a duty to mitigate damages. By the same token, a plaintiff who is injured in a car accident but fails to seek appropriate medical care may not be able to recover for injuries that have worsened due to lack of prompt treatment. The appeals court held that the trial court erred in *Ostrowski* by instructing the jury to bar – rather than reduce – recovery.

Following *Ostrowski*, the court held in *Tobia* v. *Cooper Hospital*[91] that health-care professionals as defendants could use a patient's own self neglect to limit damages. But the *Tobia* court stopped short of allowing a contributory negligence defense based on the plaintiff's health. *Tobia* involved an elderly patient who fell from a gurney while waiting in the emergency room. The patient, after initially declining assistance to use the restroom, changed her mind and tried to get down from the gurney on her own. She then fell and injured her knee. The court denied the contributory negligence claim. When a health-care professional's duty involves preventing an aged, incapacitated, and fragile patient from engaging in self-harming conduct, the professional cannot assert a contributory negligence defense. The plaintiff's self-neglect, however, could be considered in the damages phase.

In both examples, unhealthy plaintiffs did not recover full compensation for medical professionals' negligence. Had a person who had no reason to question her ability to get down from a gurney slipped and fallen, her health status would not have been part of the equation. Likewise, had a victim of medical error not suffered from post-morbid complications, at least some of which were reasonably attributable to her own lack of self-care, she would have recovered fully. The principle suggested in these two cases is that unhealthy individuals should take care of their own conditions and act reasonably with respect to them. A similar duty, however, might not be imposed on healthy victims. In that respect, the cases discriminate against the unhealthy.

[90] The avoidable consequences doctrine does not require plaintiffs to take every possible precaution or treatment for the condition, but only those that are reasonable medical recommendations. *See, e.g.*, *Komlodi* v. *Picciano*, 89 A.3d 1234 (N.J. 2014) (allowing a jury to determine "whether and to what degree" the patient, who abused alcohol and drugs, had the capacity to secure mental health treatment after she orally ingested a patch to treat back pain, which was intended to be applied to the outer skin, resulting in severe and permanent brain injury); *Steinhauer* v. *Cooper*, 2006 WL 2403439 (N.J. Super. Ct. App. Div. 2006) (entitling the defendant podiatrist to a jury instruction on avoidable consequences based on testimony that the injured plaintiff failed to take her prescribed antibiotics and "reactivated" her infection, resulting in numerous surgeries and medical costs after the defendant suggested removal of the nail from a previous fungal infection).

[91] *Tobia* v. *Cooper Hospital*, 643 A.2d 1 (N.J. 1994).

The rule seems, at first blush, similar to the physically disabled person's duty of care, which includes taking measures to account for her disability – using a cane, guide dog, or other assistance. In those cases, however, a disabled person's duty of care is adjusted *downward*; she is given a "break," or a loosening, of the Average Joe standard that takes her disability into account (as long as it is physical, not mental). In the mitigation of harm cases discussed, by contrast, the unhealthy actors' duty of self-care is adjusted *upward*. They must take reasonable steps to manage their preexisting health conditions, on pain of potentially being denied full recovery.

ASSUMPTION OF RISK. Plaintiffs' health status may also be relevant to the doctrine of assumption of risk. Assumption of risk, like contributory negligence, is an affirmative defense. Even if the defendant is liable, the plaintiff may not recover or may only recover in part if she knowingly and voluntarily encounters a risk presented by the defendant's conduct. For example, could tobacco companies avoid product liability by asserting that the plaintiff knowingly and voluntarily assumed the risk of lung cancer by smoking? If so, would denying relief constitute healthism?

Before we tackle those questions, first consider more typical examples of assumption of risk. Plaintiffs may assume the risk of a wide range of recreational activities, such as skydiving, skiing, snowmobiling, snowtubing, horseback riding, ice skating, and auto racing. For instance, in *Chepkevich v. Hidden Valley Resort, L.P.*,[92] the court denied recovery to an experienced adult skier who was injured when trying to board a ski lift with her six-year-old nephew. The plaintiff sustained her injuries after having specially instructed the ski lift operators to stop the lift to assist the child in boarding. The minor nephew also fell but was not injured. The ski resort asserted that the plaintiff assumed the risk and, therefore, should not recover for her injuries. In particular, the defendant relied on an express release of liability, which the plaintiff had signed, providing:

> Skiing, Snowboarding, and Snowblading, including the use of lifts, is a dangerous sport with inherent and other risks which include but are not limited to variations in snow and terrain, ice and icy conditions, moguls, rocks, debris (above and below the surface), bare spots, lift towers, poles, snowmaking equipment (including pipes, hydrants, and component parts), fences and the absence of fences and other natural and manmade objects, visible or hidden, as well as collisions with equipment, obstacles or other skiers. All the risks of skiing and boarding present the risk of serious or fatal injury.

[92] 2 A.3d 1174, 1190 (Pa. 1990).

> By accepting this Season Pass I agree to accept all these risks and agree not to sue Hidden Valley Resort or their employees if injured while using their facilities regardless of any negligence on their part.[93]

Similar releases of liability, also known as exculpatory clauses, are common in recreational activities and sports. And they often are not enforceable. The first issue is a matter of contract law. It turns on whether the language of the release can be reasonably understood to include the injury in question. The second issue is a matter of tort law. It turns on whether the court should choose not to enforce an otherwise valid contractual agreement because it is unfair, unconscionable, or otherwise leads to undesired results – including reducing the incentives of recreational sports operators to ensure that their activities are safe for patrons.

The *Chepkevich* court held that the release of liability was enforceable, barring the plaintiff's claim. Among other reasons, the court noted that "downhill skiing – like auto racing – is a voluntary and hazardous activity. . . . The signer [of the Release of Liability] is under no compulsion, economic or otherwise, to participate, much less to sign the exculpatory agreement, because it does not relate to essential services, but merely governs a voluntary recreational activity."[94] Extending the auto racing analogy, the court observed, "[a]utomobile racing is hazardous. It gives rise to various situations in which injury or death may result to drivers and mechanics. Experienced race drivers, such as appellant, are aware of the risks attending the sport of automobile racing."[95] The court noted that courts have upheld similar releases for other inherently dangerous activities, like stock-car racing, motorcycle club participation, and snowtubing.

Chepkevich and similar cases represent one end of the spectrum, holding plaintiffs accountable for engaging in risky behavior. That approach could disfavor the unhealthy by denying them tort recovery. That said, a number of courts have found similar recreational releases of liability unenforceable on various grounds. Some draw distinctions based on the nature of the activity or business, with a greater willingness to enforce exculpatory clauses for activities that are open to the public, discretionary, nonessential, and less highly regulated, among other factors.[96] Applying those factors, waivers of liability for snow-skiing or race car-driving would seem to be enforceable. By contrast, a

[93] Ibid. at 1176.

[94] Ibid. at 1191.

[95] Ibid. at 1190.

[96] *See, e.g., Tunkl* v. *Regents of Univ. of Cal*, 383 P.2d 441 (Cal. 1963) (discussed more thoroughly in the contracts section of this chapter).

waiver of liability in a hospital emergency room would more likely be deemed unenforceable.[97]

Other courts take a broader view, not turning on the services or activity in question, and hold that recreational releases of liability should not be enforced. Recent cases have scrutinized exculpatory clauses in a wide range of contexts, often declining to enforce them even when pertaining to arguably discretionary, nonessential services or activities. The reasoning for hospitals and ski resorts is the same, namely, that those businesses are open to the public and heavily regulated by states.[98] Moreover, customers have similar expectations that the activities will be reasonably safe and entrust themselves to the care and control of the recreational facility, just as they do a hospital. This increased reluctance to enforce exculpatory clauses, regardless of context, represents a trend toward protecting safety and avoiding accidents. This trend is arguably health-status neutral, allowing recovery for a broad class of plaintiffs, including those who engage in risky activity.

Our definition of health status, which includes health-related conduct, covers participating in risky activities. Using tobacco and racing cars can both affect health. Hence, the recreational conduct at issue in cases like *Chepkevich* could count as health status. However, that alone does not make the assumption of risk doctrine healthist.

WRONGFUL BIRTH. Another set of cases involve claims related to medical sterilization, either through tubal ligation or vasectomy. If a physician negligently performs the procedure, the patient, as well as the patient's partner, could have an unplanned pregnancy. The difficult issue here is not whether the physician breached the standard of care or caused the pregnancy. Rather, courts struggle with damages.[99] Plaintiffs can usually recover past and future medical expenses, pain and suffering, lost wages associated with the ineffective medical procedure, and the repeat surgery to complete the sterilization.[100] Courts also may award noneconomic damages for pain and suffering related to the unplanned pregnancy and the spouse's loss of consortium, as well as medical costs for prenatal care, delivery, and postnatal care.[101]

97 *See* ibid.

98 *See, e.g., Hanks* v. *Powder Ridge Restaurant Corp.*, 885 A.2d 734 (Conn. 2005); Dalury v. S-K-I Ltd., 670 A.2d 795 (Vt. 1995).

99 *See, e.g., Emerson* v. *Magendantz*, 689 A.2d 409 (R.I. 1997).

100 *See, e.g., Schloss* v. *Miriam Hosp.*, 1999 WL 41875 (R.I. 1999); *Frisina* v. *Women & Infants Hosp.* of R.I., 2002 WL 1288784 (R.I. Super. Ct. 2002).

101 *See, e.g., Pitre* v. *Opelousas Gen. Hosp.*, 530 So.2d 1151 (La. 1988); *Kingsbury* v. *Smith*, 442 A.2d 1003 (1982).

The harder question, however, is whether plaintiffs should receive any damages for the costs of rearing the unplanned child.[102] The approaches vary. Some courts allow recovery for the rearing costs but offset them against the benefits, tangible and intangible, of having a healthy child. That reasoning comes from an older line of cases that presume that a child is a "blessing" and, thus, not a "harm" for torts purposes. Other courts allow full recovery with no offset for the value of having a child. That approach better comports with the goal of tort law to make plaintiffs whole, recognizing that but for the defendant's tort, the plaintiff would not have incurred these expenses, no matter how delightful or successful the child turns out to be.

A further issue – and the one implicating healthism – arises with some courts' differential accounting if the unplanned pregnancy results in a healthy child versus an unhealthy child. If parents bear a *healthy* child, courts may decline to award rearing costs based on the presumption that the child should not be considered a loss.[103] Parents could "mitigate" their damages from an unplanned pregnancy through adoption or abortion. Thus, courts could consider the decision to raise the child further evidence that the benefits of having the child outweigh the costs. However, if a child has a health condition, then courts may award the full costs of rearing the child.[104] That result is especially justified if the parents sought to avoid the pregnancy because of the risks of having a child with a particular health condition. The troubling implication of this approach is that courts deem a child with a health condition a tort damage, while a healthy child is assumed to be a net benefit to her parents. That result seems healthist in the starkest terms.

Alternatively, that approach could be seen to *favor* the unhealthy by allowing greater recovery. However, the fact remains that the tort award nonetheless communicates that a disabled child is a liability and a burden, while a healthy child is a joy and blessing. The wrongful birth cases are also arguably healthist toward the mother, who – unlike other medical error victims – does not recover fully for losing her reproductive autonomy. By denying rearing costs, parents must bear costs they would not have otherwise.

Wrongful birth presents a number of opportunities for health-status discrimination. The preference for freedom of action in tort law may favor the healthy over the unhealthy. Moreover, the reasonable person standard fails to accommodate age, mental and cognitive impairments, or other health statuses short of full-blown physical disabilities. Also, in various cases, courts

[102] *Compare Lovelace Med. Ctr.* v. *Mendez*, 805 P.2d 603 (N.M. 1991), *with Univ. of Ariz. Health Scis. Ctr.* v. *Super. Ct. of Ariz.*, 667 P.2d 1294 (Ariz. 1983).

[103] *See* Emerson, 689 A.2d 409, 411–14; *McKernan* v. *Aasheim*, 687 P.2d 850, 852–5 (Wash. 1984).

[104] *See* Emerson, 689 A.2d at 414; *Fassoulas* v. *Ramey*, 450 So.2d 822, 823–4 (Fla. 1984).

have held unhealthy actors liable when their conditions harm others. At the same time, unhealthy victims may find their health status held against them when recovering for tort injuries. Tort law has persistently been skeptical of mental conditions, creating a subcategory of mental healthism. Just as academic literature has highlighted various instances of race, gender, and other discrimination in tort law, our objective is the same. We attune the reader to these possibilities to create new sensitivity to the issues.

5.3. HEALTHISM AND CONTRACT LAW

Opportunities for health-status discrimination also abound in contract law. Contract law essentially allows private parties to write their own laws, by allowing people to make legally enforceable promises. In that sense, contract law is highly libertarian and promotes individual autonomy. At common law, one party makes an offer. The other party can respond by accepting, outright rejecting, or proposing a counteroffer. The law gives weight to that decision, even if it is based on personal preference, bias, animus, or whim. Accordingly, contract law provides ample opportunity to discriminate based on a wide variety of features, including health status.

Contract law is also consistent with free market, laissez-faire theories that suggest the market will remedy discrimination because it is inefficient. For example, if a building contractor initially prefers not to work with a minority-owned painting company, as a rational economic actor, she may change her mind if that painting company provides superior service at a competitive price.

Market theory aside, the law – particularly health law – has widely recognized market failures. Nobel laureate Kenneth Arrow noted these imperfections, as well as the perils of regulating them, in his 1965 essay, "Uncertainty and the Welfare Economics of Medical Care."[105] If markets are not working the way that economic theory says they should, one solution is to regulate them. But that solution runs awry of strong free-market norms and preferences. Take, for example, a frequent protestors' slogan around the 2010 federal health-care reforms that culminated in the ACA: "Take your government hands off my Medicare!" The protesters are calling for the government to stay out of the business of health care. Of course, the irony is that Medicare is itself a government program designed to remedy market shortcomings. In fact, it is one of the largest federal public benefits programs, providing essential medical

[105] Kenneth J. Arrow, *Uncertainty and the Welfare Economics of Medical Care*, 53 Am. Econ. Rev. 941, 948–54 (1963).

insurance to more than fifty-five million elderly and disabled Americans, for whom the market for health insurance otherwise failed.

This section proceeds by first highlighting the persistence of freedom of contract in medical contracts, particularly physician contracts. We then discuss a few examples of statutory limits on freedom of contract, illustrating that law-makers have precedent for recognizing that at least some forms of discrimination, in at least some types of contracts, offend our values, morals, and priorities. We then turn to existing common law contract doctrines to trace opportunities for health-status discrimination that may warrant legislative or other response.

5.3.1. *Freedom of Contract in the Medical Context*

We begin with the common law no-duty rule by returning to the case of the doctor who refused to make a house call to a pregnant woman, who then died during a complicated delivery. While we first examined the case through the lens of tort law, it would come out the same under the common law of contracts. The doctor had no contractual obligation to treat the woman,

That said, in some instances, statutes alter the common law baseline, by creating an affirmative duty where one does not exist at common law. For example, federal law imposes a limited duty to provide emergency care. The Emergency Medical Treatment and Labor Act (EMTALA) applies to hospitals that participate in Medicare and have emergency departments. The statute does not require them to provide comprehensive care under any circumstances. However, it does obligate them to assess and to stabilize patients with emergency medical conditions. EMTALA also prohibits hospitals from delaying treatment or otherwise *discriminating* based on patients' ability to pay, insurance status, or various other criteria.[106] Even so, EMTALA's duty is very narrow and would not apply to the doctor's making a house call.

Congress aimed EMTALA's obligations primarily at hospitals, rather than physicians working in or on-call to the emergency department. Physicians may face government, but not private, enforcement actions, but those cases are relatively rare. Because hospitals may be on the hook for their physicians' behavior, even though the doctors themselves may not face EMTALA liability, hospitals have struggled with ensuring that physicians comply with EMTALA. These efforts have had varying degrees of success and faced considerable resistance from the medical community, who views them as intrusions on their professional autonomy. As a matter of contract law, for example, the

[106] Emergency Medical Treatment and Active Labor Act (EMTALA), 42 U.S.C. § 1395dd (1986).

hospital might condition medical staff privileges on physicians' participating in the on-call rotation. Federal fraud and abuse laws make it difficult to simply pay physicians for taking EMTALA patients.[107] More typically, hospitals resort to employing "hospitalists" who handle the otherwise unassigned patients admitted to the emergency department.

All of this is to say that physicians, outside of rare Good Samaritan statutes and limited duties under federal law, remain free to differentiate based on health in deciding whom to treat. Even after entering into a treatment relationship, they may withdraw for any reason as long as they do not "abandon" the patient. To avoid abandoning a patient, a doctor must notify the patient before terminating the relationship to give the patient enough time to secure another provider without interrupting her care. This theme of autonomy also characterizes government health-care programs, including Medicare and Medicaid. Those programs operate on insurance models that allow patients free choice of providers. They do not restrict beneficiaries to government-owned-and-operated facilities or government-employed physicians. The corollary of that free choice of providers is that the programs do not compel providers to accept Medicare or Medicaid patients and, increasingly, many do not. Medicaid patients may be particularly undesirable due to lower government reimbursement rates and perceived higher intensity patient needs. Customers shopping in the state health insurance "exchanges" also often encounter restricted networks and a limited choice of providers. Physicians and other health-care providers can therefore freely "cherry pick" on an individual patient basis, or they can decline to accept particular forms of government or private insurance. Absent any common law or statutory overlay restricting their freedom of contract, health-care providers could engage in healthist practices.

5.3.2. *Statutory Limits in Other Contexts*

Outside of the medical context, statutes have limited the common-law freedom of contract. This discussion illustrates that the law can limit or prohibit discrimination in contracting. Federal law covers the "making, performance, modification, and termination of contracts, and the enjoyment of all benefits, privileges, terms, and conditions of the contractual relationship."[108] That provision is part of the Civil Rights Act of 1866, and the US Supreme Court has interpreted it to forbid all "racial" discrimination in the making of private

[107] *See* Ethics in Patients Referrals Act, 42 U.S.C. § 1395nn (1990); The Anti-Kickback Statute, 42 U.S.C. § 1320a-7b (1972).

[108] 42 U.S.C. § 1981 (1870).

as well as public contracts. Thus, it covers people of all races.[109] Another law of the same era protects all citizens' rights to inherit, purchase, lease, sell, hold, and convey real and personal property.[110] That protection bars all racial discrimination, private as well as public, in the sale or rental of property. For example, denying a lease to an apartment or membership in a recreational club on the basis of race would violate the law.[111] Other antidiscrimination protections, like the Fair Housing Act (FHA) and the Civil Rights Act of 1968, similarly prohibit refusing to sell or to rent a dwelling to any person because of race, color, religion, sex, familial status, or national origin.[112] The FHA was the culmination of a civil rights campaign against housing discrimination in the United States. Congress approved it, at the urging of President Lyndon B. Johnson, one week after Martin Luther King Jr.'s assassination. As originally enacted, the FHA prohibited discrimination based on age, color, religion, and national origin. Congress added sex in 1974 and disability and family status in 1988.[113] Similarly, the Equal Credit Opportunity Act (ECOA) forbids credit discrimination on the basis of race, color, religion, national origin, sex, marital status, age, or whether the applicant received income from a public assistance program.[114]

Other laws restrict freedom of contract in particular contexts, including employment. As described in Chapter 4, the Americans with Disabilities Act and the Rehabilitation Act protect disability.[115] The Age Discrimination in Employment Act (ADEA) covers applicants and employees forty years of age and older.[116] Beyond their value as antidiscrimination protections, these statutes demonstrate that the law can limit freedom of contract to outlaw particular forms of discrimination. Similar laws could likewise address healthism either broadly or in particular settings. Before considering whether to address healthism in this area, we turn now to identify further examples of health-status discrimination in existing contract law doctrine.

[109] *See, e.g.*, Civil Rights Act of 1866, 42 U.S.C. §§ 1981–1982 (1866); *Saint Francis College* v. *Al-Khazraji*, 481 U.S. 604 (1987).

[110] § 1982.

[111] *See, e.g.*, *Jones* v. *Alfred H. Mayer Co.*, 392 U.S. 409 (1968); *Tillman* v. *Wheaton-Haven Recreation Ass'n, Inc.* 410 U.S. 431 (1973).

[112] Fair Housing Act, 42 U.S.C. § 3601 (1968).

[113] Pub. L. No. 93–383, § 808, 88 Stat. 633, 729 (1974) (amending the Fair Housing Act to include sex discrimination); Pub. L. No. 100–430, 102 Stat. 1619 (1988) (amending 42 U.S.C. §§ 3601–3619 [1982]).

[114] Equal Credit Opportunity Act (ECOA), 15 U.S. Code § 1691(a)(1), (2).

[115] Americans with Disability Act (ADA) of 1990, 42 U.S.C. § 12101 (1990); Rehabilitation Act of 1973, 42 U.S.C. § 701 (1973).

[116] Age Discrimination in Employment Act (ADEA) of 1967, 29 U.S.C. §§ 621–34 (1967).

5.3.3. *Health-Status Discrimination in Contract Law*

Health-status discrimination exists in contract law, although it is somewhat more obscure than in tort law. Courts have demonstrated general skepticism about the legal relevance of various health conditions in contracts disputes. The issue typically arises with respect to certain defenses to contract enforcement, as well as in calculating damages. In those cases, health status seems to get little deference. However, the courts may be more willing to scrutinize contracts that implicate health-care rights and remedies, recognizing that the subject matter is particularly sensitive. Those cases might be said to be pro-health, rather than anti-health or health-neutral.

Mental Incapacity and Undue Influence

Two related contract doctrines, incapacity and undue influence, implicate health status. Under each, a contracting party seeks to avoid the enforcement of an otherwise seemingly valid contract by arguing the contract did not form properly. A person might lack the legal capacity to enter a contract based on age or mental capability. People who are underage may not be bound by contracts they signed.[117] The law protects minors from liability for contracts that they are too immature to negotiate on public policy grounds. Similarly, people with cognitive impairments of various kinds may be unable to comprehend the nature and consequences of the contract at the time it was formed. Bases for mental incapacity may include schizophrenia, senility, Alzheimer's disease, mental retardation, and drug or alcohol dependency.

Finding a contracting party incapacitated could discriminate against that person based on health status because it deems her incapable of entering a legally enforceable agreement. Contracts for employment, housing, cell phone service, medical treatment, and a host of other daily life activities are commonplace. Therefore, disallowing a class of people with mental or other health conditions from entering those contracts is arguably discriminatory.

In most cases, however, legal incapacity arises not because an individual is being denied a contract, but rather because the individual seeks to avoid obligations under the contract. In short, mental incapacity is a defense to an otherwise valid contract. Courts, however, have been reluctant to recognize mental incapacity as a basis for voiding contracts. If courts refuse to recognize legitimate health conditions as sufficiently debilitating, that may discriminate

[117] *McDonald* v. *Sargent*, 51 N.E. 17 (Mass. 1898).

in a different way – by failing to take diminished health status seriously. The following examples illustrate this point.

In *Ortelere* v. *Teachers' Retirement Board of New York*,[118] a husband sought to void his wife's irrevocable decision to take the maximum amount of retirement benefits during her lifetime, leaving him with no benefits upon her death.[119] The wife, a New York City public school teacher for many years, suffered a "nervous breakdown" at age sixty and took a leave of absence from work. The school board's psychiatrist diagnosed her with "involutional psychosis, melancholia type" and administered tranquilizers and shock therapy. Some months later, shortly before her leave of absence expired, the wife changed her retirement account. Two months later, she died from causes unrelated to her mental condition. Her husband sought to have the election voided for lack of mental capacity, and the trial court agreed. The intermediate appellate court reversed, however, finding the evidence of incapacity lacking.

The New York highest court articulated a new, "modern" standard for mental incapacity and remanded the case back to the trial court to reconsider the evidence under that standard.[120] The traditional test for mental incapacity turned on "cognition," that is, whether the mind was "so affected as to render [the contracting party] wholly and absolutely incompetent to comprehend and understand the nature of the transaction." In *Aldrich* v. *Bailey*,[121] the court found that traditional approach both too restrictive and based on a faulty factual premise, namely that all mental faculties are simultaneously affected by mental illness.[122] Applying that observation to *Ortelere*, the wife might pass the older "cognition" test even though she was incapable of making a voluntary selection about her retirement benefits due to psychosis. Under the newer, modern standard, however, she could be incapacitated. A contract is voidable if, due to a cognitive impairment, one party is not able to act reasonably with regard to the contract, and the other party knows or has reason to know of the condition.[123]

The New York court cautioned, however, that even under the more liberal standard, contracts voided for mental incapacity should be rare: "Of course, nothing less serious than medically classified psychosis should suffice or else few contracts would be invulnerable to some kind of psychological attack. Mrs. Ortelere's psychiatrist testified quite flatly that as a person with

118 250 N.E.2d 460, 464–7 (N.Y. 1969).
119 250 N.E.2d 460 (N.Y. 1969).
120 Ibid. at 465–7.
121 30 N.E. 264, 265 (N.Y. 1892).
122 *Ortelere*, 250 N.E.2d at 464.
123 Ibid. at 465.

involutional depression she was incapable of making a voluntary 'rational' decision."[124] Nevertheless, because the trial court had not considered the evidence under the new standard, the reviewing court remanded the case.[125] This case exemplifies courts' more contemporary, nuanced understanding of psychiatric conditions, but it also evidences a continuing reluctance to void contracts on mental incapacity grounds. That approach arguably is good for mentally impaired individuals' freedom of contract, but bad for the courts' willingness to accept mental impairments as "real," similar to tort law's mental health discrimination.

Undue influence is a related contract doctrine that also considers a party's mental condition. A contract may be set aside if a person in power takes advantage of another person in such a way that the subordinate person cannot exercise free will. Like incapacity, undue influence is a defense to avoid obligations under a contract. Also, like mental incapacity, cases are rare in which courts find a party's mental condition sufficiently impaired to support an undue influence claim.

A case from 1966, *Odorizzi* v. *Bloomfield School District*, involved an elementary school teacher charged with engaging in homosexual activities.[126] The plaintiff resigned from his position but later sought reinstatement on the grounds that his employer obtained his resignation by undue influence. Soon after the criminal charges, the superintendent of the school district and the principal of the plaintiff's school came to his apartment. They told Odorizzi that if he did not resign immediately, they would suspend him and publicize his dismissal proceeding, as they were required to do by statute. They told him this process would cause "extreme embarrassment and humiliation." They also told him that he had no time to talk to a lawyer and that if he resigned immediately, they would not publicize the arrest and suspension.

Odorizzi asserted that he was under severe mental and emotional strain when he resigned, having just completed the process of arrest, questioning by the police, booking, and release on bail, and having gone forty hours without sleep. Therefore, he argued that he was incapable of rational thought or action. After being cleared of the criminal charges, he asked to be reinstated in his employment. When Bloomfield refused, Odorizzi filed an action against Bloomfield, alleging duress, menace, fraud, mistake, and undue influence. The trial court dismissed Odorizzi's amended complaint, and he appealed that

[124] Ibid. at 466.
[125] Ibid.
[126] 54 Cal. Rptr. 533 (Cal. Dist. Ct. App. 1966).

decision. The court did not reconsider the duress, fraud, and mistake causes of action, but it did review the undue influence claim.[127]

The court held that a party may rescind a contract for undue influence if her weakened mental state makes her especially susceptible to persuasion, and the dominant party employs excessive pressure. In short, courts require two elements: undue susceptibility and excessive pressure.[128] For the first element, a party's judgment must be so impaired that her mental state prevents her from freely contracting. Like the newer standard in *Ortelere*, the *Odorizzi* court did not require total weakness of mind that destroys the party's understanding. Lesser weakness of mind that may not be long-lasting or wholly incapacitating could suffice. Reported cases of undue influence usually involved elderly, sick, or senile persons alleged to have executed wills or deeds under pressure.[129] The court in *Odorizzi* concluded that the plaintiff alleged sufficient facts of undue susceptibility, noting that "exhaustion and emotional turmoil may wholly incapacitate a person from exercising his judgment." Given the posture of the case, the court did not definitively decide whether the plaintiff had proven undue susceptibility.[130]

For the second element, the court also looked for various indicators of excessive pressure or over-persuasion, including discussing the transaction at an unusual or inappropriate time, entering into the transaction in an unusual place, insisting that the business be finished at once, emphasizing the negative consequences of delay, using multiple persuaders against the weaker party, lacking third-party advisers to the weaker party, and stating that there is no time to consult financial advisers or attorneys.[131] Applying those factors, the court found that Odorizzi alleged sufficient facts to state a claim for rescission due to undue influence and reversed the trial court's dismissal of the amended complaint.[132] Again, the disposition does not establish conclusively that there was undue influence, but merely that there was enough evidence for the trial court to consider it.

Another case of undue influence, *Vokes* v. *Arthur Murray Inc.*, involved a fifty-one-year-old widow who paid $31,090.45 for dance lessons.[133] After the death of her husband, Vokes hoped to find "new interest in life" by becoming

[127] Ibid. at 539.

[128] Ibid. at 540.

[129] Ibid. citing *Malone* v. *Malone*, 155 Cal. App. 2d 161 (Cal. Dist. Ct. App. 1957) (constant importuning of a senile husband); *Stewart* v. *Marvin*, 139 Cal. App. 2d 769 (Cal. Dist. Ct. App. 1956) (persistent nagging of elderly spouse).

[130] *Odorizzi*, 54 Cal. Rptr. at 543.

[131] Ibid. at 541.

[132] Ibid. at 543.

[133] 212 So. 2d 906 (Fla Dist Ct. App 1986).

an "accomplished dancer." The defendant dancing school vowed to help make that dream come true. Over the course of a few years, Vokes signed several contracts with the defendant and paid out cash for lessons and dance-related trips. The defendant assured Vokes that she had "grace and poise," that she was "rapidly improving and developing in her dancing skill," that the additional lessons would "make her a beautiful dancer, capable of dancing with the most accomplished dancers," that she was "rapidly progressing in the development of her dancing skill and gracefulness," and similar puffery. Periodically, the defendant administered "dance aptitude tests" to assure her of her progress and to recommend additional training. Eventually, after learning that she had no dancing ability, the plaintiff sought to rescind the contracts and reclaim her money.[134] She argued that certain dance instructors knew that the widow had little to no dancing ability yet encouraged her to sign up for more lessons.

The appeals court reversed the trial court, concluding that, "[f]rom the time of her first contact with the dancing school in February, 1961, she was influenced unwittingly by a constant and continuous barrage of flattery, false praise, excessive compliments, and panegyric encomiums, to such extent that it would be not only inequitable, but unconscionable, for a Court exercising inherent chancery power to allow such contracts to stand."[135] In allowing the plaintiff's claim, the court noted that the defendant misrepresented the progress Vokes was making and that the dancing school had "superior knowledge" about talent. "The large expenditures that Plaintiff made, in pursuit of her 'progress,' were not justified by the fact that she was not improving." The court cited an earlier Florida decision, which explained that "[a] statement of a party having . . . superior knowledge may be regarded as a statement of fact although it would be considered as opinion if the parties were dealing on equal terms."[136] The court concluded that the "means and methods of [the defendants] which went beyond the unsavory, yet legally permissible, perimeter of 'sales puffing' and intruded well into the forbidden area of undue influence, the suggestion of falsehood, the suppression of truth, and the free exercise of rational judgment, if what plaintiff alleged in her complaint was true."[137] Accordingly, the court reversed for a new trial.

Vokes, although not involving a cognitive impairment, exemplifies the doctrine of undue influence. The plaintiff was in an emotionally weakened,

[134] Ibid. at 908.

[135] Ibid. at 907.

[136] Ibid. at 909 (quoting *Ramel* v. *Chasebrook Construction Company*, 135 So. 2d 876, 909 [Fla. Dist. Ct. App. 1961]).

[137] Ibid. at 907.

vulnerable state following the death of her husband. The court described her as "a widow of 51 years and without family, had a yen to be 'an accomplished dancer' with the hopes of finding 'new interest in life.'"[138] The repeated and specific misrepresentations by the dance school, at a minimum, created a question for the jury on the issue of undue influence.

However, these cases represent the exception rather than the rule. Courts generally are reluctant to void contracts on the basis of undue influence absent rather extreme facts, as in *Odorizzi* and *Vokes*. That reluctance creates the potential for health-status discrimination because courts could impose demanding standards, which may prevent persons with mental, cognitive, and emotional impairments from asserting the defense of undue influence. If unable to make the requisite showings, those individuals may find themselves bound to contractual arrangements that further debilitate them financially, emotionally, and physically. That potential runs awry of both health liberty, by denying their autonomy, and health justice, by exacerbating existing disparities.

Exculpatory Clauses in Medical Services

Common law courts have singled out contracts for medical services for special consideration on various grounds. First, as we explained in our discussion of torts, courts are less willing to enforce agreements in which patients sign away their rights to sue in the medical – opposed to recreational – setting. *Tunkl* v. *University of California* classically sets out elements that courts consider regarding the enforceability of a patient's waiver of liability. *Tunkl* involved a plaintiff who was asked to sign the waiver as a condition of treatment in the emergency room of a charitable hospital. The court held the agreement unenforceable, noting that: (1) the agreement concerns a business of a type typically thought suitable for public regulation; (2) the party seeking exculpation is performing a service of great importance to the public; (3) the service is held open to any member of the public; (4) the party seeking exculpation possesses a decisive advantage of bargaining strength; (5) the contract is one of adhesion with no option to purchase additional protection against negligence; and (6) the purchasers' property or person is placed under control of the seller.[139] Outside of the medical context, however, courts have been less willing to relieve plaintiffs of otherwise valid

[138] Ibid.

[139] *Tunkl*, 383 P.2d 441 (Cal. 1963); *See also Wagenblast* v. *Odessa S.D.*, 758 P.2d 968 (Wash. 1988) (using *Tunkl* factors to strike release signed by parents related to their children's participation in interscholastic athletics).

contracts. This special solicitude for patients suggests that courts are sympathetic to the unique nature of medical services at issue and the relative vulnerability of patients asked to sign those agreements.

Viewed through a libertarian lens, that special attention to medical waivers could discriminate based on health status, by denying patients the option to contract away potential torts claims in exchange for access to more affordable health care. Consider, for example, a free dental clinic, staffed by volunteer dentists, oral hygienists, and other assistants, that requires the patient to sign a release of liability as a condition of treatment. A patient's choice may be between no dental care at all or giving up a potential tort action in exchange for free care. By overriding the patient's freedom of contract, the court may be discriminating against her and actually undermining her health status rather than enhancing it, contrary to our health liberty and health justice guiding principles.

Another basis for voiding contracts, especially in health-care settings, concerns the context in which consent is obtained. Even if a contract is fully executed and enforceable, courts may decline to enforce it based on the fairness of the conditions under which it formed. These cases involve a procedural objection, similar to undue influence, discussed above. For example, a patient who is in physical pain and under stress, moments before being wheeled into the operating room, may not fully appreciate the agreement that she is signing. Likewise, in *OB-GYN Ltd.* v. *Pepper*,[140] the court refused to enforce an agreement to arbitrate signed when the patient first went to a clinic to receive oral contraceptives. Later, when the same patient experienced a stroke and paralysis, allegedly as a result of negligently prescribed drugs, she stated that she did not remember signing or being told the terms of the arbitration agreement. On those facts, the court found no valid meeting of the minds to establish an enforceable contract.[141] It allowed the patient to seek judicial remedy.

Pepper and similar cases, again, suggest courts' willingness to consider contracts in the health-care context as warranting closer scrutiny. Declining to hold patients to contracts signing away medical malpractice actions or agreeing to certain medical procedures might be examples of positive paternalism. In those circumstances, it may be appropriate to question whether the individuals are making medical determinations that promote healthy decision-making and facilitate individual choice regarding health.

[140] 693 P.2d 1259, 1260 (Nev. 1985).
[141] Ibid. at 1261.

Health-Care Arbitration Clauses

Pepper involved an arbitration agreement that waived the parties' right to jury trial for any dispute. Courts have scrutinized arbitration clauses in the medical context closely. They have even drawn the attention of the US Supreme Court. Lower courts, historically, were hesitant to enforce those agreements in the medical arena. However, federal law recognizes a preference for arbitration, as a general matter, under the Federal Arbitration Act (FAA).[142] One medical context, in particular – nursing home care – was the subject of a case before the US Supreme Court. The Court's decision there has implications for health-care arbitration clauses more broadly.

Kindred Nursing Services L.P. v. *Clark*[143] involved a pre-dispute arbitration clause in a contract signed while being admitted to a nursing home. Either the resident herself or someone acting with legal power of attorney may sign those agreements. Courts have increasingly struck down such agreements. When a resident is injured or dies, the facility will compel arbitration of any related personal injury claims. Some cases turn on technical questions of derivative suits, that is, whether the waiver is binding on family members for their own injuries. Those cases are for wrongful death or loss of consortium damages to the "secondary" party, the family members. One view is that the signed arbitration agreement binds only the resident, not the family members. Another view is that the action by the patient must be viable before the family can recover anything.

The specific question in *Kindred* was whether a power-of-attorney agreement bound the patient to an agreement to arbitrate her own disputes.[144] The plaintiffs in *Kindred* were two residents of a nursing home, whose relatives had valid powers of attorney to act on their behalf. Their relatives used their powers of attorney to sign arbitration clauses as part of the admissions paperwork to the nursing homes. After the residents passed away, the relatives sued the nursing homes. They argued that the arbitration clauses were not enforceable because their powers of attorney to manage financial affairs or to make medical decisions did not include the ability to bind the residents to compelled arbitration. State law agreed. The applicable cases required a power of attorney instrument to expressly refer to arbitration agreements for the agent to bind the principal to arbitration. Other states have also held that agreements involving arbitration clauses receive special treatment.

[142] 9 U.S.C. §§ 1–16 (2000) (constituting [the whole comprises the parts] Chapter 1 of the FAA, dealing primarily with domestic arbitration).

[143] 137 S. Ct. 1421 (2017).

[144] Ibid.

In its May 2017 opinion, the court in *Kindred* held that the so-called "clear statement" rule violated the FAA by singling out arbitration agreements for disfavored treatment. The FAA provides that arbitration agreements are "valid, irrevocable, and enforceable, save upon such grounds as exist at law or in equity for the revocation of any contract."[145] That is, arbitration clauses may be voided upon *generally applicable* contract law principles, such as mutual mistake, duress, unconscionability, or fraud, but not upon legal rules that apply only to arbitration clauses. The state law rule requiring an explicit statement before the agent could sign away the principal's right to a jury trial did exactly what the FAA forbids. It applied a special rule of law to arbitration contracts. *Kindred*, thus, relied on the FAA to strike down the law. The holding applies to health-care contracts generally, not just nursing home contracts. Consequently, individuals may find themselves deprived of their day in court to challenge substandard care or other medical disputes.

Importantly, the decision is facially neutral, not expressly disfavoring the unhealthy. Indeed, the FAA requires equal treatment: Arbitration clauses can be treated no differently than other contracts. As many lower courts have recognized, however, medical care is an especially sensitive, critical service that differs from other business arrangements. *Kindred* ignores those concerns and, accordingly, may disparately impact the unhealthy. Under antisubordination, *Kindred*'s result could raise the specter of healthism.

Kindred notwithstanding, state courts may strike down arbitration clauses based on generally applicable contract doctrine. For example, in an earlier case, *Sosa* v. *Paulos*,[146] a state court, although generally favoring arbitration clauses, refused to enforce a written arbitration agreement on unconscionability grounds. The patient signed the agreement less than an hour before surgery, while she was undressed and already in surgical clothing. Given the short time frame and the pending surgery, she felt rushed to sign the documents and did not actually read them. In another case, *Engalla* v. *Permanente Medical Group, Inc.*,[147] the state court set aside Kaiser Permanente's medical malpractice arbitration agreement on fraud grounds. The agreement ostensibly called for each side to name an arbitrator, who together would then select a third, neutral arbitrator. In reality, however, Kaiser's defense counsel and legal department invariably selected the third arbitrator. Moreover, the process for selecting the third arbitrator was long and tedious, taking an average of 863 days.

145 9 U.S.C. § 2.

146 924 P.2d 357 (Utah 1996).

147 938 P.2d 903, 909, 911, 912–3 (Cal. 1997).

These state court decisions suggest that courts may continue to scrutinize arbitration agreements in the medical context more closely than other contexts, similar to the trend in the waiver of liability cases. Courts may recognize that contracts related to medical treatment warrant different consideration than contracts outside of the health-care setting. That view could avoid unfair discrimination against the unhealthy and promote the principles we outlined in Chapter 2. Whether *Kindred* begins to reverse that trend, favoring equal treatment of arbitration clauses regardless of the subject matter of the contract, remains to be seen.

Medical Guarantee Cases

Contracts for medical care could also create the potential for healthism. Courts may apply special rules regarding damages in those cases, particularly when health-care providers guarantee a certain medical outcome. These decisions suggest a bias against, or skepticism toward, medical guarantee contracts. If courts decline to apply standard contract damages rules, it may result in lower awards in medical guarantee cases. That tendency could disadvantage the parties to those contracts.

Take for example the infamous "hairy hand" case, *Hawkins* v. *McGee*,[148] familiar to most first-year law students and featured in the 1973 film *The Paper Chase*.[149] A doctor agreed to perform a reconstructive surgery to the palm of a young man's scarred right hand. The medical procedure involved grafting skin from the patient's chest to his hand. In addition to discussing the duration of the hospitalization and recovery period, the doctor stated, "I will guarantee to make the hand a hundred percent perfect hand or a hundred percent good hand."[150] In fact, the surgery failed to remove the scarring and resulted in the plaintiff growing thick hair on the palm of his hand.

The plaintiff asserted that the doctor's statement about the outcome of the surgery amounted to legally enforceable guarantee. The doctor tried unsuccessfully to refute that suggestion, arguing that no reasonable person would understand those words as a contractual promise but merely as "his expression in strong language."[151] The doctor further countered that, given the "common knowledge of the uncertainty which attends all surgical operations," a surgeon would not contract to make a damaged part of the human body "one hundred

148 146 A. 641 (N.H 1929).
149 *The Paper Chase* (Twentieth Century Fox 1973).
150 Ibid. at 643.
151 Ibid.

percent perfect."[152] Based on other evidence, however, the court concluded that a jury could find for the plaintiff, then turned to the proper damages.

In contract disputes, courts typically award expectation damages, meaning that the award puts the non-breaching party in the position that she would have occupied had the contract been performed. Under that rule, Hawkins would receive the difference in value between a 100 percent perfect (or good) hand and the hand that actually resulted from the operation. The judge in *Hawkins* instructed the jury to consider two additional kinds of damages: (1) pain and suffering due to the operation, and (2) "positive ill effects of the operation upon the plaintiff's hand."[153] The reviewing court held that those instructions were an error. It found that awarding pain and suffering was not proper because those damages did not relate to the difference in value resulting from the breach. The parties anticipated some pain and suffering from the surgery; thus, those results were part and parcel of the agreement. The court also held that the jury instruction to consider the worsening of the hand was not proper because expectation damages already took it into account. If anything, under that instruction, the plaintiff might have received a *lower* award, comparing the value of two imperfect hands – the presurgery scarred hand and the post-surgery hairy hand – rather than comparing a hypothetical perfect (or good) hand with the original scarred hand. Accordingly, the court remanded for a new trial.

Another cosmetic surgery case, *Sullivan* v. *O'Connor*,[154] represents a different approach known as reliance damages. Reliance damages could at once be better and worse for patients than expectation damages. They may include pain and suffering but not represent the full value of the promised medical outcome. The plaintiff, a professional entertainer, received a jury verdict of $13,500 for three plastic surgeries on her nose. She entered into a contract with a surgeon who promised he would enhance her beauty and improve her appearance. The plaintiff alleged that the defendant performed the surgery but failed to achieve the promised result. Instead, he disfigured her, leaving her nose deformed. Prior to surgery, her nose was long and prominent but straight. Following surgery, her nose was "bulbous," "flattened and broadened," and the two sides of the tip had lost symmetry.[155]

The court considered, but did not adopt, a blanket rule from other jurisdictions that agreements between patients and physicians "by which the physician undertakes to effect a cure or to bring about a given result should be

152 Ibid.
153 Ibid.
154 296 N.E.2d 183 (Mass. 1973).
155 Ibid. at 185.

declared unenforceable on grounds of public policy."[156] The court noted that, "[c]onsidering the uncertainties of medical science and the variations in the physical and psychological conditions of individual patients, doctors can seldom in good faith promise specific results."[157] However, it opined that "if these actions were outlawed, leaving only the possibility of suits for malpractice, there is fear that the public might be exposed to the enticements of charlatans."[158] Thus, the court took a middle ground, allowing medical guarantee contracts to be enforceable upon "clear proof."[159]

The court discussed various possible approaches to damages. First, it outlined the expectation damages rule applied in *Hawkins*. Second, it explored restitution damages, which merely restores the benefit paid to the defendant, for example, any fee that the plaintiff paid to the doctor. Third, a court could adopt an intermediate position, similar to tort law, that would put the plaintiff back in the position that she occupied before the parties entered into the contract. This third option, known as reliance damages, would include not only returning the benefits conferred on the doctor but compensating the plaintiff for any worsening of her condition.

A law review article by Lon Fuller and William Perdue introduced "reliance" as a theory of contract recovery.[160] The authors explained that expectation damages might be appropriate in business contexts, concerning production or distribution of goods, but inappropriate in noncommercial contexts, such as health care. The court thus adopted the reliance damages measure and, on the *Sullivan* facts, did not limit the plaintiff's recovery to out-of-pocket expenditures under a restitution theory. She also recovered for the worsening of her condition – including her mental condition and prospects as an entertainer – as well as pain, suffering, and mental distress.[161] However, she did not receive full expectation damages, which would have compensated her for the nose her doctor promised her.

Hawkins and *Sullivan* demonstrate courts' tendency to view contracts in the medical context as distinct from other kinds of contracts. Both cases took exceptional approaches to damages. The more modern approach in *Sullivan* denies patients full contract expectation damages for breach of medical contracts, allowing only recovery for reliance. The damages award puts the

156 Ibid.

157 Ibid. at 186.

158 Ibid.

159 Ibid.

160 L. L. Fuller and William R. Perdue, Jr., *The Reliance Interest in Contract Damages*, 46 *Yale L. J.* 52, 373 (1936).

161 *Sullivan*, 296 N.E.2d at 189.

plaintiff back in the position she would have occupied before the contract but not where the plaintiff would have been if the contract had been fully performed. The older *Hawkins* approach allowed expectation damages but held firm on other consequential damages, including pain and suffering as part of the loss for which the plaintiff bargained. By treating health-related agreements as distinct from other kinds of contracts, these cases differentiate based on health. Reducing recovery for breaches of medical guarantee contracts could unfairly disadvantage the unhealthy and may impede their access to medical care.

Medical contracts are increasingly commonplace; thus, the impact of the differential treatment of them is not limited to hairy hands and nose jobs. Amid a persistently market-based approach to health care, providers seeking competitive advantage may offer various service guarantees or warranties. For example, in 2007 the Geisinger Health System in Pennsylvania introduced a medical guarantee for elective cardiac bypass surgery that included a ninety-day warranty (although Geisinger did not use that term). Under its "ProvenCare" model, Geisinger charged a single price for bypass surgery, covering any preoperative, operative, and postoperative expenses up to ninety days after the surgery. Geisinger took that step after a major effort to improve its care based on a best-practice checklist. It has since expanded its fixed-price model to include a number of other types of medical treatment. Similarly, hospitals and health systems may also offer warranties on procedures, like hip and knee replacements, agreeing to cover the costs of avoidable, surgery-related complications.[162]

Providers may offer guarantees for a variety of elective treatments. For example, ophthalmologists may offer "lifetime guarantees" for refractive surgery, such as LASIK, a procedure that uses lasers to shape the cornea in order to cure near-sightedness. One provider's website, for example, offers a Lifetime Assurance Plan, promising: "If at any time you experience visual changes, you will receive a same-technology procedure free of charge when deemed medically appropriate by the surgeon. While perfection cannot be guaranteed, with the Lifetime Assurance Plan, we'll help you maintain your personal best vision throughout your life."[163] Guarantees are also common in fertility treatment. Patients with certain clinical profiles may be offered a money-back guarantee of pregnancy after a specified number of treatment cycles. For

[162] Francois de Brantes, Guy D'Andrea, and Meredith B. Rosenthal, *Should Health Care Come with a Warranty?*, 28 *Health Aff.* No. 4, at w678–w687 (July/Aug. 2009).

[163] The Lasik Vision Institute, available at: www.lasikvisioninstitute.com/affordability/lifetime-assurance-plans/ (last visited July 19, 2017) and www.lasikvisioninstitute.com/affordability/lifetime-assurance-plans/ (last visited July 19, 2017).

example, Advanced Fertility Center of Chicago claims on its website that it is "one of the few clinics in the country willing to 'put its money where its mouth is' by offering a 100 percent refund of the IVF cycle fees if treatment does not result in a live birth (for qualifying couples)."[164] While the enforceability of these contracts is hard to predict, *McGee*, *Sullivan*, and similar cases suggest that courts will treat these cases differently than more conventional contracts. Whether that special consideration favors or disfavors medical patients will depend on the facts and posture of the case.

Professors Fuller and Perdue's suggestion, adopted in *Sullivan*, foreshadows observations in Kenneth Arrow's article, discussed earlier in this chapter. Arrow explains that the "medical care industry" has a number of features that result in its failing to function according to classic, competitive market theory.[165] These factors include the nature of the product and the fact that the demand for that product may be outside the control of the person seeking it. Moreover, patients have little knowledge about the product that they wish to purchase or what treatment or intervention might be appropriate for their condition. Physicians also lack complete information, relying largely on the patient to report of her symptoms and history. And finally, a number of ethical and professional standards other than profit tend to drive physician behavior.

Third-party payers like private insurers and government health-care programs can further distort the market. The true contracting party, many times, is the payer, but the parties deciding what services to provide are the patient and physician, both of whom are largely shielded from the true costs of treatment. Adverse selection and moral hazard also distort the market. Consistent with Arrow's observations, common law courts recognize that medical contracts are unlike commercial contracts and apply different rules accordingly. That approach, on the one hand, may offend health liberty but, on the other hand, may promote health justice.

Sterilization Guarantee Cases

A special category of medical guarantee cases have received closer scrutiny. These are the so-called wrongful birth cases. Like the other medical guarantee cases, we can understand wrongful birth from either a tort law or a contracts perspective. One early case, *Shaheen* v. *Knight*,[166] considered whether the birth of an unwanted child should be a compensable harm. The plaintiff

[164] Advanced Fertility Center of Chicago, available at: www.advancedfertility.com/ivfpr100.htm (last visited July 19, 2017).

[165] Arrow, note 105, at 941.

[166] 11 Pa. D & C.2d 41 (1957).

contended that the defendant contracted to make him sterile, and that as a result of the defendant's breach, the plaintiff's wife gave birth to a fifth child. The plaintiff further alleged that he sought to limit the size of his family for economic reasons, as opposed to concerns about his wife's or a potential child's health.

The defendant responded, among other arguments, that any such contract to guarantee sterilization, when health was not at issue, violated public policy. State law did not recognize a "warranty of cure," and the complaint alleged no lack of skill, malpractice, or negligence. Moreover, the plaintiff suffered no damages but instead "ha[d] been blessed with the fatherhood of another child."[167] Importantly, the court did not hold that all contracts for sterilization are void for public policy reasons. Rather, it found that the contract claim was distinct from a torts claim for medical malpractice and the parties, as a matter of freedom of contract, could enter a binding agreement guaranteeing a certain medical outcome. The claim failed, however, on the damages point. The court held:

> To allow damages in a suit such as this would mean that the physician would have to pay for the fun, joy and affection which plaintiff Shaheen will have in the rearing and educating of this, defendant's fifth child. Many people would be willing to support this child were they given the right of custody and adoption, but according to plaintiff's statement, plaintiff does not want such. He wants to have the child and wants the doctor to support it. In our opinion to allow such damages would be against public policy.[168]

Shaheen takes the traditional stance in both contract and tort law that awarding damages against a doctor to raise a child violates public policy. But courts have evolved more nuanced approaches, generally allowing limited damages and, in some cases, full rearing costs.[169] Most courts allow recovery for all harm that is the direct result of the physician's negligence but disallow child-rearing costs. Typical rationales are similar to the torts cases – that the birth of a healthy child is a presumed joy (as in *Shaheen*) or, even if compensable, the emotional benefit outweighs any economic costs making damages too speculative. A few courts allow full recovery, including all damages incident to the unwanted pregnancy and birth, as well as full costs to raise the child. Those courts generally do not require plaintiffs to

167 Ibid. at 43.
168 Ibid. at 45.
169 Dov Fox, *Reproductive Negligence*, 117 *Colum. L. Rev.* 149, 166 n.99 (2017); Shari Motro, *The Price of Pleasure*, 104 *Nw. U. L. Rev.* 917, 961–3 (2010).

mitigate their damages by terminating the pregnancy or by placing the child for adoption.[170]

Under that final, most generous view, some courts consider the reason for the sterilization. The court in *Burke* v. *Rivo*[171] allowed full recovery of the costs for raising a healthy but unwanted child when the parents sought sterilization for economic reasons. The complaint alleged both tort and contract theories. The court rejected the presumption that the birth of an unwanted child was a blessing that outweighed any economic harms. It further noted that under both tort and contract rules, the economic costs of raising the child were the natural and foreseeable consequences of the negligence and that public policy did not require limiting recovery, at least when the parents sought sterilization for economic reasons. The court also rejected the suggestion that the damages were too speculative or unreasonably disproportionate to the physician's wrongdoing.

Instead, the court allowed recovery for the full costs of rearing a healthy child to adulthood but offset by any benefits that the parents received as a result of having a healthy child. Offsetting benefits is consistent with the Restatement (Second) of Torts[172] and requires juries to quantify and compare costs and benefits. Some courts avoid that apples-to-oranges comparison by ruling that because the benefit was not economic, it cannot offset the economic harm. The court in *Burke* took a slightly different approach and required the resulting harm to align with the reason for the sterilization. Suppose a woman sought sterilization because of concerns about either her or the baby's health, and a healthy baby and healthy mother resulted. In those cases, courts may find the justification for damages less compelling because neither of the feared outcomes happened. Suppose, instead, that the parents sought sterilization for financial reasons, like in *Burke*, namely, seeking to avoid the cost of raising another child, and precisely that result occurred. Then, the court would award full rearing costs, offset by any benefits that the parents experience from the birth of the child.

The wrongful birth cases could result in health-status discrimination. Damages turn on why parents seek sterilization. Financial motivation merits full economic costs of rearing, while health-related reasons – whether concern for the mother or the unborn child – do not. This limited recovery approach is similar to the medical guarantee cases, showing courts' reluctance to treat

[170] *See Jones* v. *Malinowski*, 473 A.2d 429, 437–8 (Md. 1984).

[171] 551 N.E.2d 1 (Mass. 1990).

[172] Restatement (Second) of Torts § 920 (Am. Law Inst. 1979).

those contracts like any other business contract. In both instances, the peculiar nature of the medical contract shapes the courts' approach.

This chapter demonstrates that the private law of torts and contract distinguishes between healthy and unhealthy litigants and between disputes in the medical context and nonmedical context. At this juncture in the book, our point is not to suggest that any of the various examples are, in fact, healthist. We do not decide whether the distinctions effect a normative wrong, despite flagging how our guiding principles from Chapter 2 might apply to some of these cases. We have placed some markers to those points throughout this discussion but will examine them systematically in Chapter 6. For now, if readers have begun thinking, speaking, and debating the concept of healthism, we have achieved our aim.

6

Testing Healthism

6.1. INTRODUCTION

By introducing healthism into the legal and policy lexicon we hope to draw attention to an all-too-familiar yet under-examined, under-theorized form of discrimination in the United States. The foregoing chapters provided detailed descriptions of various laws, policies, practices, decisions, and attitudes that treat people differently based on their health status. If you have stuck with us through that discussion, hopefully now you are spotting examples of potential healthism all around you – on grocery store shelves, television and social media advertisements, proposed federal or state legislation, the terms of your health insurance plan, a stray comment in the carpool line, your employer's recruiting materials, a newspaper headline, a court verdict, your health club's membership agreement, and the doctor's office waiting room, to name just a few possibilities. Differentiation based on health status abounds. If this book has brought that issue to the forefront of readers' minds, we have accomplished our principal goal. But we have two further objectives. First, we offer a methodology for discerning acceptable differentiation based on health status from healthism. Second, we provide some initial suggestions for law and policy to more effectively address, and avoid exacerbating, current examples of healthism.

Regarding our methodology, Chapter 1 explained that not all health-status differentiation is healthist. For other recognized categories – racism, sexism, ageism, ableism, religious discrimination – we can say more confidently, across contexts, that subordinating treatment on those bases is usually normatively wrong. For the very limited circumstances when differentiation is acceptable, the law may already provide carve-outs. For example, employment law's Bona Fide Occupational Qualification (BFOQ) defense may allow a Catholic college to require administrators and faculty to be Catholic.

Or an airline or bus company may have mandatory retirement ages for drivers and pilots. Historically, we legitimized subordinating treatment for some of these groups. For example, in tort law, before enactment of the Married Women's Property Acts, women could not sue or be sued. And we legitimized racial subordination under "Jim Crow" Laws. The Civil Rights Act of 1964 and similar laws outlawed racial discrimination. The law governing sex, gender, and sexual orientation discrimination continues to evolve. The ACA's Section 1557 extends existing federal antidiscrimination statutes to federally funded health-care programs and health insurance, as discussed in Chapter 4. Health-status discrimination, however, has not been legally recognized or protected. Our suggestion is new enough that reasonable minds may disagree about the normative rightness or wrongness of any particular example. What constitutes unacceptable discrimination, on any basis, is always contextual. We wish to push back against the tolerance for disadvantaging the unhealthy.

In addition to the fact that healthism is a relatively new idea, health is a nuanced concept. Our definition in Chapter 1 includes health conditions as well as behaviors, habits, or activities associated with lower health or health risks. Including both conditions and behaviors complicates our theory of discrimination. Multiple genetic, environmental, societal, behavioral, and other factors affect a person's relative state of health. For one, health is a combination of nature and nurture. Some of what contributes to a person's health may seem within her control, theoretically offering her an opportunity to avoid discrimination simply by changing her behavior. Voluntariness, however, does not negate the possibility for undesirable discrimination. We certainly are not the first to flag discrimination based on arguably mutable or voluntary characteristics. Moreover, in many cases, certain conduct is not clearly voluntary or involuntary conduct. Is use of an addictive substance like tobacco "voluntary"? The flexibility of our rubric for identifying healthism reflects the complexity of health itself.

Another challenge is acknowledging that health-based distinctions can be not merely tolerable but also beneficial. They can encourage people to make healthier choices, lower health risks, and reduce health-care costs. Workplace wellness programs encourage employees to adopt healthier habits. Likewise, a number of health promotion and public health strategies create incentives for people to lower their health risks. In so doing, those policies have the power to improve access to care and overall health. To simply ban all health-based classifications would then throw the baby out with the bathwater. That said, despite the potential benefits, there are times when differentiation on the basis of health status can do serious harm to individuals and society. Even well-intentioned policies can be unwittingly discriminatory.

So how do we tell the difference? Which policies are healthist, and which are health-promoting? Which merit the attention of law- and policy-makers? The preceding chapters provided not only a host of examples but also a conceptual framework for making these critical distinctions. This chapter pulls those examples and concepts together. To briefly recap.

In Chapter 1, we defined discrimination to include only the kinds of systematic disadvantage that produce normative wrongs. Possible normative wrongs include status harms like creating or perpetuating animus, as well as structural harms, like impeding access to health care and other resources. We also broke down other elements of our definition of healthism: What does it mean to be healthy? Why do we include behaviors? What constitutes a normative wrong? Then, in Chapter 2, we offered four guiding principles – health welfare, health liberty, health equality, and health justice. Applying those principles helps differentiate between "bad" healthist laws and policies and "good" health-based classifications.

Health welfare draws on utilitarianism, or creating the greatest good for the greatest number of people in society. For our purposes, health welfare focuses on the social impact of a particular law or policy. Importantly, our approach allows for paternalism in certain contexts. If the particular policy tends to improve collective health, lower overall health risks, or decrease health-care costs, then it would be consistent with health welfare. By contrast, a policy that reduces collective health, increases health risks, or raises costs would undermine health welfare.

Health liberty is all about choice. We start from the premise that each person has a right to control her own body and is the best judge of what is best for her own health and happiness. That control allows people to pursue their own desires, as long as they do not harm others in the process. Thus, laws or policies that support healthy decision-making and increase people's choices regarding their health and health care serve health liberty. By contrast, laws or policies that punish people for their private conduct or cut off access to choices subvert health liberty. In discussing health liberty, we caution that not everyone is as "free" to make decisions about their health and happiness as might initially appear. A host of social determinants – income, employment opportunities, housing, relationship status, education, caregiving obligations, access to outdoor space, ability to obtain healthy food – may all affect a person's ability to take advantage of various health-care and health-promoting opportunities.

Health equality looks to dignity and equal treatment as its benchmarks. The belief that all persons should be treated equally is among the United States' founding principles. Federal law formally recognizes race, color, national origin, religion, and sex (among other permitted categories) as impermissible grounds for unequal treatment. More recently, age, disability, pregnancy, genetic information, family status, and gender identity have been protected to varying degrees. Protecting people from disadvantage based on their health status is central to our project. Ensuring fair, nondiscriminatory treatment is the core of health equality.

We recognize that many instances of discrimination operate at a subconscious level. We therefore target both intentional and unintentional discrimination, including facially neutral laws and policies that disparately impact the unhealthy. Law- and policy-makers may have unknowingly internalized certain prejudices or preexisting judgments. We are especially concerned about health-based distinctions that are driven by stereotypes or animus toward certain groups, or that stigmatize individuals unfairly.

Finally, health justice is about distributive fairness. Health justice acts as a meta-principle, drawing together threads of welfare, liberty, equality, and other values. Social justice spans a wide variety of contexts, including environmental justice, reproductive justice, food justice, and, more recently, health justice. The critical insight of social justice is that existing biases, privileges, and other structural barriers impede full equality of opportunity in society. Laws and policies may violate health justice if they thwart health-care access, worsen health outcomes, or deepen existing health disparities even if they do not clearly reduce overall social welfare, single out certain groups, or restrict choices. In our view, such laws and policies are still healthist. They disproportionately harm already-disadvantaged individuals or groups. Accordingly, any laws or policies that improve access or reduce disparities promote health justice.

These four guiding principles – shown in Table 6.1 – are the foundation of our rubric for identifying healthism.

The current chapter applies the four guiding principles from Chapter 2. Using case studies, we demonstrate how law- and policy-makers can distinguish between socially beneficial health-based classifications and socially harmful healthism. This discussion is not exhaustive. It only touches a fraction of the examples identified in earlier chapters. We leave it for the reader to evaluate the remaining examples in the book, as well as the employer's offer of free Fitbits in exchange for access to data, federal work requirements for public health insurance, President Trump's comment on a media personality's cosmetic surgery, or myriad other examples.

6.2. HEALTH-BASED CLASSIFICATIONS

Having largely reserved judgment on the normative rightness or wrongness of the examples in this book, we now provide a way of analyzing them. Of

TABLE 6.1. *Healthism Rubric*

Characteristics of socially desirable health-status differentiation
Promotes healthy decision-making*
Facilitates individual choices regarding health#
Lowers health risks*
Lowers health-care costs*
Facilitates better health care and better health-care access°
Characteristics of healthism
Is driven by animus†
Stigmatizes individuals unfairly†
Punishes people for their private conduct#
Impedes access to health care°
Cuts off resources or otherwise limits the ability to adopt healthy life choices#
Produces worse health outcomes°
Maintains or increases existing health disparities†

*Health welfare
#Health liberty
†Health equality
°Health justice

course, social values are fluid and resist permanently fixed determinations. What is benign today may be healthist tomorrow. Thus, our approach is flexible, accommodating evolutions in science, cost-benefit analysis, social norms, and legal protections. Because of the heterogeneity of the examples, we do not purport to offer a universal remedy – such as a proposed constitutional amendment or model statute – for addressing instances of healthism. Rather, we urge law- and policy-makers, as well as the public at large, to be attuned to the pervasiveness and damaging impact of health-status discrimination. Solutions may include legislation, nonbinding resolutions, internal policies or practices, shifts in common law doctrine, federal or state constitutional amendments, or simply shifts in public attitudes about health.

To set the stage, we begin with various examples of health-status classifications, some of which seem healthist and others do not. Readers may have initial hunches or visceral reactions to the examples, which we then test in our discussion. We thoroughly dissect a few from each category and then leave it for readers to assess and debate the remaining examples after learning our methodology. Here is the list:

Employment

- Refusing to hire nicotine users or overweight workers
- Firing workers for being overweight

- Firing workers because of their or their dependents' health insurance costs
- Firing or refusing to hire workers based on health conditions or risks
- Refusing to cover or capping benefits for certain health conditions or risks
- Prohibiting workers from smoking on the job

Public Accommodations and Housing

- Refusing to provide services or charging more to overweight people
- Refusing to provide services or charging more to people with certain health conditions, such as HIV/AIDS
- Imposing taxes and bans on unhealthy foods and other goods, including tobacco, alcohol, and sugary beverages
- Banning smokers from public housing
- Charging overweight customers for multiple airline or theater tickets

Health Insurance and Health Care

- Refusing to sell health insurance policies to individuals with certain health conditions or risks
- Charging higher premiums based on individual risk profiles
- Charging higher copayments for drugs for certain health conditions, such as HIV/AIDS
- Eliminating copayments and deductibles for preventive care
- Offering premium discounts or other incentives for workplace wellness programs that include biometric screenings and health risk assessments
- Failing to provide medical exam room and other equipment that can accommodate overweight patients
- Refusing to treat patients based on race, sexual orientation, gender identity, income, or insurance type

Tort Law

- Declining to fully compensate for emotional harm, as compared to physical harm
- Capping noneconomic damages in medical malpractice cases
- Holding unhealthy defendants liable for transmitting diseases or exposing others to injury resulting from their conditions
- Disallowing or reducing recovery to unhealthy plaintiffs who fail to take care of their own health conditions
- Disallowing recovery to individuals who are injured while engaging in risky activities
- Allowing full recovery for birth of an unwanted unhealthy child but limiting recovery for birth of an unwanted healthy child

Contract Law

- Protecting physicians' freedom of contract to refuse medical care to particular patients
- Declining to recognize defenses to contract enforcement based on mental or physical impairments
- Declining to enforce contractual releases of liability in medical care contexts
- Enforcing arbitration clauses for disputes arising out of medical care
- Applying nontraditional approaches to damages in medical guarantee contracts
- Allowing breach of contract recovery for failed elective sterilization procedures when the motivation was economic but not when it was therapeutic

In some cases, existing law clearly prohibits some of those examples. For instance, the ADA prevents employers and public accommodations from discriminating on the basis of legally recognized disabilities. GINA outlaws discrimination based on genetic information in health insurance and employment. The ACA prohibits preexisting condition exclusions and discrimination in federally funded health care. Many state statutory caps on noneconomic damages in medical malpractice cases have been eliminated. EMTALA restricts certain health-care providers' ability to reject patients. But we have demonstrated that, despite these efforts, a significant amount of socially damaging healthism continues. We turn now to whether the law should intervene.

6.3. APPLYING THE MODEL

We now apply our methodology to real-life situations. We first describe examples that we deem clearly healthist. Next, we describe benign examples of health-status discrimination. Finally, we consider close calls, which invite further debate and, in some cases, require empirical research.

6.3.1. *Healthist Health-Status Classifications*

We start with the easy cases. Two clear-cut examples include employers' refusal to hire individuals who test positive for nicotine and discriminatory health insurance pricing, specifically, jacked-up prescription drug charges for HIV/AIDS patients. As we explain, these policies run awry of each of our guiding principles.

Nicotine Hiring Bans

Bans on hiring nicotine users are paradigmatic healthist conduct, potentially violating all four guiding principles. We can begin with health welfare. Clearly, using tobacco – especially smoking – creates negative welfare both by depleting a person's own health and by imposing externalities on others. At first blush, it would seem that any effort to reduce that welfare loss would be beneficial. Yet while nicotine hiring bans may seek to improve individual and collective health, this strategy may well backfire. First, nicotine use rarely, if ever, affects a worker's ability to perform the job. A discriminator therefore pays a penalty for her "taste" for discrimination because she does not select the most effective workers.[1] Of course, as we explained in Chapter 2, employers could have rational reasons for discriminating against nicotine users, such as saving on health insurance premiums and preventing absenteeism. Whether the decision to ban hiring nicotine users is efficient for a particular employer depends on whether the benefits of the policy outweigh its costs. Second, the hiring bans do not clearly generate positive welfare and could even create additional negative welfare by imposing a perverse incentive for nicotine users to seek suboptimal employment. Recall from Chapter 2 that the tobacco surcharge in health insurance did not encourage people to quit but instead caused them to forgo coverage altogether. Some nicotine users might opt to kick the habit for their dream jobs. However, given how difficult it is to quit, others may choose to simply seek alternative employment. If employers across an entire industry adopt these policies, prospective employees who use nicotine may take jobs below their skill levels. Consequently, categorically excluding nicotine users from the hiring pool could undermine health welfare. The bans shut nicotine users out of desirable jobs for reasons unrelated to their performance, potentially leading to inefficiencies and corresponding welfare losses but without offsetting those negative results by improving population health. Accordingly, such bans could actually have negative welfare effects.

The negative welfare associated with nicotine hiring bans may go beyond individual employers and employees. Counterintuitively, instead of lowering risks and costs, nicotine hiring bans – if adopted widely enough – could actually result in a net decrease in collective health. In the United States, full-time employment frequently provides health insurance coverage, access to wellness programs, and wages for purchasing health care.[2]

[1] John J. Donohue III, *The Law and Economics of Antidiscrimination Law* 7–11 (Nat'l Bureau of Econ. Research, Working Paper No. 11631, 2006), www.nber.org/papers/w11631.pdf.

[2] Jessica L. Roberts, *Healthism and the Law of Employment Discrimination*, 99 *Iowa L. Rev.* 571, 626–29 (2014).

Health care is very expensive in the United States, making most people dependent on health insurance for obtaining needed medical treatment.[3] A majority of Americans rely on their employers for health insurance.[4] Hence, denying an individual a job because she tests positive for nicotine also denies her access to the predominant source of health insurance and, derivatively, access to health care.[5] Research clearly shows that people who lack health insurance have less access to health care and are more likely to have poor health.[6] Likewise, unemployment limits a person's ability to pay for health care out of pocket, as well as to obtain the benefits of employer-provided wellness programs, which – somewhat ironically – frequently include tobacco cessation initiatives.[7] Pushing nicotine users to the margins of employable society may then result in their working in jobs that do not offer employer-sponsored health benefits or adequate compensation, or leave them unemployed altogether. Because nicotine users face greater health risks, limiting their access to needed health care and wellness programs denies these services to some of the people who could benefit most. Thus, shutting nicotine users out of employment may paradoxically produce a healthier workforce but a less healthy overall population. Accordingly, these hiring bans may not enhance welfare and could even decrease it.

Turning next to health liberty. Refusing to hire nicotine users is distinct from prohibiting employees from using nicotine at work. While an employer may have a legitimate claim to regulate an employee on the job, nicotine hiring bans govern off-duty conduct. These policies offend health liberty by exerting control over individuals' personal lives. Testing prospective employees for nicotine penalizes them for lawful, private conduct outside of the workplace. Moreover, the bans could actually limit people's abilities to make decisions relevant to their health. Americans rely on their employers for health insurance coverage, access to employer-sponsored wellness programs, and adequate wages to purchase health care and health-related goods and services, including fresh foods, gym memberships, and childcare during a daily workout. Nicotine bans therefore cut off resources and limit a person's ability to

[3] Roberts, note 1, at 571, 627–8.

[4] Employer-provided health insurance covers up to 55.7 percent of the population. *See* Jessica C. Barnett and Marina S. Vornovitsky, *Health Insurance Coverage in the United States: 2015, U.S. Census Bureau Current Population Reports* 1 (September 2016).

[5] Roberts, note 1, at 571, 627–8.

[6] Agency for Healthcare Research and Quality, *National Healthcare Quality and Disparities Report: Chartbook on Access to Healthcare* 3 (2016).

[7] Roberts, note 1, at 571, 627–8.

adopt healthier life choices. Nicotine hiring bans are then also anti-libertarian because they punish people for their private conduct and limit their range of choices related to both their health care and their health.

Bans on hiring nicotine users most clearly violate health equality. Such policies are facially and intentionally discriminatory and based on stereotypes and animus. Nicotine users – particularly smokers – are the targets of widespread social stigma.[8] Surveys show that significant portions of the population think less of smokers and view smoking as a personal failure.[9] In fact, stigmatization, or "denormalization," of smokers has even been the explicit goal of various public health initiatives.[10] Smokers themselves internalize these negative social attitudes, reporting that they feel shame about their smoking and keep smoking-related secrets.[11] Recall Elizabeth Emens's observation from Chapter 2 that "[a] person discriminates based on animus if she [or he] treats someone differently because of dislike or hostility towards the protected class of which that person is a member."[12] Given the negative perceptions that people hold about smokers, it is highly likely that nicotine hiring bans are driven – at least in part – by animus.

To reach that conclusion, consider possible alternative rationales for the bans. Employers may assert that they do not want to hire nicotine users because they are more expensive to insure, more likely to miss work due to health reasons, take more frequent work breaks, or project a negative image inconsistent with the employer's business model. Employers may even assert that they simply want to encourage their employees to be healthier.[13] Even assuming those reasons are genuine, they could still be linked to stereotyping and potential animus. To be sure, nicotine users may be more costly to employ because their risk profiles may drive up premiums and miss work more often. But any number of other off-duty behaviors – including alcohol consumption, sunbathing, sedentary lifestyles, a Twinkies habit, night-owling or insomnia, marital stress, or skydiving – could also increase health risks and absenteeism. Singling out nicotine use implies that something more than a simple cost-benefit analysis

[8] Jessica L. Roberts and Elizabeth Weeks Leonard, *Stigmatizing the Unhealthy*, 45 *J.L. Med. & Ethics* 484 (2017).

[9] Jennifer Stuber et al., *Smoking and the Emergence of a Stigmatized Social Status*, 67 *Soc. Sci. & Med.* 420, 424 (2008); Jennifer Stuber et al., *Stigma and Smoking: The Consequences of Our Good Intentions*, *Soc. Serv. Rev.* 585, 598 (2009).

[10] Kristen Bell et al., *Smoking, Stigma, and Tobacco "Denormalization": Further Reflections on the Use of Stigma as a Public Health Tool*, 70 *Soc. Sci. & Med.* 795, 795–96 (2010).

[11] Sei-Hill Kim and James Shanahan, *Stigmatizing Smokers: Public Sentiment Toward Cigarette Smoking and Its Relationship to Smoking Behaviors*, 8 *J. Health Comm.* 343, 349 (2003); Stuber et al., Stigma and Smoking, note 8, at 585, 598.

[12] Elizabeth Emens, *The Sympathetic Discriminator: Mental Illness, Hedonic Costs, and the ADA*, 94 *Georgetown L.J.* 399, 409 (2006).

[13] Roberts, note 1, at 571, 579–90.

is at play. With respect to promoting a healthful workplace image or culture, the employer could outlaw using nicotine products at work – which plenty of employers lawfully do – without infringing on an employee's ability to use nicotine products in her private time. Finally, the paternalistic urge also begs the question, why only ban hiring nicotine users? Why not ban hiring heavy drinkers, motorcycle riders, sunbathers, non-yoga-practitioners, or people who have unprotected sex?

In addition to potentially being animus-based, nicotine hiring bans themselves further stigmatize nicotine users. These policies reduce people who use nicotine to a single characteristic – nicotine use – without regard to other attributes that could make them good employees. Recall from Chapter 2 that stigma forms in four phases: (1) acknowledging difference, (2) associating that difference with negative characteristics, (3) classifying people based on that difference, and (4) devaluing people based on the classification.[14] Targeting nicotine users with hiring bans is exactly the kind of distinction that can lead to negative stereotyping and status loss. Nicotine hiring bans thus offend health equality.

Finally, nicotine hiring bans can also impede health-care access, worsen health outcomes, and exacerbate existing disparities, thereby undermining health justice. We have already highlighted how these policies can create access barriers and lead to poor health outcomes. Health welfare looks to the net impact of these policies. If nicotine hiring bans harm only a small subset of society but offer even a minor corresponding benefit to enough people, they might generate positive welfare. Health justice, however, is about more than the welfare calculus. Even if nicotine bans do not produce net welfare losses, they could still offend health justice by entrenching biases and social stratification. Nicotine hiring bans could even deepen existing health disparities. Multiracial populations and Native Americans, people with disabilities, and lower-income individuals are all more likely to use nicotine.[15] These same groups already face significant health disparities.[16] By further cutting off access

[14] Bruce G. Link and Jo C. Phelan, *Conceptualizing Stigma*, 27 *Ann. Rev. Socio.* 363, 367–75 (2001).

[15] Brady Dennis, *Who Still Smokes in the United States – in Seven Simple Charts*, *The Washington Post* (Nov. 12, 2015), available at: www.washingtonpost.com/news/to-yourhealth/wp/2015/11/12/smoking-among-u-s-adults-has-fallen-to-historic-lows-these-7-charts-show-who-still-lights-up-the-most/?utm_term=.ac7981009d8e.

[16] Recall from Chapter 1 that nonwhites and people with disabilities tend to have less access to health care and poorer health outcomes. *See* Agency for Healthcare Research and Quality, *National Healthcare Quality and Disparities Report: Chartbook on Access to Healthcare* (2016); *Disability and Health, Healthy People* 2020, available at: www.healthypeople.gov/2020/topics-objectives/topic/disability-and-health.

to health care and other resources to these already-disadvantaged populations, nicotine hiring bans may perpetuate and exacerbate existing inequalities. Their potential to impede health-care access, lower health outcomes, and worsen health disparities puts nicotine hiring bans at odds with health justice.

Of course, our healthism rubric looks at benefits as well as costs. On the positive end of the equation, very little is clearly redeeming about banning nicotine users. In theory, they may appear to promote health by giving nicotine users one more reason to quit. However, similar kinds of incentives, like tobacco surcharges, have not been effective. And far from facilitating choices about health, nicotine bans limit employment opportunities, access to benefits, and other resources. Even assuming a net social benefit, nicotine hiring bans will still have negative impacts on health-care cost and access for nicotine users.

For all these reasons, employers' bans on hiring nicotine users are healthist. They also fall outside of the protection of existing laws described in Chapters 3 and 4. Smoking is not a disability – even though some conditions resulting from smoking may be. The ACA clearly does not prohibit and, indeed, expressly *allows*, discrimination against tobacco users, with respect to health insurance premiums.[17] Having thus recognized a clear-cut case of healthism, how should law- and policy-makers respond?

In this case, we advocate a legislative response. State or federal law-makers could enact a statute prohibiting employers from refusing to hire based on off-duty nicotine use, as several states already have. Some state statutes include other forms of "lifestyle discrimination." While we would not oppose more expansive legislation, our priority is health-related attributes. We would then also advocate similar statutes related to weight and other health statuses. Beyond addressing the health justice, health welfare, health liberty, and health equality concerns directly, these statutes would signal public disapproval of healthism. That expressive value could have a desirable spillover effect on public attitudes and norms by opposing health-status discrimination.

Discriminatory Pricing in Health Insurance

Another easy case of healthism is discriminatory pricing in health insurance. In Chapters 1 and 4, we explained that health insurers historically use health status for underwriting and ratemaking. That approach makes sense if we view health insurance primarily as a risk-pooling mechanism to protect individuals from unexpected financial loss. Health insurers would no more want

[17] *See* 45 C.F.R. § 147.103(iv) (allowing premium rates to vary based upon tobacco use).

to sell an insurance policy to someone with a cancer diagnosis than an automobile insurer would want to sell to a person who just got her third DUI. Those customers present risks that the amount of premiums they pay will exceed the costs of their claims. But law-makers and the public have largely reconceptualized the purpose of health insurance. Instead, health insurance is now a mechanism to get more people access to needed health care. Making this vision of health insurance work requires cross-subsidization. The "good" risks pay more than they would under experience rating, resulting in more affordable coverage for the "bad" risks. The "bad" risks pay less than they would under experience rating, making insurance more affordable for them.

Even with this vision of health insurance, opportunities for health-status discrimination remain. As detailed in Chapter 4, the ACA specifically allows pricing based on tobacco use, age, and wellness program participation in different contexts. In addition, although mandating a package of EHB for health plans, the ACA does not regulate pricing for specific goods or services. The law cabins annual out-of-pocket charges but does not specify particular limits on billed charges, copayments, and the like.[18] This issue may arise in out-of-network charges, or "surprise billing," which have recently garnered legislative attention.[19] For example, an individual may go to an in-network emergency room but receive treatment from an out-of-network specialist, who subsequently bills the patient astronomical charges.

At least one example of discriminatory pricing in health insurance is clearly healthist. Insurers may charge more for medications to treat a particular illness, for example, HIV/AIDS.[20] A group of patients in need of the overpriced drugs challenged this practice in Florida. According to the lawsuit, health insurers charged higher copayments and coinsurance for drugs to treat HIV/AIDS than for other conditions. The plaintiffs further alleged that the increased

[18] *See* 42 U.S.C.A. §§ 18022(c)(1)(B), 18071(c)(1)(A) (2012) (detailing the procedure for out-of-pocket limits); *see also Out-of-Pocket Maximum/Limit*, available at: www.healthcare.gov/glossary/out-of-pocket-maximum-limit/ (Accessed Feb. 1, 2018) (citing the out-of-pocket limits for health care plans in 2016 and 2017).

[19] *See* Margaret Darling et al., *Receive a Surprise Medical Bill? Here are Three Federal Actions That May Address Surprise Bills, Brookings: Up Front* (Aug. 8, 2017), available at: www.brookings.edu/blog/up-front/2017/08/08/receive-a-surprise-medical-bill-here-are-three-federal-actions-that-may-address-surprise-bills (discussing steps taken in legislatures to prevent surprise billing); *How to Avoid Surprise Medical Bills, Wall Street Journal: How-To Guide* (last visited Feb. 1, 2018), available at: http://guides.wsj.com/health/health-costs/how-to-avoid-surprise-medical-bills (providing guidance on how patients should respond to unexpected medical bills).

[20] Jane Perkins and Wayne Turner, *NHeLP and The AIDS Institute Complaint to HHS Re HIV/AIDS Discrimination by Florida Insurers, HealthLaw.Org* (May 29, 2014), available at: www.healthlaw.org/publications/browse-all-publications/HHS-HIV-Complaint#.VcUqNnggNUS.

costs impaired their ability to obtain medical treatment.[21] The effect, if not the goal, of the policy was to discourage patients from enrolling in those particular health plans and push them instead toward other plans. HIV/AIDS patients may have considerable prescription drug costs and can live long lives maintained on them. Thus, insurers who want to save costs might like to avoid fully covering those treatments by shifting the costs on the policyholders or driving people with HIV/AIDS to select other insurers' plans. However, that latter goal assumes there are other health insurers offering alternatives – that is, assuming any other insurers in the relevant market offer nondiscriminatory policies. If not, those pricing strategies would effectively deny any access to care for HIV/AIDS patients.

Turning to our guiding principles, while discriminatory pricing might preserve or generate welfare for the individual health insurer, those policies could reduce the welfare of society as a whole. As explained, copayments and coinsurance safeguard insurers against moral hazard. Having to pay even a fraction of the expense out of pocket may encourage patients to think more carefully before seeking medical care. The goal is to reduce unnecessary or excessive medical spending. However, there is no good reason for HIV/AIDS patients to think twice before taking their medications. If these policies discourage HIV/AIDS patients from filling prescriptions, their health likely will deteriorate. A particularly cold utilitarian might assert that denying access to drugs means that sick people will die faster, thus costing health insurers less. However, that view ignores the possibility that the pricing policy could produce significant negative welfare by worsening health outcomes and costing more for treatment, potentially undermining health welfare. Moreover, if HIV/AIDS patients suffer from more debilitating symptoms as a result of not taking medication, their own ability to enjoy life and contribute to society goes down. Reducing access to drugs that can maintain an individual relatively symptom-free is hard to justify from a health welfare perspective.

The pricing policy also does not comport with health liberty. Restricting access to drugs that allow people with HIV/AIDS to participate fully in society limits their choices about health care, healthy behaviors, or any number of other activities or preferences. Although affected individuals may be able to choose other health insurance policies without the higher co-payments – assuming other options remain on the market – they still have limited choices. Moreover, the premiums on those remaining policies will likely rise, further disadvantaging those policyholders. People with HIV/AIDS may then find themselves without access to health insurance and unable to attain medical

[21] Ibid.

treatment, which would allow them to live longer, more productive lives. Thus, the discriminatory pricing policy offends health liberty by limiting an individual's ability to make meaningful choices.

Discriminatory health-insurance pricing also violates health equality. The policies challenged in Florida were facially discriminatory, placing HIV/AIDS sufferers in one category subject to higher prescription drug copayments. Given the highly stigmatized history of HIV/AIDS, the discriminatory pricing regime may very well have been animus-driven and could reinforce stigma. Whether it is accurate or not, the public may blame people for contracting HIV/AIDS from unprotected sex – particularly unprotected gay sex – or intravenous drug use. If there is any doubt that certain forms of sexual conduct continue to face significant stigma, consider that conservative commentators have attributed recent natural disasters to human sexuality![22] Singling out HIV/AIDS – opposed to other potentially fatal conditions managed with regular prescription drug regimens, such as heart disease, diabetes, asthma, cancer, Parkinson's disease, multiple sclerosis – treats similarly situated people differently. Moreover, by imposing higher copayments, insurers perpetuate stigma by reinforcing the suggestion that HIV/AIDS patients are somehow different and perhaps to blame. However, the individual responsibility narrative, while seemingly consistent with health liberty, can actually be the product of stigma and animus because we hold some individuals accountable for their actions but not others.

Finally, charging HIV/AIDS patients more for their prescription drugs falls squarely within the concerns driving the health justice movement. That population has long faced prejudice, bias, and structural disadvantage.[23] Thus, even if the policy somehow improved collective health welfare, it would certainly

[22] *See* Jeremy B. White, *Ann Coulter Says Storm Harvey Is More Likely God's Punishment for Houston's Lesbian Mayor Than a Result of Climate Change, Independent* (Aug. 30, 2017), available at: www.independent.co.uk/news/world/americas/us-politics/ann-coulter-harvey-climate-change-god-punishment-more-credible-tweet-a7919301.html (discussing Coulter's claims that Hurricane Harvey was God's punishment for Houston's gay mayor); *Katrina "Divine Retribution" Pastor Promoted, NBC: News* (updated Jan. 31, 2009, 9:48 PM), available at: www.nbcnews.com/id/28952871/ns/world_news-europe/t/katrina-divine-retribution-pastor-promoted/#.WnNXAJM-fRo (discussing an Austrian priest who made comments in 2005 that Hurricane Katrina was "divine retribution" for New Orleans' laid-back attitudes toward sex).

[23] *See, HIV in the United States: At a Glance,* Ctr. for Disease Control and Prevention (last updated Nov. 29, 2017), available at: www.cdc.gov/hiv/statistics/overview/ataglance.html (noting that 77 percent of those infected with HIV were homosexual and bisexual men and intravenous drug users); *see also, HIV/AIDS, World Health Organization: Global Health Observatory Data* (last visited Feb. 1, 2018), available at: www.who.int/gho/hiv/en (observing that sub-Saharan African remains the area of the world that is the most severely affected by HIV).

perpetuate existing disparities for those groups. Indeed, it could worsen those inequalities. For all these reasons, the discriminatory pricing appears to be another clear example of healthism, again warranting legal intervention.

Thankfully, the ACA addresses this issue. The law prohibits health status-based underwriting and health status-based ratemaking with some exceptions. The law, however, says nothing direct about variable copayments or coinsurance for particular benefits. At some point, the patient might hit the out-of-pocket limits, meaning that the insurer would cover any additional benefits without cost sharing. Section 1557 also offers some protection. Federal law recognizes HIV/AIDS as a disability. Section 1557 extends existing federal disability discrimination laws to federally funded and operated health-care centers, health-care programs, and the individual market health insurance exchanges.[24] In those settings, insurers cannot discriminate against people with HIV/AIDS. Employer-sponsored and other health plans, however, may have more latitude.[25]

Fortunately, Florida insurance regulations offered an even clearer fix. They expressly prohibited discrimination in insurance on the basis of HIV/AIDS.[26] Based on those protections, the Florida Office of Insurance Regulation issued a memo to health insurers, capping the price of certain HIV/AIDS drugs and warning that the agency will screen all health plans for discriminatory pricing.[27] Lawsuits likely prompted those regulations, demonstrating that civil rights advocacy can highlight discrimination and lead to a legal response. That sort of recognition and change is precisely what we hope this book can inspire.

[24] Section 1557 provides that

> [a]n individual shall not, on [the basis of race, color, national origin, sex, age, or disability], be excluded from participation in, be denied the benefits of, or be subjected to discrimination under, any health program or activity, any part of which is receiving Federal financial assistance, including credits, subsidies, or contracts of insurance, or under any program or activity that is administered by an Executive Agency or any entity established under this title.

42 U.S.C. § 18116(a); *see also* www.npr.org/sections/health-shots/2014/07/08/329591574/complaint-says-insurance-plans-discriminate-against-hiv-patients.

[25] *See McGann* v. *H & H Music Co.*, 946 F.2d 401, 404 (5th Cir. 1991) (holding, pre-ACA, that an employer did not unlawfully discriminate against an employee with AIDS when they reduced their employer-sponsored maximum payable medical benefits for AIDS within seven months from the employee's claim for AIDs).

[26] Ron Hurtibise, *State Tells Insurers to Limit Co-pays for HIV/AIDS Drugs, Sun Sentinel* (July 1, 2015), available at: www.sun-sentinel.com/business/consumer/fl-hiv-drug-review-20150630-story.html.

[27] Informational guidance on Florida's form and rate filing process for ACA-compliant products in the small-group and individual markets, Fla. Off. of Ins. Reg., available at: www.floir.com/siteDocuments/PPACANoticeToIndustry03242015.pdf.

6.3.2. *Benign Health-Status Classifications*

Next, consider two examples that fall on the other end of the health-status discrimination spectrum. We conclude these policies are health-neutral or health-promoting. In other words, they are classifications based on health status that are *not* healthist.

Tobacco Cessation Programs

Despite our analysis of the nicotine hiring bans, not all smoking-related employment policies are healthist. An employer might, for example, prohibit smoking on the job without violating smokers' liberty. The policy would also not violate health equality because the employer may prohibit various other activities at work, thus treating smokers similarly to their nonsmoking colleagues. Although we acknowledge entrenched biases and stigma against smokers, on-duty smoking ban does not exacerbate existing health disparities or impede smokers' access to health care in the way that the hiring ban does. The policy also does not relegate smokers to second-class citizenship or perpetuate existing social stratification. Thus, this health-status classification would not be healthist under our rubric.

By the same token, an employer could readily construct a nonhealthist tobacco cessation program to address nicotine use among its employees. The ACA distinguishes between wellness programs that are participation-based, which are subject to fewer requirements, and programs that are standard-based, which are subject to more requirements.[28] Workplace wellness programs may include financial incentives, styled as rewards or penalties, including premium discounts, surcharges for employer-sponsored health plans, bonuses, or prizes for achieving certain goals. Participation-based programs might require the employee to complete a health-screening questionnaire, have an annual check-up, or attend a smoking cessation class. Standard-based programs might require the employee to achieve a certain body mass index (BMI), weight, or blood pressure, or successfully complete a tobacco cessation program by quitting.

Tobacco cessation programs necessarily target smokers, technically constituting differentiation on the basis of health status. But as long as all employees can participate fully – that is, so long as there are no structural barriers to participation, such as requiring individuals to attend meetings after work hours, which could require childcare – the intervention would be consistent with

[28] *See* 42 U.S.C. § 300gg-4(j)(2), (3) (2012) (discussing which wellness programs are and are not subject to requirements).

health liberty. Employees could freely choose whether to participate or not, with the only risk being the loss of the reward or imposition of the penalty. Federal law specifies that for standard-based programs, the discount or reward cannot amount to more than 30 percent of employee-only health plan premium.[29] The ACA, therefore, supports wellness programs.[30] Moreover, program designers can be careful to avoid stigmatizing participants. Yet even with the risk of stigma, the benefits of those initiatives, *if effective*, also could lower workers' health risks and, accordingly, their potential health-care costs.

But even without clear evidence of the effectiveness, our other guiding principles support tobacco cessation programs, as long as certain parameters are followed. To take the most benign example, consider a workplace wellness program that rewards tobacco users with a $10 Amazon gift card for participating in a brief, telephone health-counseling session regarding strategies to quit. That program targets smokers and other tobacco users, but it would not be healthist under our methodology. From a health welfare perspective, merely encouraging tobacco users to think about their habit or addiction and providing them with information about quitting could improve their health. Moreover, it certainly does not reduce their health by cutting off access to health insurance and health care.

The policy also does not compromise health liberty because the incentive – $10 – is relatively low and unlikely to impinge on the workers' free choice to participate or not. Moreover, participation is private, conducted via one's own telephone. The employer might further enhance liberty by allowing the counseling sessions to occur during work hours, thereby removing any barriers to participating, including evening and weekend family responsibilities or telecommunications technology impediments.

The program singles out tobacco users but does not clearly violate health equality. Bias or animus does not seem to motivate the program and, if conducted properly, it would not further stigma. Employers could enhance the

[29] *See* 42 U.S.C. § 300gg-4(j)(3)(A) (2012) ("The reward for the wellness program . . . shall not exceed 30 percent of the cost of employee-only coverage under the plan."). While that provision seeks to avoid overly coercive incentives, a court recently vacated the EEOC's implementing regulations for wellness programs under the ADA and GINA, finding that the agency failed to explain why 30 percent was an appropriate incentive level. *See AARP v. EEOC, D.D.C.*, No. 16-2113 (Dec. 20, 2017).

[30] The ACA's inclusion of incentives for wellness programs capitalized on their increasing popularity, "analogous to putting a car on a train that was already running down the rails." Judy Peres, *Workplace Wellness Programs Popular, But Do they Improve Health?*, *Chicago Tribune* (Dec. 13, 2014), available at: www.chicagotribune.com/news/ct-workplace-wellness-met-20141212-story.html#page=1 (quoting Janet Coffman, associate professor of health policy at the University of California, San Francisco).

equality of the program by offering similar incentives for participating in brief phone counseling regarding other health risks or overall health. Health justice also seems minimally implicated because the possibility of receiving a modest gift card does not derive from existing structural inequities or perpetuate existing disparities for nicotine users. Thus, the law should not only permit but also encourage these kinds of helpful health-status classifications.

Holding Unhealthy Defendants Liable

Some of the instances of differentiation based on health in private law may also not be healthist. We consider the case of the impaired physician in more detail. While holding providers who abuse substances liable for their torts arguably punishes a form of health-related conduct, it is not healthist. First, consider health welfare, derived from classical utilitarianism. Various authors have analyzed tort law through a utilitarian lens.[31] The case against the impaired physician might be brought as a negligence action, either for breach of the applicable medical standard of care or for failing to disclose the substance-abuse problem to the patient. In utilitarian terms, the negligence standard balances the costs of additional precautions against the value of additional safety to determine the net welfare effect of holding the defendant liable.[32] If the cost of the precaution outweighs the safety gained, then the utilitarian calculus would deem the defendant *not* liable for failing to take the precaution. To hold otherwise would create incentives for overly cautious behavior at a net cost to society. It is possible that holding the doctor liable would not improve welfare if the cost of informing the patient were too high – perhaps due to the loss of physician privacy or the potential for "warning pollution," which provides too much information that patients then ignore – or the risk of harm is too low – perhaps if the physician is in recovery and highly compliant with the program. While juries are not instructed in

[31] *See, e.g.*, Richard A. Posner, *Utilitarianism, Economics, and Legal Theory*, *J. Legal Stud.* (Jan. 1979) at 103 (arguing for the economic norm of "wealth maximization" to replace utilitarianism in tort law); Mark A. Geistfeld, *Efficiency, Fairness, and Economic Analysis of Tort Law, in N.Y. Univ. L. & Econ. Working Papers* (Apr. 2009) at 6, available at: http://lsr.nellco.org/cgi/viewcontent.cgi?article=1189&context=nyu_lewp (claiming that economic analysis can be fully compatible with welfare economics and, therefore, integral to rights-based tort systems).

[32] *See United States* v. *Carroll Towing Co.*, 159 F.2d 169, 173 (2d Cir. 1947) ("Liability depends upon whether [the burden of adequate precautions] is less than [the gravity of the resulting injury] multiplied by [the probability of that injury occurring]."); *The T. J. Hooper*, 60 F.2d 737, 740 (2d Cir. 1932) (using industry customs of precaution and ideas of common prudence to determine if the defendant was properly diligent).

utilitarian terms, tort law may implicitly incorporate a cost-benefit analysis into determinations of liability.

Turning now to health welfare, a tort verdict could improve health welfare if it encourages a physician to clean up her act. That incentive could then improve her individual health status, if she gets help for her problem. Although creating incentives is a common justification for the torts system, there is also good reason to question whether people really act rationally in the face of liability.[33] Nevertheless, a judgment against the physician could improve collective health by bringing an unsafe provider to light and perhaps preventing further harm if she loses her license. Private law can therefore act as a supplement for more formal regulations of professional conduct, including licensing and credentialing laws.[34]

Health liberty also tips in favor of holding a substance-abusing physician liable. A libertarian view of tort law values freedom of action, as discussed in Chapter 5. Thus, actors should be held liable when they choose to expose others to risk, either intentionally or by failing to act reasonably. A libertarian might say that a liability verdict against an impaired physician is not contrary to health liberty as long as she was aware of the risk she was taking. Even if we accept a degree of involuntariness related to addictive substances, the physician still knew of her impairment and proceeded anyway. It becomes a harder question, however, if the substances impaired her ability to make a rational choice. Given that tort law generally does not exempt people with mental impairments from the reasonably prudent person standard, the physician might be liable even under those circumstances. Setting aside that wrinkle, the torts verdict would not seem to limit the physician's ability to access health care or to make decisions about her health or wellness. It is possible that the size of the judgment or losing employment could affect the ability to pay for health care; however, balanced against the other criteria, that attenuated possibility does not warrant deeming this example healthist.

33 *See, e.g.*, Christine Jolls et al., *A Behavioral Approach to Law and Economics*, 50 *Stan. L. Rev.* 1471, 1497 (arguing that, according to Coasian principles, parties will bargain for a different outcome in the face of a court judgment, if there is a preferable outcome); *but see also* Michael G. Faure, *Calabresi and Behavioural Tort Law and Economics*, 1 *Erasmus L. Rev.*, no. 4, 2008, at 75, 76 (arguing that decision-making involves cognitive biases that do not always end in actions predicted by traditional economic models).

34 *See* Michael D. Green, *Safety as an Element of Pharmaceutical Quality: The Respective Roles of Regulation and Tort Law*, 42 *St. Louis Univ. L.J.* 163, 163–4 (stating that the application of the juncture between law and economics has only accentuated the deterrent role that tort law plays); *see also* Thomas G. Shearman and Amasa A. Redfield, *A Treatise on the Law of Negligence* at v–vi (5th edn. 1898) (arguing that private actions for negligence and the damages recovered in those actions are powerful deterrents).

With respect to health equality, we might take a step back and reconsider whether this example truly differentiates based on health status. Although the physician may be held liable for operating under the influence, the law does not treat her differently from similarly situated defendants *based on* a health-related attribute. To be sure, her health status may have contributed to the patient's injury. However, she is not being held liable for using substances but rather for failing to meet the applicable standard of care – the same standard that applies to all physicians, healthy or unhealthy. A physician who performed a delicate operation despite her relative inexperience or even an experienced physician who had a bad day could be likewise liable. The law would treat those healthy physicians the same as our similarly situated, substance-using physician.

Health justice is also not obviously in play. While addiction may face significant stigma, doctors typically have high social status. Thus, holding physicians liable for professional negligence – even if that negligence relates to substance use or addiction – is not a problem that exacerbates existing disparities or that calls for structural fixes. Moreover, courts tend to be especially deferential to physician privacy. In summary, holding doctors liable when their health status had a role in the negligent conduct may not be a classification based on health status. They are simply expected to act reasonably, like everyone else. But even if those verdicts differentiate on the basis of health status, they do not seem to be healthist.

6.3.3. *Close Cases*

While some health-based classifications are clearly healthist and others are clearly not, most fall somewhere in the middle. Although our four guiding principles may not always yield a definitive answer, they can nonetheless help employers, corporate actors, law-makers, policy-makers, and our readers think through these sticky issues. Here we examine some close cases: plaintiffs engaged in health-risky activities, different kinds of workplace wellness programs, and a policy banning smokers from public housing. In these examples, our analysis cuts both ways.

Disallowing Recovery to Unhealthy Plaintiffs

We concluded that holding unhealthy defendants – specifically impaired physicians – liable for their torts is not healthist. We now turn to unhealthy plaintiffs. If a plaintiff engages in unhealthy activity, the defendant may raise an affirmative defense, arguing that even if she unreasonably exposed the plaintiff to risk, the plaintiff either contributed to that negligence or assumed the risk with her behavior in the first place. For ease of analysis, we use an example of an express assumption of the risk: A plaintiff signs a release of liability to enter a ski resort. While skiing, she is injured and then sues the resort. As a defense to its alleged negligence, the resort points to the signed release, in which the plaintiff acknowledged the risks and agreed not to sue the resort.

Assuming it negligently maintained its facilities, should the resort be held liable? Does healthism have anything to offer this issue? On one hand, failing to enforce the waiver would protect individuals who engage in health-risky activities from signing away their tort remedies. Engaging in paternalism to deter people from risky activities could arguably be discriminatory but not necessarily normatively wrong. On the other hand, disallowing tort recovery may create an incentive for people to avoid risky activities, potentially improving their individual and collective health. Avoiding risky activities could lower accident rates, thereby also lowering health-care costs. Allowing people to recover fully, despite knowingly and voluntarily engaging in dangerous activities, presents a moral hazard problem. People may opt to take on a risk they otherwise would not if they do not have to bear the full costs of an injury. While it may be fair to conclude that no one is conscripted to go skiing, should it matter if the facility is a health club, and a waiver of liability is required as a condition of membership? Suppose, further, that the plaintiff's physician has recommended an exercise regime? Or suppose the waiver is presented at a hospital emergency room? The welfare effects of enforcing the waiver may very well change depending on the nature of the activity.

Which view is most consistent with health liberty? The answer, again, depends. Holding individuals, including unhealthy individuals and individuals engaged in health-risky activities, to their bargains respects their liberty and autonomy. Upholding those contracts could offer more choices of health-care providers and recreational facilities because those individuals and businesses could shield themselves from potentially exorbitant torts judgments. If they are able to operate free from that financial threat, they can keep their costs and, thereby, prices, down for all customers.

Moreover, if there is sufficient market demand for the same services, *without* the waiver of liability, then competing facilities will offer the same services, plus full rights to sue. One ski resort could offer cheaper lift tickets in exchange for signing an enforceable waiver, while another may not require guests to sign a waiver but would charge more for lift tickets. Having alternatives enhances freedom of choice. To that extent, waivers of liability across contexts, *including* medical contexts, could promote access to health care. Recall from Chapter 5 that courts are increasingly reluctant to enforce waivers of liability, especially when offered in exchange for essential services, such as health care. If hospitals could offer more affordable care to patients willing to sign waivers, enforcing waivers could provide an avenue to health care that otherwise would not exist. That argument underlies much of tort reform: If health-care providers did not face unlimited staggering liability, health-care costs would decrease, and providers would be more widely available, not deterred out of the business by malpractice fears. Empirical evidence on that suggestion, however, points in both directions.[35]

That said, expecting a patient undergoing medical treatment to sign away her right to a medical malpractice action hardly seems voluntary or consistent with freedom of action, especially if she needs the treatment and has no alternative. If the patient's consent does not seem truly voluntary – for example, if she signs moments before being wheeled to the operating room – the contract may not be enforceable. And as the contracts cases regarding medical guarantees recognize, health care is different and may warrant more delicate consideration. Depending on the circumstances, medical waivers could also implicate health justice. If patients in poorer health must sign waivers to afford care while healthier patients can preserve their right to sue, that system could impede access to health care and increase existing disparities.

Moreover, if waivers shelter health-care providers from tort liability, they might not perform at the same standard of quality. However, that outcome is unlikely. In addition to personal injury law, state licensing boards, professional codes of conduct, the Hippocratic Oath (in the case of doctors), and personal morality all create incentives for providers to treat patients with their full competence. Thus, waivers of liability may not produce any meaningful impact one way or another. The same may not be true of recreational facilities. Protecting the ski resort operator from liability through enforceable waivers could remove an incentive for maintaining the facility in safe working order, which could lead to more accidents, worse health outcomes, and increased health-care costs. That very concern animates courts' decisions to decline to enforce waivers of liability even for nonessential services context.

[35] *See* Michelle M. Mello et al., *National Costs of the Medical Liability System, Health Aff* (Millwood) (Sept. 2010), at 8, available at: www.ncbi.nlm.nih.gov/pmc/articles/PMC3048809/pdf/nihms269333.pdf; Myungho Paik et al., *Will Tort Reform Bend the Cost Curve? Evidence from Texas, J. Empirical Legal Stud.* (June 2012) at 174; J. William Thomas et al., *Low Costs of Defensive Medicine, Small Savings from Tort Reform, Health Affairs: Med. Malpractice & Errors* (Sept. 2010) at 1578–9, available at: www.healthaffairs.org/doi/abs/10.1377/hlthaff.2010.0146; Michael B. Rotherberg et al., *The Cost of Defensive Medicine on 3 Hospital Medicine Services, Jama Internal Medicine: Research Letter* (Sept. 15, 2014), available at: https://jamanetwork.com/journals/jamainternalmedicine/fullarticle/1904758.

For reasons discussed more fully in Chapter 1, we include both static health conditions and health-related conduct within our definition of health. Nevertheless, case law distinguishes appropriately among types of voluntary activities when it comes to enforcing waivers of liability. Likewise, we probably would not consider enforcing a recreational waiver of liability healthist. But we might give more pause to a similar waiver in the health-care context, based on the more limited choice and the essential nature of the services. Alternatively, we could carve out the health-care settings by stipulating that a medical procedure is not "unhealthy" conduct in the same way that skiing, snow tubing, sky diving, racecar-driving, or bungee jumping is. Thus, the medical waiver cases arguably may not classify based on health.

To sum up, our criteria point in both directions on whether denying plaintiffs full tort recovery for engaging in health-risky activity is healthist. Sticking to the examples of recreational activities, the guiding principles suggest that the assumption of the risk defense promotes healthy decision-making, facilitates individual choice about health care and health risks, and increases the availability of recreational facilities. Whether those waivers actually lower health risks and health-care costs, however, is less clear. If participants take more precautions or engage in more deliberation, they may lower their health risks. But if waivers lead facility operators to take fewer precautions, there could be more accidents.

Regarding health liberty, plaintiffs in the recreational activity cases are in some sense "punished" for their private conduct by being unable to recover fully. However, from the health equality perspective, animus does not appear to drive the assumption of the risk doctrine, and enforcing waivers does not seem likely to stigmatize risk-preferring individuals. Regarding health justice, denying tort recovery could cut off resources to pay for medical treatment for the injuries (to the extent the victim did not otherwise have health insurance), which could result in worse health outcomes. But the rule does not cut off resources or limit the individuals' ability to adopt safer, healthier lifestyles, nor does it create or exacerbate health disparities. Therefore, on balance, enforcing recreational waivers does not seem healthist. Nonetheless, we would be more concerned about the potential for healthism with medical waivers to the extent that they differentiate based on health status.

Biometric Screening

Next consider a case that the EEOC filed against two employers for requiring their employees to submit to biometric testing as part of their wellness programs.[36] The employees who refused the testing faced losing their health insurance, receiving disciplinary action, and taking on the full cost of their insurance to maintain coverage. The agency alleged that those penalties effectively compelled employees to participate, rendering the programs involuntary. The EEOC further alleged that the programs violated the ADA's limitations on workplace medical examinations and inquiries. Both arguments strike a health liberty chord.

Regarding the other guiding principles, the biometric screening does not seem to violate health equality because it does not appear animus-driven or stigmatizing. All employees, regardless of health status, were eligible to participate. Moreover, the policies could serve health welfare and perhaps health justice by encouraging employees to identify and address health issues. Some individuals might not otherwise have had access to similar opportunities to improve their health, thus creating more choices pursuant to health liberty. But the policy could also offend health liberty by punishing people for their private conduct. For example, if the program is attainment-based, not participation-based, it could penalize people for their diets and their level of physical activity.

Health justice is harder to assess. It is unclear how to measure whether the biometric screening might cut off access to health resources, produce worse health outcomes, or create or exacerbate health disparities. Employers typically kick in 80 percent or more of employee's premiums.[37] Losing that support poses a real threat. If individuals with certain health conditions refuse to participate, they could end up without health insurance and, as a result, access to health care. While an employee wellness program that requires medical testing could encourage healthy decision-making and perhaps facilitate choice, it remains to be seen whether such programs are actually consistent with health welfare by lowering costs, reducing risks, or producing better health outcomes.[38]

36 *See* EEOC, *EEOC Lawsuit Challenges Flambeau Over Wellness Program*, Press Release (Oct. 1, 2014), available at:www.eeoc.gov/eeoc/newsroom/release/10-1-14b.cfm (last visited Feb. 2, 2018); Lewis Krauskopf and Mica Rosenberg, *U.S. Judge Denies EEOC Bid to Stop Honeywell Wellness Penalty*, *Reuters.Com* (Nov. 3, 2014), available at: www.reuters.com/article/2014/11/03/honeywell-intl-eeoc-idUSL1N0ST26K20141103 (last visited Feb. 2, 2018).

37 *See 2017 Employer Health Benefits*, Kaiser Family Foundation (Sep. 19, 2017), available at: www.kff.org/report-section/ehbs-2017-summary-of-findings/ (noting in summary of findings, "[o]n average, covered workers contribute 18 percent of the premium for single coverage").

38 Al Lewis, *Workplace Wellness Produces No Savings*, *Health Aff. Blog* (Nov. 25, 2014), available at: http://healthaffairs.org/blog/2014/11/25/workplace-wellness-produces-no-savings; Soeren Mattke, *Workplace Wellness Programs Study: Final Report*, *RAND Corp.* (2013), available at: www.rand.org/content/dam/rand/pubs/research_reports/RR200/RR254/RAND_RR254.sum.pdf; Peres, note 29.

Our analysis, in some cases, necessarily turns on empirical evidence of cost savings, risk reduction, or health improvement. Time may tell whether some apparently healthist policies are, in fact, socially desirable. This uncertainty is challenging for law- and policy-makers because it is unclear whether they should intervene. They are left instead to implement the programs and wait and see whether they are healthist. We acknowledge that this approach makes planning difficult. But we nevertheless believe that the law can address healthism when it manifests, regardless if negative outcomes were not apparent at the outset.

While leaving open questions complicates the analysis, our approach is not unique in that regard. Consider, for example, the doctrine of reasonable care. A utilitarian view of negligence requires predictions and estimates of costs that may be in flux at the time of the trial. Even under a more nuanced, less formulaic approach to negligence, what a jury considers "reasonable" at one point in time may shift based on new information, scientific studies, and social mores. Likewise, administrative policies and priorities shift as scientific evidence becomes available. And, even there, controversy surrounds how to understand, interpret, and apply scientific evidence, like in the context of climate change.[39] Although we recognize the difficulty of having our analysis remain uncertain in some cases, we believe our rubric provides a sound basis for having these important discussions.

Public Housing Smoking Bans

Next, take the US Department of Housing and Urban Development (HUD) regulations banning tobacco use in public housing, discussed in Chapter 3.[40] Under this policy, public housing agencies must make their properties smoke-free. Smokers cannot light up in units, common areas, or even outdoors within twenty-five feet of the buildings.[41] HUD was careful, however, to emphasize that it does not prohibit public housing residents from smoking,[42] nor does it

[39] *See* Dan M. Kahan, *The Polarizing Impact of Science Literacy and Numeracy on Perceived Climate Change Risks*, *Nature Climate Change* (May 27, 2012), available at: www.nature.com/articles/nclimate1547; *see generally*, Mike Hulme, *Why We Disagree about Climate Change: Understanding Controversy, Inaction and Opportunity* (2009).

[40] 24 C.F.R. § 965.653.

[41] 24 C.F.R. § 965.653(a) (banning tobacco use "in all public housing living units and interior areas (including but not limited to hallways, rental and administrative offices, community centers, day care centers, laundry centers, and similar structures), as well as in outdoor areas within 25 feet from public housing and administrative office buildings.").

[42] 81 Fed. Reg. 87430, 87432, 87434.

prohibit leasing to smokers.[43] It simply bans smoking on or near the properties. At first blush, the policy may seem similar to banning smoking at work. Yet deeper analysis reveals that the smoking ban raises other serious issues.

First, smoking in public housing has important welfare effects. Remember that one way of thinking of welfare is in terms of externalities – costs or benefits imposed on third parties. In the context of the nicotine hiring bans, employers do not need to refuse to hire nicotine users in order to prohibit smoking at work. They can keep the workplace smoke-free and still let employees smoke or use tobacco on their own time. The negative externalities associated with smoking are limited to the potential costs of absenteeism or heightened premiums. Fellow employees do not need to deal with second-hand smoke, poor air quality, or coworkers who smell like smoke and take frequent breaks. More negative externalities arise, however, when it comes to housing. Unlike coworkers, fellow tenants must bear the costs of lowered air quality, second-hand smoke,[44] and fire hazards associated with smoking. In other words, third parties must bear even more of the potential costs of smoking when they share living space with smokers.

Not surprisingly then, justifications for smoke-free housing policies like HUD's include the effect of second-hand smoke – especially on particularly vulnerable parties like children, pregnant women, chronically ill people, and pets.[45] In issuing the final rule the agency explained, "[t]his rule improves indoor air quality in the housing; benefits the health of public housing residents, visitors, and PHA staff; reduces the risk of catastrophic fires; and lowers overall maintenance costs."[46] HUD Secretary Julian Castro asserted, "Every child deserves to grow up in a safe, healthy home free from harmful second-hand cigarette smoke . . . . HUD's smoke-free rule is a reflection of our commitment to using housing as a platform to create healthy communities."[47] The ban on smoking in public housing then seems designed to promote welfare. But do the benefits of this policy outweigh its potential costs?

[43] 81 Fed. Reg. 87430, 87443 (explaining that "[t]his rule is not to be interpreted as making smoking a bar to public housing tenancy").

[44] For research on the health effects of second-hand smoke, see David M. Homa et al., *Vital Signs: Disparities in Nonsmokers' Exposure to Secondhand Smoke – United States, 1999–2012*, 64 *Morbidity & Mortality Weekly Report* 103 (2015); *Chapter 4: Advances in Knowledge of the Health Consequences of Smoking: From 1964–2014, Surgeon General's Report* 63–106.

[45] U.S. Department of Housing and Urban Development Office of Lead Hazards and Healthy Homes, *Change Is in the Air: An Action Guide for Establishing Smoke-Free Public Housing and Multifamily Properties* 10 (October 2014).

[46] 81 Fed. Reg. 87430 (2016).

[47] Nereida Moreno, *Chicago, Public Housing Agencies to Implement Federal Smoking Ban, Chicago Tribune* (Jan. 4, 2017), available at www.chicagotribune.com/news/ct-public-housing-smoking-met-20161229-story.html.

In terms of the financial impact, the answer seems to be "yes." Researchers from the Centers for Disease Control and Prevention estimate that HUD's new rule could save a whopping $496.82 million per year, including $310.48 million in health-care expenses related to second-hand smoke, $133.77 million in renovation costs, and $52.57 million in losses from smoking-related fires.[48] Of course, these benefits are not without their costs. HUD estimates that implementing and enforcing the smoke-free policies may require an investment of upwards of $30.2 million in the first year and $7.7 million per year in subsequent years.[49] Yet even with this high price tag, the benefits more than outweigh the costs.

However, there could be more to the story. Smokers in public housing may find themselves in a catch-22. While smokers only make up about 17 percent of the general population, they make up 30 percent of the population living below the poverty line.[50] Consequently, many smokers may not be able to afford private housing. For example, one person affected by the new ban explained that she did not have the money to leave public housing but wondered if she could ever successfully kick the habit.[51] If a person is truly addicted and has difficulty quitting on her own, and violations of the smoke-free housing policies could lead to eviction, then smokers who live in public housing may end up homeless and sick. This result would not only compromise their health and well-being but also impose an unexpected drain on public resources. Furthermore, some comments noted that the smoke-free policy might create a perverse incentive to hide smoking, leading to the improper disposal of cigarettes and, as a result, *more* fires.[52]

Prohibiting smoking in public housing also runs afoul of health liberty by infringing on people's private lives. Specifically, those policies forbid tenants from engaging in otherwise legal conduct in the sanctity of their homes.[53] Some individuals commenting on the rule referred to the prohibition as "an invasion of civil rights" and called it "authoritarian and invasive."[54] One person living in public housing explained: "You kind of feel like you're in jail

[48] Brian A. King et al., *National and State Cost Savings Associated with Prohibiting Smoking in Subsidized and Public Housing in the United States*, 11 *Preventing Chronic Disease* 1, 1 (2014).

[49] 81 Fed. Reg. 87430, 87431.

[50] Veronica E. Helms et al., *Cigarette Smoking and Adverse Health Outcomes among Adults Receiving Federal Housing Assistance*, 99 *Preventive Med.* 171, 171 (2017).

[51] *See e.g.* Moreno, note 49, (reporting that a smoker "can't afford to leave public housing but wonders if she can ever truly quit tobacco").

[52] 81 Fed. Reg. 87430, 87440.

[53] Commentators also made this point. *See* 81 Fed. Reg. 87430, 87434.

[54] 81 Fed. Reg. 87430, 87439, 87440.

because you have to follow all these different rules and orders. But you have to do what you have to do to keep your apartment."[55]

Although they target conduct in the home, arguably smoke-free housing policies could raise fewer problems for health liberty than nicotine hiring bans. Whereas nicotine hiring bans effectively outlaw smoking and other nicotine use across the board in any context, HUD's new policy simply means smokers will have to go outside their homes. In other words, people will not lose their leases if they test positive for nicotine. They are free to smoke as much as they want. Thus, while at first blush smoke-free housing policies might seem *more* intrusive than nicotine hiring bans, upon closer inspection, they are actually *less* invasive.

Like nicotine hiring bans, smoke-free housing policies also offend health equality by singling out an already highly stigmatized group: smokers. However, the housing ban introduces yet another level of social isolation and stigmatization. Smokers become literal outsiders, forced outside into the elements. They cannot even stand *near* the housing units, common areas, or administrative buildings. They must be at least twenty-five feet away. As one set of authors observes, "one need only look outside at the huddle of smokers commonly seen outside public buildings in inclement weather to witness the decreased social standing of smokers relative to non-smokers."[56] Comments responding to HUD's rule asserted that banning smoking "demonize[s] and dehumanize[s] smokers" and "discrimate[s] against smokers."[57] Thus, while smoke-free housing policies technically ban "smoking" but not "smokers," they nonetheless hold the power to be highly stigmatizing, even more so than nicotine hiring bans. Some have outright proposed that the policy might be animus-driven, stating that if HUD was going to prohibit smoking, it should ban all things that could cause harm, produce unsavory odors, create smoke, or lead to health risk, including pet dander, smelly food, scented candles, and alcohol.[58]

And, finally, smoke-free housing policies create complicated health justice concerns. While smoking can be construed as voluntary, we do not want to adopt an oversimplified account of choice. One public housing resident facing the upcoming HUD policies told a reporter, "I know that I have a trace of lung cancer as we speak, and I still have a pull on a cigarette. It's the hardest thing ever."[59] As discussed at length throughout this book, many smokers

[55] Moreno, note 49 (quoting Etta Davis).

[56] Stuber et al., *Smoking and the Emergence*, note 8, at 420, 422 (2008).

[57] 81 Fed. Reg. 87430, 87440.

[58] 81 Fed. Reg. 87430, 87440, 87442.

[59] Moreno, note 49, available at: www.chicagotribune.com/news/ct-public-housing-smoking-met-20161229-story.html.

would prefer to quit. Eighty-five percent of smokers have tried to stop smoking and failed.[60] Threatening them with penalties, including potential eviction, adds yet another layer of disadvantage to this already-burdened population. For example, when faced with the tobacco penalty, several individuals simply decided to go without insurance.[61] Being without health insurance puts an already-disadvantaged population at even greater risk, since so many Americans must rely on health insurance to access care.

The possibility of compounding existing risk is especially troubling in the context of public housing. First, the smoke-free policy could have a particularly devastating impact on certain already-disadvantaged populations. Comments responding to HUD's rule cautioned that it could disproportionately impact people with disabilities and the elderly, who might face difficulty leaving their units to comply with the policy, as well as individuals who use nicotine to cope with pain or ease other more harmful addictions.[62] Commentators also feared that using eviction as a possible enforcement mechanism would end up forcing the people who most need stable housing out of their homes.[63]

Moreover, smoking disproportionately affects poorer communities. While smoking used to be widespread, low-income individuals are the last holdouts regarding this once-ubiquitous habit.[64] One possibility for the correlation between income and smoking is that poorer individuals lack the support and resources to quit.[65] In response to HUD's smoke-free policy, a volunteer tenant patroller and former smoker explained that residents will need classes in smoking cessation to comply with the regulations and to stay in their apartments.[66] As a result, several people commenting on the rule urged HUD to include smoking cessation support in the final rule to help residents with limited resources.[67]

The possibility of eviction could further exacerbate the health disparities already faced by low-income smokers. Because they may not be able to afford private housing, tenants may face homelessness as the result of the HUD

60 Frank Newport, *Most U.S. Smokers Want to Quit, Have Tried Multiple Times, Gallup* (July 31, 2013), available at: www.gallup.com/poll/163763/smokers-quit-tried-multiple-times.aspx.

61 Abigail S. Friedman et al., *Evidence Suggests that the ACA's Tobacco Surcharges Reduced Insurance Take-Up and Did Not Increase Smoking Cessation, Health Affairs* 35, no. 7, 1176, 1181 (2016).

62 81 Fed. Reg. 87430, 87434. 87440.

63 81 Fed. Reg. 87430, 87434.

64 Stuber et al., *Smoking and the Emergence*, note 8, at 420, 422.

65 Bell et al., *Smoking, Stigma, and Tobacco*, note 9, at 795, 796–7 (2010).

66 Moreno, note 49, available at: www.chicagotribune.com/news/ct-public-housing-smoking-met-20161229-story.html.

67 81 Fed. Reg. 87430, 87434.

policy.[68] Comments on the rule pointed out that the smokers themselves would not be the only people to suffer. Entire families, including children, could find themselves without a place to live.[69] Homelessness leads to substantial health risks. Not only do health-related factors such as poverty, domestic violence, addiction, and mental health conditions contribute to homelessness, but homelessness itself brings with it a whole host of health risks, including susceptibility to infectious disease, mental health issues, and substance abuse.[70] Perhaps the most tragic consequence of homelessness is the increased likelihood of an untimely death, either from suicide or from unintentional injuries.[71] Moreover, once sick, homeless individuals experience substantial barriers to accessing health care. Beyond the obvious issues like the lack of health insurance or other means to pay for health care, homeless people may also have difficulty establishing treatment relationships – due to either structural instability or stigma by providers – and adhering to care plans. Not surprisingly, the absence of low-cost housing is the strongest determining factor for homelessness.[72] Pushing smokers out of public housing and onto the streets runs the risk of not only worse health outcomes for that population – which is already at heightened health risk – but also a potential reduction in collective welfare.

Of course, smokers are not the only parties worth considering. Allowing smoking in public housing raises health concerns for the people and animals who are exposed to second-hand smoke but are also unable to relocate. Poor air quality, fire hazards, and other risks plague individuals who live near smokers.[73] Those factors could negatively impact health. Thus, when considering the health welfare and health justice concerns of smoke-free housing policies, we must think of the effects on not only the smokers but also on those around them.

We can now take a step back and examine how the guiding principles operate together. Outlawing smoke-free housing policies would avoid singling out

68 81 Fed. Reg. 87430, 87436.

69 Ibid.

70 Seena Fazel, John R Geddes, Margot Kushel, *The Health of Homeless People in High-Income Countries: Descriptive Epidemiology, Health Consequences, and Clinical and Policy Recommendations*, 384 *Lancet* 1529 (2014).

71 Ibid.

72 Jason Wilson Klein and Simha Reddy, *Care of the Homeless Patient*, 99 *Med. Clin. N. Amer.* 1017 (2015); Cheryl Zlotnick et al., *Health Care for the Homeless: What We Have Learned in the Past 30 Years and What's Next*, 103 *Am. J. Pub. Health* S199 (2013).

73 U.S. Department of Housing and Urban Development Office of Lead Hazards and Healthy Homes, *Change Is in the Air: An Action Guide for Establishing Smoke-Free Public Housing and Multifamily Properties* 10–11 (October 2014).

smokers (health equality), honor their "choices" (health liberty), and possibly prevent further smoking-related health disparities (health justice). Yet permitting smoking in public housing could undermine the health of people who live near smokers (health welfare and health justice). Health welfare remains particularly ambiguous. Whether smoke-free housing policies lead to welfare gains or welfare losses depends on a few other factors. One, will smokers face eviction and potential homelessness if they fail to comply? Two, will smokers receive any support in quitting?

We have already discussed the ways that smoke-free housing policies could produce worse health outcomes and lead to increased disparities for smokers. The impact on smokers alone is sufficient to raise health justice concerns. But if those problems balloon, smoke-free housing policies could have a negative health welfare impact. Factoring eviction into the equation further exacerbates those risks. The negative consequences of homeless smokers could outweigh the benefit of not having roommates or neighbors who smoke.

Subjecting smokers to potential eviction without offering any help to quit raises concerns related to not only health welfare and health justice but also health equality and health liberty. If forcing smokers to huddle in the cold offends health equality and demonstrates their lowered social standing, surely pushing them into homelessness would have the same – if not a greater – effect. Moreover, having nowhere to live certainly limits a person's choices and resources, thereby impeding free choice and offending health liberty. If smokers will not end up on the streets and will have help kicking the habit, then prohibiting smoking in public housing looks a lot like tobacco cessation programs, making them sound health policy. But if smokers are left to their own devices and risk ending up homeless, then smoke-free housing policies appear healthist.

Unfortunately, the answers to these two key questions – whether smokers will face eviction and whether smokers will have support – remain unclear. For instance, Chicago Housing Authority Spokesman Matthew Aguilar indicated he did not want to resort to evictions, explaining: "Many of the details have yet to be finalized. However, we will work to ensure that the new HUD rules will not adversely impact CHA residents or result in punitive actions."[74] Not all federal, state, or local agencies may be similarly inclined. While the HUD policy is federal, individual public housing agencies and lease terms will ultimate dictate how to enforce the ban on smoking in public housing. Despite advocating "a graduated enforcement approach," HUD has referred

[74] Moreno, note 49, available at: www.chicagotribune.com/news/ct-public-housing-smoking-met-20161229-story.html.

to "lease enforcement actions" by public housing agencies as "the best way to ensure compliance with such policies."[75] Regarding the availability of support to kick the habit, that issue too remains unclear. HUD at present will not provide direct smoking cessation assistance, instead offering online resources and looking to Medicaid and public housing agencies to provide much-needed support.[76]

This is where our theory of healthism with its guiding principles provides useful input for law-, policy-makers, and other decision-makers. On one hand, smoke-free housing policies may offer the promise of lowered costs and improved health. On the other, if administered wrongly, they could further disadvantage smokers by reducing their well-being, increasing the stigma that they face, limiting their choices and resources, and exacerbating health disparities, perhaps even causing a greater drain on social resources. Limiting the use of eviction as an enforcement mechanism and providing support could mitigate these potential dangers. Although smokers would still be singled out for regulation, they would have access to more choices – via tobacco cessation programs – and have a real shot at both improving their health and keeping their apartments.

6.4. CONCLUSION

In writing this book, we sought to start a public conversation about health-status discrimination and to introduce the concept of healthism. Yet we did not want to leave the question of potential solutions unaddressed. We therefore also provided a framework to guide law- and policy-makers who wish to promote health. Our four guiding principles may sometimes tip all in favor of – or all against – a given policy. Those easy cases are probably the exception, not the rule. Far more likely, a particular policy will promote some guiding principles while transgressing others. Even in these cases, our rubric remains useful. It can still guide law- and policy-makers – as well as corporations, employers, physicians, and the public – in crafting policies and interventions that are likely to improve health, while avoiding discrimination. Our theory of healthism provides a powerful tool for negotiating the potential pitfalls of crafting sound, nondiscriminatory health policy in an era when health and health care remain among our nation's most contentious issues.

75 81 Fed. Reg. 87430, 87437.

76 81 Fed. Reg. 87430, 87435.

Index